Advance Praise for *No Room of Her Own*

"After reading *No Room of Her Own*, I'm more convinced than ever that unless we bend toward justice, years hence, our children will look back upon current policies—that are producing poverty and homelessness alongside peopleless homes—as a societal experiment that is far worse than the Tuskegee study, in which the ravages of syphilis were studied while the individuals were left untreated."

—Stephen Bezruchka M.D., M.P.H.,
School of Public Health, University of Washington

"Hellegers carefully and contextually places the reader into the individual lives of un-housed women who unmistakably form the very subtext for social justice."

—Neil J. Donovan, Executive Director,
National Coalition for the Homeless

"*No Room of Her Own* is a gift to readers who want to understand the lives of women who have no home. Hellegers provides a platform for each woman to tell her story in her own vivid, heart-wrenching language. As I read the book I felt as if I trudged uphill with each woman as she searched for a place to shower, a chance at a job, a safe bed—or even a doorway—for the night. Any image I had of homelessness as a position of inert helplessness has been dispelled by reading the stories of women on the move to improve their situations. Violence, depression and anger are potent parts of the women's struggles. External threats to safety and health frequently erode confidence. But hope and courage regularly rise up to triumph over despair."

—Ginny Nicarthy, author of *Getting Free:
You Can End Abuse and Take Back Your Life*

"The reality that sings out from Desiree Hellegers's remarkable book is that women who lack a roof to sleep under at night are not lacking in competence, will-power, a way with words, and a generous spirit of activism. The first-hand stories gathered here, framed by Hellegers's cogently political introduction, show how in the USA's grossly class-divided, racist, and sexist society, housing is not a right but a privilege. Homelessness is a punishment for being already disadvantaged. *No Room of Her Own* will be an inspiration to activist women, both homeless and housed."

—Cynthia Cockburn, feminist researcher and writer, member of
Women in Black London, author of *From Where We Stand:
War, Women's Activism and Feminist Analysis*

"Desiree Hellegers presents fifteen heart-wrenching portraits of the lives of homeless and formerly homeless women. These women's stories are not sanitized to elicit sympathy from the reader. Rather, Hellegers offers us multidimensional narratives that resist the objectifying tendencies of other portrayals of the unhoused. In doing so, she aids the women's persistent struggle to assert value in their lives in the midst of constantly being undermined by a society that treats them as disposable commodities. This book will be an important contribution towards understanding the reality of those who struggle on a daily basis to survive on the streets."

—Daniel Kerr, Assistant Professor of History,
American University

"*No Room of Her Own: Women's Stories of Homelessness, Life, Death, and Resistance* is a well researched piece of work, and sobering reminder that for women who experience homelessness in the United States, they face many of the same horrid injustices as their sisters around the globe. By recording and presenting the voices of women who have struggled through the trauma of the streets, we can better understand the beautiful and tragic story of the human experience. It's also a call to action, and a reminder we all have a part to play."

—Israel Bayer, Executive Director of *Street Roots*,
a street newspaper in Portland, Oregon, and former board
chair of the North American Street Newspaper Association (NASNA)

"Heartbreaking and inspiring stories of courageous women enduring and triumphing over adversity few of us can imagine. Desiree Hellegers brilliantly collates and connects the stories of disparate homeless women. We learn much about these citizens with no addresses. They have been studied to death but rarely do we hear their voices. Hellegers skillfully and with compassion weaves the tapestry of these women's testimonies. From Sweet Pea to Debra and Marlowe, their accounts of survival and dignity reveal hidden truths of gender relations and our political and social culture. *No Room of Her Own* breaks the silences surrounding the national disgrace of homelessness. These women must be heard."

—David Barsamian, founder and director of Alternative Radio

"*No Room of Her Own* will take its place next to Liebow's *Tell Them Who I Am* as a definitive contemporary human document on the lives of homeless women."

—Mitchell Duneier, Maurice P.
During Professor of Sociology, Princeton University

"Some of my deepest conversations have been with wise homeless sisters of all colors on the underside of America—yet they have a rich understanding of America! Don't miss this book!"

—Cornel West, Princeton University

PALGRAVE *Studies in Oral History*

Series Editors: Linda Shopes and Bruce M. Stave

The Order Has Been Carried Out: History, Memory, and Meaning of a Nazi Massacre in Rome, by Alessandro Portelli (2003)

Sticking to the Union: An Oral History of the Life and Times of Julia Ruuttila, by Sandy Polishuk (2003)

To Wear the Dust of War: From Bialystok to Shanghai to the Promised Land, an Oral History, by Samuel Iwry, edited by L. J. H. Kelley (2004)

Education as My Agenda: Gertrude Williams, Race, and the Baltimore Public Schools, by Jo Ann Robinson (2005)

Remembering: Oral History Performance, edited by Della Pollock (2005)

Postmemories of Terror: A New Generation Copes with the Legacy of the "Dirty War," by Susana Kaiser (2005)

Growing Up in The People's Republic: Conversations between Two Daughters of China's Revolution, by Ye Weili and Ma Xiaodong (2005)

Life and Death in the Delta: African American Narratives of Violence, Resilience, and Social Change, by Kim Lacy Rogers (2006)

Creating Choice: A Community Responds to the Need for Abortion and Birth Control, 1961–1973, by David P. Cline (2006)

Voices from This Long Brown Land: Oral Recollections of Owens Valley Lives and Manzanar Pasts, by Jane Wehrey (2006)

Radicals, Rhetoric, and the War: The University of Nevada in the Wake of Kent State, by Brad E. Lucas (2006)

The Unquiet Nisei: An Oral History of the Life of Sue Kunitomi Embrey, by Diana Meyers Bahr (2007)

Sisters in the Brotherhoods: Working Women Organizing for Equality in New York City, by Jane LaTour (2008)

Iraq's Last Jews: Stories of Daily Life, Upheaval, and Escape from Modern Babylon, edited by Tamar Morad, Dennis Shasha, and Robert Shasha (2008)

Soldiers and Citizens: An Oral History of Operation Iraqi Freedom from the Battlefield to the Pentagon, by Carl Mirra (2008)

Overcoming Katrina: African American Voices from the Crescent City and Beyond, by D'Ann R. Penner and Keith C. Ferdinand (2009)

Bringing Desegregation Home: Memories of the Struggle toward School Integration in Rural North Carolina, by Kate Willink (2009)

I Saw It Coming: Worker Narratives of Plant Closings and Job Loss, by Tracy E. K'Meyer and Joy L. Hart (2010)

Speaking History: Oral Histories of the American Past, 1865–Present, by Sue Armitage and Laurie Mercier (2010)

Surviving Bhopal: Dancing Bodies, Written Texts, and Oral Testimonials of Women in the Wake of an Industrial Disaster, by Suroopa Mukherjee (2010)

Living with Jim Crow: African American Women and Memories of the Segregated South, by Anne Valk and Leslie Brown (2010)

Gulag Voices: Oral Histories of Soviet Incarceration and Exile, by Jehanne M. Gheith and Katherine R. Jolluck (2011)

Detained without Cause: Muslims' Stories of Detention and Deportation in America after 9/11, by Irum Shiekh (2011)

Soviet Communal Living: An Oral History of the Kommunalka, by Paola Messana (2011)

No Room of Her Own: Women's Stories of Homelessness, Life, Death, and Resistance, by Desiree Hellegers (2011)

Oral History and Photography, edited by Alexander Freund and Alistair Thomson (2011)

Place, Writing, and Voice in Oral History, edited by Shelley Trower (2011)

No Room of Her Own

Women's Stories of Homelessness, Life, Death, and Resistance

Desiree Hellegers

palgrave
macmillan

NO ROOM OF HER OWN
Copyright © Desiree Hellegers, 2011.

First published in 2011 by
PALGRAVE MACMILLAN®
in the United States—a division of St. Martin's Press LLC,
175 Fifth Avenue, New York, NY 10010.

Where this book is distributed in the UK, Europe and the rest of the world,
this is by Palgrave Macmillan, a division of Macmillan Publishers Limited,
registered in England, company number 785998, of Houndmills,
Basingstoke, Hampshire RG21 6XS.

Palgrave Macmillan is the global academic imprint of the above companies
and has companies and representatives throughout the world.

Palgrave® and Macmillan® are registered trademarks in the United States, the
United Kingdom, Europe and other countries.

ISBN: 978–0–230–11657–3 (hardcover)
ISBN: 978–0–230–11658–0 (paperback)

Library of Congress Cataloging-in-Publication Data

No room of her own : women's stories of homelessness, life, death, and
resistance / Desiree Hellegers.
p. cm.—(Palgrave studies in oral history)
ISBN 978–0–230–11657–3
1. Homeless women—United States—Case studies. I. Hellegers, Desiree,
1961–

HV4505.N56 2011
362.5092'273—dc22   2011009888

A catalogue record of the book is available from the British Library.

Design by Newgen Imaging Systems (P) Ltd., Chennai, India.

First edition: August 2011

10 9 8 7 6 5 4 3 2 1

Printed in the United States of America.

This book is dedicated to homeless people everywhere

Contents

List of Illustrations   xi

Acknowledgments   xiii

Series Editors' Foreword   xvii

CHAPTER 1
Introduction   1

CHAPTER 2
"Mama Pam"   29

CHAPTER 3
Annamarie Tailfeathers   39

CHAPTER 4
Elizabeth Thatcher   49

CHAPTER 5
"Sweet Pea"   59

CHAPTER 6
Debra Martinson   69

CHAPTER 7
Anitra Freeman   79

CHAPTER 8
Roxane Roberts   93

CHAPTER 9
Delores Loann Winston   105

CHAPTER 10
Mona Caudill Joyner   115

CHAPTER 11
Jessie Pedro   127

CHAPTER 12
"Marie"   137

CHAPTER 13
Janice Connelly   147

CHAPTER 14
"Flower"   157

CHAPTER 15
Arnette Adams   165

CHAPTER 16
Marlowe   173

CHAPTER 17
Conclusion   183

CHAPTER 18
Afterword   189

Notes   195

Index   213

Illustrations

Cover Photograph of Roxane Roberts

1	WHEEL/Women in Black Vigil	14
2	Anitra Freeman at a Women in Black cleansing	79
3	Photograph of Roxane Roberts	93
4	Photograph of Mona Caudill Joyner	115
5	Photograph of Jessie Pedro	127
6	Photograph of Arnette Adams	165

Acknowledgments

Thanks, in alphabetical order, to Arnette Adams, Janice Connelly, "Flower," Anitra Freeman, Mona Joyner, "Marie," Marlowe, Debra Martinson, Pam, Jessie Pedro, Roxane Roberts, "Sweet Pea," Annamarie Tailfeathers, Elizabeth Thatcher, and Loann Winston. Without their willingness to share their stories, and without their honesty, righteous anger, patience, and good humor, this book would not have been possible.

The incomparable Michele Marchand cannot be thanked enough. She introduced me to WHEEL and the Women in Black, supplied photographs and sources, fact-checked drafts, weighed in on my analysis at various critical moments, and sent links to newspaper articles.

I owe a debt of gratitude to Linda Shopes for insights and questions she brought to bear early on that crucially shaped my research. Thanks also for editorial comments and insights supplied by Bruce Stave and Chris Chappell and for the assistance of Sarah Whalen and Erin Ivy at Palgrave, and Rohini Krishnan and the team at Newgen Imagining Systems.

This book would not have been possible without the assistance of staff at the Lutheran Compass Center Women's Program. Thanks are particularly due to M.J. Kiser and Beverly. My analysis was shaped at various points by conversations with women who lived and worked at the Compass Center in the 1980s, including Grace Brooks, Ann Barney, Patty, Kandy, Maude, and the late Mary Witt, who died too young but left a hell of a mark. Thanks also to Josephine Archuleta and the staff of Sacred Heart Shelter. Marty Hartman, Rev. Pat Simpson, Rev. Marcia McLaughlin, Kim Tanner, and the staff and women of Mary's Place provided important insights, leads, and resources along the way.

Michael Stoops of the National Coalition for the Homeless offered critical insights and sources, as did Israel Bayer of *Street Roots*, and the staff of *Real Change* at various points. Thanks are due also to Mitch Duneier, and Ginny Nicarthy who read and commented on the introduction.

I'm grateful to Mike Buchman and Martha Swain for the hospitality they provided during numerous trips to Seattle; Mike also generously read and commented on a draft of the introduction. I'm grateful also for insights into Seattle history and organizing provided by Scott Morrow, John Fox, and Elmer and Aaron Dixon. And thanks to the staff at the *Daily Evergreen* at the University of Washington for making their archives and Xerox machine available to me. My research is also indebted to articles and archival material accessed through the Seattle Civil Rights and Labor

History Project, coordinated by Professor Quintard Taylor of the Department of History at the University of Washington.

I have benefited over the years from conversations with organizers and residents who built Dignity Village from the ground up: Ibrahim Mubarak, Jack Tafari, J.P., Gaye Reyes, Tim Brown, Tim McCarthy; with Genny Nelson of Sisters of the Road Café; with Wendy Kohn and Heather Mosher; and with Marjorie Philips and Sister Cathie Boerboom. Friends in the Portland peace movement, including Mikel Clayhold the tireless (though very tired) Mr. Dan Handelman, Yvonne Simmons (who ran with the beatniks and banned the bomb in London), Ann and Bruce Huntwork, Regina Hannon, Linda Tomassi, Will Seaman, Peter Miller, Max White, and Cecil Prescod have at various points provided important insights into organizing, and, in the weeks before she died, Pat Hollingsworth, peace activist and potter extraordinaire, weighed in with important insights into links between war, women, and violence.

I'm grateful to colleagues in the Department of English at WSU Vancouver and in Pullman, including Carol Siegel, Kandy Robertson, Wendy Olson, Wendy Johnson, Thabiti Lewis, David Menchaca, and TV Reed for insight and encouragement they've supplied along the way. I owe a debt of thanks also to Shari Clevenger. WSU provided a sabbatical and travel funds that made this research possible. Thanks are due also to editors and readers at *Rhizomes: Cultural Studies in Emerging Knowledge,* which published an article based on earlier version of the introduction.

I owe a particular debt of gratitude to the faculty of the Center for Social and Environmental Justice at WSU Vancouver, for the intellectual and political community they've provided over the years, their commitment to WSU's land grant mission, and to closing the gap between mission statements on diversity and global education and the everyday material practices of teaching, service, and research.

I'm grateful particularly to Clay Mosher, whose insights on drug and alcohol policy and on the prison-industrial complex have been invaluable over the years, and who read and commented on the introduction and suggested sources on numerous occasions; to Marcelo Diversi and Susan Finley, whose research, teaching, and service have continually emphasized the agency, creativity, and rights of homeless people; and to Paul Thiers and Dan Jaffee, whose work on globalization has fed my own analysis. Conversations with Luz Maria Gordillo and Jorge Lizarraga on immigration policy enabled me to suggest connections that merit far deeper exploration. I can never do justice to the contributions of Laurie Mercier, who provided invaluable guidance and insight over the years into the theory and practice of oral history; and the incomparable Pavithra Narayanan, who has served as an example of intellectual courage and as a continual reminder of the ongoing need to link theory and praxis.

My sister-in-law Deborah Cornaire read multiple drafts of the book with the keen eye of a poet and provided invaluable insights and encouragement. I'm thankful to Kay Bockman, who donated time and services that made the afterword of this book possible. Chris Clayhold is also owed a debt of gratitude in that regard. Thanks are due also to Bob and Sandy Shulman, who kept me from losing faith in academia and in myself, to Angela Redinger, and to my amazing acupuncturist Angela Parson.

I'm deeply grateful for the love, patience and friendship of Debra Hill, a founding member of Dignity Village, whose insights into the lived experience of homelessness have proven invaluable over the years, who critiqued and commented on a number of passages and spurred me toward completion of this project.

Finally, this book could never have been completed without the friendship, support, love, and encouragement of friends and family, including Jeanne Yeasting, Linda Cargill, Roxane Hill, Jason Reynolds, Meg Vogt, Don and Jeff Clayhold, Jill Petty, my sister Cammie Hellegers; and the endlessly patient, ever curious Mikel Clayhold, who learned early on from the late Theda Clayhold, to rise with the ranks, not from them.

Series Editors' Foreword

What better way to put a human face on the unhoused than oral history? Although they may be divested of tangible possessions, homeless people continue to own their remembered life experience. In *No Room of Her Own*, an oral history of unhoused women in Seattle, Washington, Desiree Hellegers recounts the multiple, dehumanizing, often dangerous challenges these women face daily. She reveals an unusual capacity to situate herself in the world of the unhoused, to cultivate their trust patiently, to elicit and listen to their stories respectfully, and to render the stories lucidly and sympathetically. The narratives she has recorded demonstrate how this group of women do what they can for themselves; seek community among one another and their allies; work, sometimes successfully, to find a permanent home; and join with others to advocate publically for their interests.

More importantly, Hellegers is an incisive critic and passionate ally in the struggle to overcome the structural obstacles to homelessness. In her view, homelessness is not the result of individual failings, but rather a social condition resulting from the dismantling of the social safety net and the progressive erosion of civil society in recent decades, as well as a long tradition of Social Darwinism in this country and the utter exclusion of the poor from public discourse. Standing alone, the narratives might elicit an armchair pity. Contextualized as they are, they illuminate the human consequences of our nation's policies. In sum, this volume, rooted in a passion for social justice, offers for a respectful view of homeless women and a gendered analysis of homelessness.

In doing so, it joins several other contributions to this series that concern human rights and human dignity. These touch on such diverse topics as those affected by Hurricane Katrina, internment of Japanese Americans during World War II, and survivors of the Soviet Gulag. Overall, the Palgrave Studies in Oral History series seeks to bring to publication on a variety of topics the best in oral history, both in substance and in method, so that students, scholars, and the general reader reap the benefits of cutting-edge research.

Bruce M. Stave
University of Connecticut
Linda Shopes
Carlisle, Pennsylvania

CHAPTER 1

Introduction

I arrived in Seattle from the East Coast in 1984, and within a few weeks, I stumbled on my first job—and my first home—in the Pacific Northwest. The shelter where I lived and worked during my first year in the city was in an old convent in the shadows of that space age spire, monument "to the era's belief in commerce, technology and progress," that makes its stock appearance in every movie and sitcom ever shot in the city.[1] Built by private developers for the 1962 World's Fair at the cost of $4.5 million, the Space Needle would be refurbished for another $20 million in 1999, the year that Mayor Paul Schell would make the mistake of inviting the World Trade Organization to town.[2] The year that the first U.S. astronaut orbited the earth, the first visitors to the Space Needle, accompanied by "female elevator attendants dressed in skin-tight gold 'spacesuits,'" made their way to the top of the structure to dine in the "Eye of the Needle," a restaurant that every fifty-eight minutes makes a full revolution above the city.[3]

After a year, I moved on to work at the Lutheran Compass Center, in an old mission on a prime piece of real estate overlooking the Puget Sound, at the edge of Pioneer Square, the city's original downtown. From its very beginnings, downtown Seattle was a contested space. When the city's first white settlers staked their claim to Pioneer Square in 1852, it had long been the wintering grounds of the Duwamish Indians.[4] While the 1855 Treaty of Point Elliott disposed of the original villagers' rights to the land, when they resisted their removal from downtown in 1856, launching an attack against the settlers, they were no match for the cannonballs lobbed from the deck of the U.S.S. *Decatur* anchored in Elliott Bay.[5] Two white settlers died in the fighting, but apparently the settlers did not bother to record the body count of the Duwamish and their indigenous allies.[6]

A few blocks south of the Lutheran Compass Center is Yesler Way, named after Henry L. Yesler, the city's first millionaire and one of its first mayors. Head up the hill on Yesler, and you come to Yesler Terrace, the "first racially integrated housing project in the nation."[7] Head back down the hill on Yesler, and you're traveling on the paved over path of the country's first "Skid Road," where the ancient forests of the Pacific Northwest, ringed by choke chains, skidded down through the center of Pioneer Square to Yesler's mill. Yesler would serve, for a time at least, as the dividing line between the city's rich and poor. By the 1890s, "the city's center of banking and commerce" was concentrated north of Yesler Way, where "[m]en in top hats and tails escorted wasp-waisted ladies to admire fanciful terra-cotta, intricate ironwork, and luminous marble halls."[8] South of Yesler became home to "boardinghouses and cheap working men's hotels," to the men who fashioned the "intricate ironwork," laid the tile, and the marble floors, and the women who fed them, laundered their clothes, and worked in bars and brothels around the city.[9] Though most of the Chinese workers, who would spent the better part of the 1870s laying the railroad tracks into Seattle, were expelled from the city in 1886 by an angry mob, by the turn of the twentieth century, Chinese workers made their homes once again in the city, beside "Japantown" south and east of Yesler.[10]

At the turn of the twentieth century, Pioneer Square was home to grand hotels and storefronts, as well as saloons and brothels. But by 1920, when the Lutheran Compass Center was built on Washington Street, just a block away from the original site of Yesler's mill, the square was losing ground as the city's economic center and becoming synonymous with "sin and ruin" in the public rhetoric of temperance crusaders.[11] The mission hadn't existed for long when the Depression hit, and the region's disposable workers, the broke and the broken, the disabled and the elderly came to roost amid the flophouses, the bars, pawnshops, and missions of Pioneer Square and gave new meaning to the business of going on the skid. Just south of the square, a few blocks from the Lutheran Compass Center and Yesler's mill, the city's unemployed, including a large number of immigrant workers, organized a multiethnic self-governing "Hooverville" that became home to more than 600 men and a handful of women.[12]

When I went to work at the Lutheran Compass Center Women's Program in 1985, Ronald Reagan was entering his second presidential term, and he was well into the business of implementing a succession of neoliberal "reforms." Neoliberalism was pioneered during the New York debt crisis of 1975, and in Chile in the 1970s, where the privatization of public assets, and the elimination of social security, was initiated by University of Chicago–educated economic and political advisors.[13] By the mid-1980s in the United States, labor, safeguards against corporate greed, and the social safety net forged in the New Deal—including public and subsidized housing programs first inaugurated under the auspices of the Housing Act of 1937—and in the Johnson Era "War on Poverty," were under attack. The fallout from these policies, exacerbated by the effects of deinstitutionalization and urban "renewal," was radiating across the country, and the ranks of the working poor, the elderly, and the disabled swelled the shelters and sidewalks of every major city in the country from Washington, D.C. to Los Angeles.[14]

In 1985, I worked graveyards, and while ferries moved back and forth across the Sound lit like private parties, I listened for hours to the stories of homeless women who had grown up in Seattle, mainly in and around Yesler Terrace, and the stories of women from cities, farmlands, and reservations from all over the United States, women who spoke of surviving experiences that were more domestic terrorism than domestic violence, of hitchhiking across country and riding the rails, working as RNs and CNAs, as carnies and in canneries, as secretaries, store clerks, as beauticians and construction workers, prostitutes, dancers, and writers, and the vast majority as mothers, wives, or caretakers of one sort or another.

Riding the bus one day in Seattle, I sat next to a homeless man who carried nothing but a brown paper bag, from which he pulled a hefty photo album—the kind you might find on a coffee table in someone's living room—and in the space between Yesler Avenue and Union, he showed me pictures of his past. The one that stands out in my memory is the portrait of him, circa 1969 or 1970, in his army uniform, all spit and polish. Among the few and heavy things homeless people carry, their stories about their lives and experiences are the most precious. Whatever Maslow might have to say about the hierarchy of needs, we cannot do without our stories. They are our lifelines, the cords that connect us with community and with ourselves; they are what enable us to thread together the past and the present.

I began the interviews for this book in 1991, in the immediate aftermath of the first Gulf War, out of a desire to explore oral history as a vehicle and medium that might serve to counter, challenge, and interrogate dominant beliefs about homelessness in the United States and the underlying assumptions that shape them. I came to this project with critical questions about the disparity between the truncated, and somewhat clinical, notes I was compelled to draft at the end of every shift at the Center, and the variety and complexity of the stories that women conveyed about their own lives. Along with personal stories that were variously poignant and profane, ribald, tragic, and hilarious, were recommendations about cooking, parenting, and operating heavy machinery; there were queries and insights on making meaning out of the suffering and violence the women witnessed and experienced, and about religion, spirituality, and sexuality. The women turned their analytical gazes on the many institutions they encountered in their lives that were variously charged with assisting, treating, domesticating, reforming, and rehabilitating "them." And they offered observations about and critiques of civil society in the United States and of the institutions, discourses, and policies that create and sustain homelessness and poverty in the United States.

Since the early 1980s, homeless people have been studied to death, and despite the existence of extended memoirs by homeless people, street newspapers, and publications like *Poor Magazine*, the voices of homeless people are rarely heard in public, academic, and mainstream media representations of homelessness except at best in brief quotes and fragments.[15] While notable exceptions exist, the disembodied analytical and homogenizing voice of the privileged "expert" more often than not drowns out the lived experience and situated knowledge of homeless and formerly homeless people. In embarking on this book, I wanted to not only help amplify these voices and perspectives, but also to move outside the narrative arc that typically shapes stories about homeless people. I didn't want to confine interviews to tracing experiences that seem to lead inexorably toward shelters or the streets. I wanted to provide narrators the space to represent their lives on their own terms, rather than assuming that homelessness defined their lives or identities. I began with the goal of conducting all the interviews with women who were current or former residents of the Lutheran Compass Center to demonstrate the richness and complexity of lives that might converge in any given shelter in the United States. My move to Portland, Oregon, in 1993 complicated work on the book, and after a decade-long hiatus between 1996 and 2006, I made the decision to more actively seek out and include the voices of women who'd been involved in some of the multiple—and intersecting—sites of cultural and political organizing that emerged within the ranks of homeless people in Seattle in the 1990s.

Public discourse on homelessness in the United States represents homeless people as the fitting objects of the expert clinical gaze, as "other." Single homeless people, whose family ties may be torn or tangled, who reject normative gender roles or the constraints of the nuclear family, are, moreover, arguably most apt to be alternately criminalized or pathologized in debates and policy discussions on homelessness. They are represented, implicitly or explicitly, as incapable of analyzing their own situation, as devoid of historical understanding and political agency. As David Wagner has observed, single homeless people are frequently seen as "vulnerable and dependent people worthy perhaps of sympathy but judged to be socially disorganized, disaffiliated and disempowered."[16] With notable exceptions, like Mitch Duneier's groundbreaking book *Sidewalk*, and Elliot Liebow's *Tell Them Who I Am, The Lives of Homeless Women*, the stories told about homeless people more often than not reduce their complex life experiences and social roles—as children, parents, spouses, partners, workers, artists and intellectuals, as political and cultural agents—to "case studies," and one-dimensional narratives that lead inexorably to shelters or to the streets.[17]

For the past thirty years in particular, public debates and policy discussions on homelessness have persistently overstated the pervasiveness of mental health issues and substance abuse problems among homeless people, in the face of substantial evidence to the contrary. While people with "severe and persistent" mental health issues and substance abuse problems are among the most visible and most studied of homeless people, and chronic homeless people, in particular, collectively they have long constituted less than half of homeless people in the United States.[18] And, as many researchers, along with advocacy groups like the National Coalition for the Homeless, have long contended, while mental illness and substance abuse certainly complicate individuals' ability to maintain stable housing, they do not in themselves *cause* homelessness. Homelessness is caused by lack of housing that is affordable, accessible, and appropriate for all of those who need it.[19] The situation is akin to a game of musical chairs in which "not only are seats gradually removed, but the number of players is progressively increased."[20] As Anitra Freeman puts it in my interview with her, "Personal problems don't dig the hole in the sidewalk; they just influence who is going to fall into it. It's systemic factors that create the hole." And those who are most likely to fall into the hole—to become homeless—are those who are least able, for a variety of reasons, to compete for scarce affordable housing and resources.

Housing, like health care, is a fundamental human right acknowledged in the Universal Declaration of Human Rights, adopted by the General Assembly of the United Nations in 1948, which includes the provision that:

> Everyone has the right to a standard of living adequate for the health and well-being of himself and of his family, including food, clothing, housing and medical care and necessary social services, and the right to security in the event of unemployment, sickness, disability, widowhood, old age or other lack of livelihood in circumstances beyond his control. (Article 25, Section 1)[21]

Mainstream media accounts and public policy debates on homelessness in the United States frequently fail to capture the gravity of the consequences for those who find themselves without a means of meeting the fundamental human need for housing. While mental health and substance abuse issues do not cause homelessness, with all its attendant forms of physical and psychological trauma, homelessness can—and does—cause and exacerbate mental health and substance abuse issues.[22]

The Structural Roots of Homelessness

While notable exceptions exist, and a wealth of critical literature has been generated on the subject, racist and classist assumptions about the individual pathologies of low-income and homeless people continue to strongly inform the practices of the social services and shelter providers. As Vincent Lyon-Callo, Jean Calterone Williams—and countless homeless people—have argued, homeless men and women are routinely subject to multiple and intersecting forms of surveillance and policing.[23] Shelters and social services routinely anatomize the behaviors and personal stories of homeless people, subjecting them to "refined diagnostic tools, statistical record keeping," and "categories of pathology."[24] Access to services is, more often than not, contingent upon demonstrating compliance with this framework, and noncompliance is invoked as further evidence of deviance and pathology.[25] Invasive and demeaning, these practices reinforce the feelings of guilt, shame, and vulnerability that routinely accompany homelessness.

For the past three decades, the emphasis on the individual pathologies of homeless people has provided a dose of rhetorical Prozac to middle- and working-class people in the United States. This emphasis has soothed our collective anxieties as we've stepped over bodies in doorways and anesthetized us in the face of early warning signs about the effects of the incremental structural adjustment of civil society in the United States. As the most vulnerable members of society, homeless people, as Anthony Marcus has observed, serve as "social barometers or canaries in a coal mine":

> They measure the amount of competition, the level of functioning that is necessary to survive, the displacement of those who must labor to live, and the degree

of comfort and security that we can claim…The question that the existence of poverty raises is: Do we really want to live in a society based on such severe competition?…Can we as a society really justify commodifying and parceling out such huge rewards and such stern punishments for social accomplishment and social failure?[26]

As a form of social punishment, homelessness is far sterner in many respects than sentences handed out in court for most criminal offenses. Particularly for those who are new to the research on homelessness, it is important to understand some of the policies and skewed public priorities that are sentencing more and more Americans by default to a condition, which, though cruel, is becoming far from unusual.

Over the past thirty years, deregulation, the financialization of the economy, corporate tax cuts and tax cuts to the wealthy, deunionization, and the loss of living wage jobs following the passage of North American Free Trade Agreement (NAFTA) in 1993, have all contributed to the development of an income gap nearly unprecedented in U.S. history. According to data released in a 2010 report by the Congressional Budget Office, between 1979 and 2007, "[t]he gaps in after-tax income between the richest 1 percent of Americans and the middle and poorest fifths of the country more than tripled," with "greater income concentration at the top of the income scale than at any time since 1928."[27] Over the last three decades, moreover, among Blacks in the United States, many of the hard-won economic—as well as political—gains of the civil rights movement have been eroded. A 2010 study by the Institute on Assets and Social Policy at Brandeis University documents a fourfold increase in the wealth gap between Blacks and whites between 1984 and 2007, from $20,000 to $95,000.[28]

The past several decades, moreover, have seen the progressive redirection of federal spending from investment in education, housing, social services, and domestic infrastructure to investment in the military and the prison industrial complex. The high domestic costs of war emerged as a theme in my 1996 interviews with Debra Martinson, and again ten years later in my interviews with Anitra Freeman, and with Marlowe, who demanded to know, "If they can spend billions to make a freaking weapon, why can't they help people?" In 1961, outgoing Republican president Dwight D. Eisenhower cautioned the nation that "the total influence—economic, political and even spiritual" of an "immense military establishment and a large arms industry," while "new in the American experience" was already "felt in every city, every State house, every office of the Federal government."[29] Eisenhower went on to warn against the dangers of "mortgag[ing] the material assets of our grandchildren," as well as "their political and spiritual heritage," to subsidize these interests.[30] Over the past five decades, we have seen the country's material, political, and spiritual assets repeatedly mortgaged, in wars fought disproportionately by poor people and people of color, with even more disastrous costs meted out on the succession of countries the United States has bombed and invaded. In his 1967 speech at Riverside Church, Martin Luther King spoke of seeing Johnson's poverty program "broken and eviscerated as if it were some idle political plaything of a society gone mad on war," concluding that "America would never invest the necessary funds or energies in rehabilitation of its poor so long as Vietnam continued to draw men and skills and money like some demonic, destructive suction tube."[31]

In 2011, a conservative estimate places the combined cost of the wars in Iraq and Afghanistan at over a trillion dollars.[32] This figure is in addition to baseline military spending. Economists Joseph Stiglitz and Linda Belmes estimate the long term cost of the war in Iraq to be considerably higher, at over $3 trillion. They note, moreover, that $1 trillion directed at domestic social spending "could have built 8 million additional housing units," covered a year of Head Start for 120 million children, "insured 530 million children for health care for one year; or provided 43 million students with four-year scholarships at public universities."[33] Factoring in interest on military expenditures, the cost of veterans' benefits, and other expenses routinely masked by federal estimates of tax expenditures, the War Resisters League estimates that 48 cents of every federal tax dollar is devoted to military expenditures.[34]

With workers increasingly struggling to stave off the threat of homelessness, more are compelled by the "economic draft" to look to the military as a way of keeping a roof overhead. Combat veterans—and their families—are disproportionately drawn from working class and poor communities and communities of color. Historically ineligible for draft deferments predicated on access to higher education, they are now compelled into service by the economic or "poverty draft" and by promises of job training, secure housing, and health care. Meanwhile, the Veterans Administration estimates that "one out of every three homeless men who is sleeping in a doorway, alley or box" in the United States on any given night is a veteran, and the "vast majority...come from poor, disadvantaged communities..."[35] Despite the organizing efforts of groups like the Western Regional Advocacy Project (WRAP), discussion of the economic impacts of the interminable and ever-expanding "War on Terror" are still routinely relegated to the fringes of public debates and policy discussions of homelessness and the economic crisis.[36]

Since the 1980s, prisons have increasingly served as one of the largest purveyors of publicly subsidized housing in the United States for low-income people, and people of color, with a corresponding massive transfer of wealth to corporations that increasingly serve as the cornerstone of the prison industrial complex.[37] The United States has seen "a dramatic escalation of the numbers of drug offenders in prisons and jails—a rise from 41,000 persons in 1980 to 500,000 today," an increase of more than 1200%.[38] "Nonviolent drug offenders now account for about one-fourth of all offenders behind bars, up from less than 10 percent in 1980." [39]

The fact that costs incurred by "the War on Drugs" and for housing nonviolent offenders in the prison industrial complex far outstrip expenditures for public and subsidized housing goes routinely unremarked in debates on homelessness and in conservative indictments of "big government." As Michelle Alexander has most recently argued, Reagan's War on Drugs, now entering its fourth decade, has been a singularly effective response to both the Johnson Era "War on Poverty," and the civil rights movement, which was rapidly evolving, at the time of Martin Luther King's assassination, into a "poor and working-class movement that cut across racial lines."[40]

In 2008, nationwide, the average operational cost per prison bed, not including the capital costs of prison construction, was almost $29,000.[41] In 2006, in Washington State the average operational cost of a prison bed was estimated at $27,000, with an additional "$11,000 per year per bed to amortize capital costs" of prison construction, for a total of $38,000 a year,[42] enough to cover four years of in-state undergraduate tuition at the University of Washington in 2010 with enough to cover the estimated costs of a year's room and board at the university.[43] An estimated $4 billion a year, or nearly three times the federal funds devoted to emergency services for homeless people, is spent on prosecuting "minor offenses" for marijuana possession alone.[44]

While for the present, homelessness is the focus of considerable media attention, the primary focus of the mainstream media is on "the new homeless," the embattled middle- and working-class people facing the prospect of foreclosure, and on families, in particular. These narratives implicitly, if not explicitly, construct "the new homeless" in opposition to the "other," older less worthy—if not criminal—class of "homeless people."[45] In the face of yet another "crisis" of American capitalism, such distinctions invoke myths about American meritocracy that are becoming more and more unsustainable, and that, as Anthony Marcus has argued, mystify the deep and persistent roots of social Darwinism in the United States.[46]

For all the public sympathy ostensibly directed toward "the new homeless," city governments have responded to the current economic crisis by enacting *more* statutes aimed at criminalizing poor and homeless people and excluding them from public spaces. A 2009 report by the National Law Center on Homelessness and Poverty and the National Council for the Homeless documents a 7 percent increase between 2006 and 2009 in laws prohibiting "camping," an "11% increase in laws prohibiting loitering" and "6% increase in laws prohibiting begging," in "particular public places."[47]

Similar measures were enacted in response to rising rates of homelessness during the economic recession in the 1980s and 1990s. It was in 1993, with unemployment at 11 percent that Rudy Guiliani was elected mayor of New York and began sweeping homeless people from the streets of New York City with a constellation of new statutes against loitering and camping in public places.[48] The increased mobility of capital in the 1990s, accelerated by the passage of NAFTA in 1994, saw the emergence of what Don Mitchell has termed a "war against homeless people in the name of global competitiveness."[49] In Seattle, as in New York, as Timothy A. Gibson has explored at length, the disorderly bodies of the poor and homeless were represented by developers, city administrators, and the media as undermining the comfort and safety of high-end shoppers, theater goers and condo dwellers in the city's increasingly upscale downtown core. Homeless people, in effect, undermined the image of Seattle as a "spectacular city," and a magnet for global capital.[50] City governments in Seattle and other major cities in the United States progressively responded in the 1990s to the swelling ranks of unemployed, underemployed, and underpaid workers—and their performance of "private" behaviors in putatively "public space"—by outlawing behaviors necessary for human survival, effectively outlawing homeless people themselves.

No definitive estimates exist of the number of homeless people in the United States at the turn of the decade; the most recent data—from January 2009's one-night count—identified 643,067 sheltered and unsheltered homeless people on a single night in the United States.[51] The widely cited estimate of 2.3 to 3.5 million homeless in any given year in the United States is based on data gathered in 1996, and does not reflect the upsurge in homelessness in response to the current economic crisis.[52] And while the U.S. Conference of Mayors Hunger and Homelessness Survey of December 2009 cited a nationwide increase of homeless families, reports of a "leveling or decrease" in homeless individuals in 16 out of 25 cities surveyed[53] have met with skepticism from homeless advocates and service providers. There can be little doubt, in any case, that the economic crisis—if not permanent economic decline in the United States—coupled with the foreclosure crisis, which impacts both renters and homeowners, is pushing more and more Americans into poverty and homelessness.[54]

Nationwide, more than 2 million households confronted foreclosure in 2007 and at least an equal number was projected in 2008–2009.[55] It may be some time before reliable data exists on how many people will end up homeless as a result. While corporate beneficiaries of multibillion-dollar bailouts under the auspices of the Troubled Asset Relief Program and the Obama foreclosure bailout post record profits in 2010, ordinary Americans have accrued few benefits from the federal expenditures.[56] Meanwhile, the effects of the foreclosure and broader economic crisis on ordinary Americans are intensified by the ever-expanding gap between wages and "fair" market rents (FMRs), and by cuts in subsidies to—and the progressive erasure of—low-income housing stocks.

In at least fifty cities across the country, FMRs were already far beyond the range of minimum wage workers in 2007. With the FMR at $670, a one-bedroom apartment averaging $756 and a two-bedroom $900,[57] at the national median income of $16, an individual needed to work only a couple of extra hours a week to afford a two-bedroom apartment at the federal standard of 30 percent of her or his gross income going toward rent. However, even with the seventy-cent increase in the federal minimum wage in July 2008, *a minimum wage worker*, by contrast, needed to work 90 hours a week to support a two-bedroom apartment, 79 hours a week for a one-bedroom apartment, and a "mere" 70 hours a week for a studio apartment.[58] A sudden reduction in work hours, or a trip to the emergency room—let alone job loss or a catastrophic illness—could easily tip the scale toward homelessness. The 2007 U.S. Conference of Mayors' Report on Hunger and Homelessness estimated the number of employed among the nation's single homeless at 13 percent, but these figures do not include those who were able to stave off homelessness—at least temporarily—by doubling up or couch surfing.[59]

The situation was and is even more dire for millions of unemployed workers and for the elderly and disabled on fixed incomes. At the *maximum* $637 a month in 2008, a Supplemental Security Income (SSI) check barely covered the rent of a studio apartment, let alone utilities and food.[60] It can take years for even severely disabled individuals to be approved for either SSI or Social Security Disability Insurance. As *The Oregonian* reported in 2008, "Portland's Social Security office has some of the nation's longest delays for benefits." In Portland—as in Seattle, and any number of other places around the country—"in the years-long waits some die before seeing a dime."[61] Washington is one of the few states to provide "general assistance unemployable" (GAU) benefits for people with short-term disabilities and for those who have not yet qualified for SSI or Social Security disability payments. Having narrowly escaped elimination in the 2009 round of state budget cuts, at $339 a month, the payments have remained virtually static since I worked at the Compass Center in the 1980s.[62]

If "fair" market rents are beyond the reach of millions of Americans, low-income housing stocks, which took a lethal hit during the Reagan administration, have been steadily declining ever since.[63] Between 1978 and 1983, the Department of Housing and Urban Development (HUD) budget was virtually gutted, dropping from $83 to $18 billion in constant dollars; in 2008, at $35.2 billion, the HUD budget was less than half the amount allocated in 1978.[64] Between 1978 and 2005, however, tax deductions for home mortgages—*which apply to not simply first, but second homes*—ballooned from $37 billion in 1978 to $122 in 2005.[65] And while from 1976 to 1982, HUD presided over the development of some 755,000 new public housing units, between 1982 and 2006, HUD built only 256,000 new units.[66] At the same time, single-room-occupancy hotels (SROs)—more commonly known as "flophouses"—long the mainstay of the urban poor, disappeared in droves in the 1970s and 1980s, with an estimated 1 million units lost across the country to "urban renewal, gentrification and the 'revitalization' of downtown areas."[67]

With allocations for Section 8 vouchers (which subsidize rents to private landlords) lagging far behind, and old units lost to condo conversions and demolition, Seattle is among the many cities nationwide that have adopted the grotesque practice of holding a lottery to see who will be awarded the privilege of a spot on the *waiting* list for Section 8 housing. In 2008 Chicago held a lottery for a shot at one of the 40,000 spots on a waiting list for Section 8.[68] It was the first time the waiting list had been opened in ten years. The estimated wait time? Depending on the number drawn, anywhere from a few weeks to ten years.[69] In Seattle in 2006, when the waiting list was opened up for the first time in four years, during a two-week window, 5,949 people competed for a chance at one of the 4,000 spots on the waiting list. Once on the list, the estimated wait was projected at anywhere from a few months to three years.[70] In both cities, as in many cities across the country, the long waiting lists mean that elderly and medically frail individuals in particular can—and do—die homeless before they secure a spot in publicly subsidized housing, even if they're lucky enough to win "the lottery."[71]

But the good news is that once you've been on the waiting list long enough to be deemed "chronically homeless," you may well qualify for emergency assistance provided under the auspices of the 1987 McKinney-Vento Act.[72] Since 2001, every city government seeking access to McKinney-Vento funds has been compelled to draft and promote its own "Ten-Year Plan to End Homelessness." But, as the 2006 report by WRAP observes, the plans are, in fact, quite limited in scope. Far from "ensur[ing] adequate, affordable and universal housing for all," the plans focus on providing housing—as well as supportive services—to *chronically* homeless people.[73] And while there is some evidence that the plans have, in fact, helped reduce chronic homelessness in urban cores in the United States,[74] the programs fall far short of providing a comprehensive solution to the growing crisis in public and affordable housing in the United States.[75]

While one might expect HUD to be at the forefront of efforts to shore up existing stocks in public housing, in 2010 HUD sponsored the most comprehensive legislation to date aimed at privatizing public housing in the United States, the "Preservation, Enhancement, and Transformation of Rental Assistance [PETRA] Act." The act would effectively auction off the remaining stocks of public housing in the United States to private landlords and corporations. The legislation would transform public housing into a profit-driven enterprise with taxpayers picking up the tab for jacked up rents, while more and more low-income people are forced into homelessness.[76]

The War against the Poor

Despite the spike in the numbers of homeless people in the last few years, in more than fifty cities—including Portland, Oregon, and San Francisco, considered two of the most progressive and "livable" cities in the United States—it's illegal to sleep outside. According to a 2009 joint study by the National Coalition for the Homeless and the National Law Center on Homelessness and Poverty, in almost a third of 235 cities in the United States, people can be charged for sitting or lying in "certain public spaces."[77] While courts have ruled it "cruel and unusual" to "criminally punish a homeless person for necessary life activities in public...if the person has nowhere else to perform the activity," cities continue to routinely enact and enforce ordinances against public sleeping.[78]

Sweeps of homeless encampments are routine in most cities; among the things that may get swept away along with your few remaining personal effects—your journals or the last of your family photographs—are "important personal documents and medication."[79] When you're homeless, "losing" your I.D. guarantees that your stay on the streets will be extended. It can set back your search for housing, a job, and social services for months. Lose your heart or blood pressure medication or your insulin and you just might lose your life or suffer a disabling heart attack or stroke.

Forty-seven percent of the 235 cities surveyed for the 2009 report, including Seattle, Portland, and San Francisco, "prohibit loitering in particular public places," and 19 percent "prohibit loitering city-wide."[80] Loitering laws selectively target homeless people and people of color. Every morning, I have to move to the edge of the sidewalk to dodge the crowd of diners obstructing the sidewalk as they linger over lattés at the corner cafe. If you're white and well-dressed enough, you can linger without loitering. You can camp on the sidewalk for days waiting for the release of a new Harry Potter book, the opening of a new Ikea Store, or tickets to the Rolling Stones "Postmortem Tour." The sidewalk is your oyster. If you're homeless and sleeping or sitting on the sidewalk, you can be arrested and charged, and if that happens, it is more than likely that you're going to rack up fines, more debts you can't pay, along with a criminal record, "making it more difficult to obtain employment or housing."[81]

As Kim Hopper has observed, the roots of contemporary welfare policies and practices toward homeless people lie in Elizabethan England, and the belief that "relief must be made so onerous and degrading that even the lot of the most menial laborer would seem preferable...If idleness could be turned to profit, or at least assured subsistence, how then could the ranks of 'free labor' be harnessed to arduous and ill-paid jobs?"[82] In sixteenth-century England, when peasants were forced off their land en masse to allow wealthy wooliers to fatten their flocks, poor laws—designed to preempt protest and ensure a docile pool of surplus labor—meted out penalties for pan handling and vagrancy that included "branding, enslavement, and execution for repeated offenders."[83] African Americans in the United States risked physical branding, torture, and death for trying to escape slavery, an institution that itself legalized systematic rape, sexual trafficking, and the torture of both women and men. To be homeless in the United States is to be branded both psychologically and physically. To be homeless is to confront daily reminders that you don't count for much in the world, that your life is disposable. For some, the recognition comes as a shock; but it's hardly news to those who are most likely to suffer permanent injury when they drop through the frayed social safety net to streets and alleys, the ones who are already wounded, who were beaten, raped, or psychologically abused in childhood, in their families of origin, in foster care, in juvenile detention facilities and mental hospitals.

The causal link between financial stress, sleep disorders, and "negative coping behaviors," including gambling and drug and alcohol abuse, is broadly acknowledged during periods of economic crisis, when the impacts are visited on the denizens of Wall Street and Silicon Valley dotcoms. But the effects of intergenerational poverty and homelessness are the stuff of long-term study, with action ostensibly to be deferred until the problematic of the chicken and the egg can be definitively resolved.[84] More often than not, "treatment" for the manifestations of poverty and its myriad traumas takes the form of incarceration; at best, the antidotes offered are individual—community mental health and drug treatment—rather than collective and structural. Predictably, moreover, mental health services and drug treatment programs have been among the first programs to get axed to balance local and federal budgets. Still, anyone who's experienced homelessness can attest to the fact that homelessness can, and does, cause mental illness and drive people to drink. Lose your housing in the United States and you run the risk of losing both your mind and your life.

While the effectiveness of sleep deprivation has gained considerable visibility in recent years as a preferred strategy among the various torture tactics practiced at Abu Ghraib, Guantanamo, and Bagram to break the minds and wills of prisoners of war, its disabling effects on homeless people are rarely, if ever, addressed in debates about and studies of homelessness. Documented effects of sleep deprivation range from "irritability, moodiness and disinhibition," "apathy, slowed speech, and flattened emotional responses," impaired memory and impaired decision-making, to "emotional irrationality," hallucinations, and bipolar disorder.[85] Even in cities where loitering laws and laws against public sleeping are only sporadically enforced, homeless people are frequently roused from their sleep and set on forced marches that can last all night and into the day.

When you're homeless, your bags are one of the things that brand you. Lockers are a precious commodity among homeless people. In the post-9/11 era when every bag is a suspected terrorist, bus station lockers are a thing of the past, and even if you're one of the lucky ones with a shelter bed to return to at night, the majority of shelters prohibit "residents" from storing their belongings during the day. Being homeless is like being on the longest most grueling shopping—or backpacking—trip of your life. And to compound the misery, like a number of the women whose stories are included in this book, there's a good chance you have already suffered a stroke, have sickle cell anemia, epilepsy, fibromyalgia, arthritis, or hypertension, or you are on the verge of liver or kidney failure.

Under the auspices of discouraging homelessness, countless cities across the country refuse to provide public bathrooms accessible to homeless people, and then prosecute homeless people for public urination. When your body or your bags brand you as homeless, your need for a bathroom renders you a regular supplicant to security guards at the library or city hall. Fast-food joints are the pay toilets of the homeless, and it can cost you an order of fries or a small coke every time you have to go. Use the same bathroom often enough and whether or not you're a paying customer, you're likely to find yourself barred. If you're homeless, an anxious night on the street, coupled with a bit of borderline mission food, can easily bring on a bad case of diarrhea. If you have irritable bowels, chronic incontinence, or something as pedestrian as the flu or food poisoning, the chances are good that you're going to soil yourself on the street, and you're going to have to wait at least until morning to shower it off. The chances are good that you're going to have to navigate through a gauntlet of gazes and verbal barbs as you walk or ride the bus to the mission, where you'll stand for an hour or more in one of those long lines that snake around the city blocks outside missions in the time-honored public pageantry of the poor, your marked body on public display.

Homeless people are moving targets, and the longer you're on the street, the more visible you become. Spend a single night homeless and you catch on quickly. You recognize the obvious: that a single night on the street can kill you. Stories about murders by "transients" are familiar enough in the mainstream media, but homeless people are far more likely to be prey than predator, and when they are murdered, the stories are more often than not buried in the back pages. In 2004, two teenagers in Milwaukee, Wisconsin, beat to death a homeless man named Rex Baum, using rocks, bricks, a pipe, a baseball bat, and the barbeque grill from Baum's campsite, smeared their own feces on his face, "cutting him with a knife 'to see if he was alive.'" They wedged Baum's head in his barbeque grill before heading off to dinner at McDonalds.[86] The 2009 report of The National Coalition for the Homeless, "Hate, Violence and Death on Main Street USA," is filled with accounts of homeless people assaulted—or killed—for sport. The report documents 880 assaults against homeless people between 1999 and 2008, including 244 murders.[87]

The spike in incidents in recent years seems to be fueled in part by the popularity of "Bumfights," a series of videos that feature footage of chronically homeless men pummeling each other for the price of a bottle; a popular spin on Crocodile Dundee, with a "Bum Hunter" in safari gear, shows a man "'tagging' homeless people by pouncing on them and binding their wrists."[88] Until recently, you could rent copies at Hollywood Video. The director of a homeless shelter in Fort Lauderdale, and publisher of the monthly street newspaper, *Homeless Voice*, reported that "Kids are even starting to videotape themselves hurting homeless people."[89] In 1999, a forty-seven-year-old homeless man named David Ballenger was stabbed and beaten to death in Seattle by three teenagers, one of whom reportedly told a friend, "Let's just say there is one less bum on the face of the Earth."[90]

You don't have to watch "Bumfights" to get the message that homeless people are nothing more than garbage, human litter, a public sanitation problem. Many of the women I interviewed spoke of the way in which their own experiences of homelessness had fundamentally altered their perspective on "civil" society in the United States, calling into question truths they had once held as self-evident about fundamental rights to life, liberty, and the pursuit of happiness. As my former housemate, Debra Hill, a founding member of Portland's Dignity Village, who was homeless off and on for more than two decades in Portland, puts it, "You don't feel like anybody gives a shit. You don't feel like you're human, and you feel like as far as far as [people who are housed] are concerned, you could die out there and nobody'd give a damn one way or another."

Seattle Organizing:
SHARE/WHEEL, Women in Black and *Real Change*

Figure 1   WHEEL/Women in Black Vigil

When I began interviews for this book, street newspapers were springing up around the country, challenging stereotypes about homeless people and catalyzing political organizing among the unhoused and their supporters. Focusing on the issues of poverty, homelessness, and housing policy, and featuring work by homeless reporters, columnists, poets, and short fiction writers, street newspapers now exist in some forty cities throughout the United States, and in many more cities internationally.

With a circulation of over 18,000 in 2010, Seattle's street newspaper *Real Change* provides a source of income, purpose, and dignity for more than fifty homeless and formerly homeless vendors.[91] For almost two decades, *Real Change* has provided a critical counterpoint to the city's "aggressively pro-development mainstream media,"[92] keeping the struggles for economic justice and affordable housing, the preservation of public space, and the civil rights of homeless and low-income people at the forefront of public debates around the future of Seattle's urban core. And together with the Women's Housing Equality and Enhancement League (WHEEL)—and Women in Black—*Real Change* has been instrumental in raising public awareness of violence against homeless people and of the deaths of homeless people on the streets of Seattle.

WHEEL's roots go back at least as far as Thanksgiving of 1990, when an ad hoc group of homeless and formerly homeless supporters erected the city's first tent city in decades, not far from the site of Seattle's original Hooverville. The inhabitants of Seattle's tent city dubbed their group SHARE—or Seattle Housing and Resource Effort—and over the space of two or three weeks, according to WHEEL's only paid organizer Michele Marchand, their encampment just south of the King Dome (the site now of "Safeco Field") had grown to 180 residents. SHARE members refused to disband the tent city until the city government agreed to provide shelter for all 180 tent city participants.

In 1993, WHEEL was officially born when an anonymous community member, observing that the leadership of SHARE was predominantly male, donated money for an organizer to work exclusively with women and ensure that homeless women's needs and perspectives were taken into account in organizing campaigns. Under the auspices of WHEEL, with support from SHARE and allies in the social service providers, the women mounted letter-writing campaigns and organized rallies to pressure the Seattle's mayor and the Seattle City Council to expand the operating hours for shelters and day centers and provide women-only floors in subsidized housing. As Michele Marchand recalls, "within six months they won every single plank in their platform. Every single one of them." Over the course of the next few years SHARE and WHEEL successfully pressured the City Council to cede buildings and funds to support several more shelters.

When in 1993, the Seattle City Council, bent on creating a more hospitable climate for shoppers—and investors—in the city's downtown core, followed New York and Los Angeles in adopting a series of ordinances targeting various forms of "incivility" among homeless people, including "sitting on the sidewalk,"[93] SHARE/WHEEL were at the forefront of challenging the laws. When the City Council moved to more aggressively prosecute individuals in violation of Seattle laws against public camping,

SHARE/WHEEL organized public sleep-outs, with homeless campers and housed supporters risking arrest and jail time to challenge the laws and agitate for more shelter to address the city's homeless crisis.

From 2005 to 2006 WHEEL and SHARE waged a campaign to enable residents of SHARE/WHEEL shelters to withhold personal identifying information required by "Safe Harbors," King County's computerized "homeless population information system."[94] The information is routinely required of homeless people around the country as part of the federally-mandated "Homeless Management Information System" (HMIS). HUD identifies the purposes of the HMIS system as enabling "unduplicated count[s] of homeless persons, understand[ing] patterns of service use, and measur[ing] the effectiveness of homeless programs."[95] Despite assurances that "all personal client information is encrypted and is not identifiable in the database, thereby ensuring privacy for clients,"[96] SHARE/WHEEL resisted participation in the program and in so doing confronted the possibility of the total loss of city funding. "[T]he Safe Harbors computerized tracking program," SHARE/WHEEL argued, was discriminatory and violated the right to privacy of homeless people seeking services; activists also cited "the impossibility of peer-run organizations facilitating such tracking."[97] The City and SHARE/WHEEL ultimately agreed that in lieu of participating in the Safe Harbors system, SHARE/WHEEL would undertake "voluntary monthly surveys of shelter participants."[98]

In 2008, twelve Seattle churches served as home to self-governing SHARE/WHEEL shelters. While "Tent City One" and "Tent City Two," as they are now known, were relatively short-lived, "Tent City Three" and "Tent City Four" have for several years now rotated among the parking lots and grounds of some fifty area churches, synagogues, and secular organizations. Seattle University has also hosted Tent City Three on campus. Today SHARE/WHEEL is arguably the largest and most cost-effective provider of emergency shelter in the Pacific Northwest.[99]

In addition to working with SHARE to coordinate the tent cities and shelters, WHEEL coordinates the Women's Empowerment Center, a self-managed organizing arts and cultural center. The organization publishes a twice-monthly newsletter, and in 2007, a joint effort with the Seattle-based Whit Press culminated in the publication of *Beloved Community: The Sisterhood of Homeless Women in Poetry* (Seattle, WA: Whit Press, 2007), which features poems by women interviewed here, including Anitra Freeman, Janice Connelly, Mona Joyner, and Roxane Roberts. WHEEL sponsors an annual women's forum, which recognizes the skills and contributions of homeless women to the city and serves as a platform to launch the group's political campaigns. WHEEL's 2008 campaign focused on the expansion of emergency shelter and on the creation of a "homeless place of remembrance," to commemorate the deaths of Seattle's homeless and raise public awareness of the lethal consequences of homelessness.

The murder of David Ballenger and the serial killings of three women camped in Pioneer Square prompted WHEEL to begin organizing under the auspices of the international Women in Black movement to call attention to the deaths of homeless people in one of the most livable cities in the United States. The Women in Black movement began in Israel in 1988 when Jewish women, who were subsequently joined by Palestinian women, began protesting against Israel's occupation of the West Bank and Gaza. Vigils have since sprung up in countries in Africa, in India, Colombia, and Mexico, and all over Europe, to protest war and violence, especially violence against women.[100] Women in Black is a decentralized movement, rather than an organization with a "constitution or a manifesto," and as such the focus of the vigils varies somewhat from place to place.[101] The Seattle vigils are the only Women in Black vigils internationally to focus exclusively on the deaths of homeless people. As a whole, the movement is rooted, however, in a "feminist understanding: that male violence against women in domestic life and in the community, in times of peace and in times of war, are interrelated," and in the understanding that "[v]iolence is used as a means of controlling women."[102]

While many communities across the country have long held annual services to mark the deaths of homeless people in their midst—with the National Coalition for the Homeless designating December 21 as "National Homeless Persons' Memorial Day"—Seattle's WHEEL/Women in Black has, since 2000, held vigils *each time* a homeless individual dies outside or by violence. The group has now stood to honor the lives—and call attention to the deaths—of more than 400 people. WHEEL/Women in Black vigils spurred Health Care for the Homeless in Seattle-King County to begin publishing a "King County Homeless Death Review" in 2003.[103]

Participants in the Women in Black vigils regularly congregate before and after at Mary's Place, which until its demolition in 2008, was located in the basement of a Methodist Church directly across the street from the Columbia Tower and just a few short blocks from City Hall. The church was also the site of a men's shelter operated by the Compass Center. Founded by Jean Kim, a Presbyterian minister, who worked as a social worker at the Compass Center in the 1980s and experienced homelessness first hand as a child growing up in Korea, Mary's Place has long been a partner in WHEEL's organizing efforts. On Saturdays, Mary's Place transforms into the Church of the Mary Magdalene, an ecumenical Christian community that embraces lesbian, bisexual, and transgendered women as congregants and as ministers, and returns again and again to the parallels between the suffering of Christ and the struggles of homeless people, and of homeless women in particular.

Like so many of the women that I encountered during my years of working at women's shelters, the women that I interviewed for this book, whether or not they were explicitly involved in political organizing around homelessness, were, with few exceptions, concerned not simply with their own struggles, but with the broader struggles of women, men, and children confronting homelessness, poverty, and violence.[104] If, as Jessie Pedro observes in my interview with her, there ought to be a "school that prepares women to be homeless," in the absence of a formal training program, women often stepped up to help orient other women new to homelessness.

Homeless and low-income women often provide countless hours of uncompensated social services, advising each other on which agencies can be counted on to help and which can be counted on to serve up condescension, blind alleys, and bad leads. They know, as only those who've experienced homelessness first hand can, the potentially catastrophic consequences of a wasted bus ticket or a wasted afternoon. From their standpoint in shelters or on the streets, they glean situated knowledge that is invaluable to others struggling to survive homelessness. And they know that the struggle is immeasurably compounded by daily reminders that their lives are disposable.

Disposable Lives: Workers, Women, War, and Violence

The treatment of homeless people as disposable commodities is inextricably linked to the treatment of workers as disposable resources. The history of institutionalized racism in the United States has played no small role in maintaining a captive workforce of low-wage workers. In pitting whites against people of color, the racial caste system in the United States has served as a crucial impediment to labor organizing, while severely constraining educational, employment, and investment opportunities for people of color in particular.

Racism emerges as a theme in my interview with Janice, who grew up on a reservation in the Southwest, and Loann speaks of the reminders she encountered growing up of the long history of state-sanctioned terrorism against Blacks in the United States. Roxane, Loann, Flower, and Arnette all came of age in Seattle's Central District, which, like the city's Chinatown, was shaped by racially restrictive real-estate codes, redlining, and systemic housing discrimination.[105] The GI Bill, including Veterans Housing Administration loans and educational loans, has been credited with the expansion of the middle class in the United States in the aftermath of World War II. However, few African Americans, Native Americans, Latinos, and Asian Americans were able to access these benefits, which have continued to provide long-term, intergenerational economic benefits to white families in the United States. The persistence of racial discrimination in housing, banking, and home loans is, of course, well-documented,[106] along with the disproportionate impacts of the subprime lending and foreclosure crises on Black communities throughout the country.

Mona and Jenny come from mining families in predominantly white communities, in Harlan, Kentucky, and Butte, Montana, respectively, where workers weathered black lung and mining explosions to put food on the table. While mining has long been the locus of union struggles, in the age of deindustrialization, access to health care remains limited for mine workers and their families, who bear the costs of corporate practices that exploit both workers and land with impunity. Like reservations throughout the West, which are scattered with toxic mining debris and military ordinance, the mining towns in which they grew up have been treated as "national sacrifice zones."

Mona's story, which touches on the unsolved 1999 murder of her fiancé, José Lucio, a Mexican day laborer, speaks to the economically precarious status—and progressive dehumanization—of low-wage indigenous workers who have been driven north in increasing numbers in the wake of neoliberal policies beginning in the

1980s. Accelerated by the passage of NAFTA in 1994, neoliberal policies have devastated the Mexican economy, flooding it with cheap U.S.-produced corn, imported crops and goods, and opened up indigenous communal lands for mining, logging, and other environmentally devastating practices by transnational corporations bent on economic "development."[107] Like early English poor laws, the primary function of policies that criminalize undocumented workers, while mystifying the root causes of Northern migration, is to maintain a captive, exploitable, and stigmatized pool of surplus labor.

A number of the interviews raise questions about the impact of military service on working families. While an extensive body of research exists on the effects of posttraumatic stress disorder (PTSD) on military veterans, far less attention has been paid to the impact of domestic violence on wives, partners, and children of veterans and on the intergenerational impacts of military-related PTSD. However, a 1992 study of 1,200 Vietnam veterans and 376 of their wives and female partners found that "children of veterans with PTSD were substantially more likely to have behavior problems" and concluded that "a veteran's PTSD is a major source of family dysfunction."[108] A 1999 segment on *60 Minutes* ignited a fire storm of controversy in claiming that "the rate of spousal assault in the military is significantly higher than the national average," citing "Pentagon records from 1992 through 1996," which indicate that "military spouses were victims of domestic violence [at] a rate five times higher than the civilian population when compared to Justice Department records for the same five years."[109]

A number of the stories collected here speak to the power that normative gender roles exercise in women's lives. They speak to the strength and pervasiveness of myths about white knights and picket fences and about the nuclear family as a safe space, rather than at its worst, a space of coercion, abuse, and terror.[110] Results of a 2005 survey by the Centers for Disease Control (CDC), the most comprehensive survey to date on intimate partner violence in the United States, indicate that nearly a quarter of *all* women in the United States (23.6 percent) have experienced sexual or physical assault at the hands of husbands, boyfriends, or girlfriends.[111] Battering cuts across socioeconomic lines, but women living below the poverty line suffer from the highest rates of intimate partner violence (35.5 percent).[112] While control is a central motivation in battering, economic stress is believed to exacerbate domestic conflict.[113]

Many of the women I interviewed spoke of having been beaten, raped, or psychologically abused in childhood, in their families of origin, in foster care, or in juvenile detention facilities and mental hospitals. Studies have demonstrated that women—and men—who have experienced childhood sexual and physical abuse are more likely to suffer from mental health and substance abuse issues and end up in abusive relationships as adults.[114] Women—and men—who are abused by intimate partners are also at substantially higher risk for "'disability and activity limitations, [including] asthma, stroke, arthritis, and, in women, heart disease."[115] Any one of these factors can undermine a person's ability to walk the economic tightrope that is the lot of more and more Americans.

Every year battered women's shelters are forced to turn away thousands of women; they necessarily prioritize women facing imminent threats of violence and in need of a confidential location.[116] Battered women from the ranks of the working poor who are lucky enough to access space at domestic violence shelters face the same long waits for low-income housing that confront other women among the ranks of the working poor, the disabled, and the elderly. The absence of living wage jobs, coupled with a lack of affordable and low-income housing, can trap women into a seemingly endless cycle of abusive relationships.

Tens of thousands of women who are forced to sleep outside on any given night in the United States are at risk of being raped or murdered, whether it's by a boyfriend, husband, partner, or stranger. In a 2001 survey of 974 homeless women, 34 percent of the women surveyed reported having experienced major violence—defined as "being kicked, bitten, hit with a fist or object, beaten up, choked, burned, or threatened or harmed with a knife or gun."[117] Half of the women moreover "were assaulted no less than twice that year."[118] In a separate study, 13 percent of homeless women surveyed reported having been raped in the past year, with more than half having been raped at least twice.[119]

Homeless women are studied in the art of urban camouflage; both their physical and psychological survival depends on looking like they have a home to return to.[120] Women who are visibly homeless are subject to continual sexual harassment and sexual assault on the street. Every "offer" of money for sex carries the threat of rape on the street. These kinds of daily threats and indignities are routine in the lives of homeless women, and they exact a heavy psychological toll. Those who are forced to sleep outside and don't have men to protect them (which can easily create its own set of problems) work hard to make themselves invisible at night, which makes one-night street counts wholly unreliable at estimating the numbers of women on the street. Seatttle's one-night street count of homeless people in January 2008 identified 1,976 people sleeping in cars and motor homes, in doorways and alleys, under bridges and overpasses, in the bushes and in the brush throughout the city, including 141 women and 1,158 people whose gender was undetermined.[121]

Women who cope with homelessness by "couch surfing"—who go uncounted in one-night street counts and are excluded altogether from federal definitions of homelessness—end up being pressured into sex and relationships; they are battered, sexually assaulted, and/or murdered—by men who offer them safe haven from the streets. It should come as no surprise that some women who end up homeless are coerced into prostitution. In a study involving 130 people who had engaged in prostitution in San Francisco, 84 percent "reported current or past homelessness." Of those surveyed, "Fifty-seven percent reported that they had been sexually assaulted as children and 49% reported that they had been physically assaulted as children."[122] Working in prostitution, they were repeatedly raped, beaten, and retraumatized. Between 1982 and 1998, forty-eight women who'd worked as prostitutes were murdered in Washington by the "Green River Killer," a man who later professed," I wanted to kill as many women I thought were prostitutes as I possibly could."[123] How many of those women were homeless and would be alive today if they'd had a roof over their head on the night they were murdered, we'll likely never know.

Adults who have little or no access to mental health treatment, therapy, or anti-depressants often resort to illegal drugs to cope with trauma, grief, or feelings of hopelessness. Those who try to excise their bad memories with a needle or a pipe find themselves in an endless cycle of abuse, addiction, and incarceration. Canadian physician Gabor Maté illuminates the link between childhood trauma, and addicts' attempts to numb, medicate, and distance themselves from deep-seated feelings of worthlessness and despair. A Hungarian-born child of holocaust survivors, who has spent two decades as a physician working with addicts on Vancouver's skid row, Maté draws connections between the intergenerational traumas borne by children of Holocaust survivors and those borne by skid row addicts, including the institutional and state-sanctioned abuse suffered by First Nations people. Connections between broader forms of political violence and addiction are, however, largely ignored or marginalized to specialized subfields in the dominant—and largely ahistorical—theories on the links between addiction and homelessness.

Roxane Robert's story in particular raises questions about both the human and economic costs of incarcerating nonviolent drug offenders. Since Reagan picked up the mantle of Nixon's "War on Drugs" in 1982, two years prior to the emergence of the much-publicized crack cocaine "epidemic," rates of incarceration in the United States have quadrupled; "the number of people incarcerated for a drug offense is now greater than the number incarcerated for *all* offenses in 1980."[124] Rates of incarceration in the United States now exceed those of every other country in the world,[125] outstripping Poland, our nearest "competitor" by more than a three-to-one margin.[126] "According to U.S. Department of Justice statistics, from 1986 to 1996 the number of women sentenced to state prison for drug crimes increased tenfold, from 2,370 to 23,700."[127]

The primary, if not exclusive casualties of the "War on Drugs" have been poor people and poor people of color in particular. "As a result of a variety of law enforcement practices and policies, people of color are far more likely to be subject to drug arrests than are whites who use or sell drugs" and garner harsher sentences.[128] Until the passage of the Fair Sentencing Act of 2010, despite the fact that the drugs have identical pharmacological effects, "simple possession of 28 grams of crack cocaine yield[ed] a five-year mandatory minimum sentence for a first offense; it [took] 500 grams of powder cocaine to prompt the same sentence."[129] People of color represent more than 60 percent of those incarcerated for drug-related offenses in the United States.[130] The 884,500 African Americans incarcerated in the United States in 2009 represented a ninefold increase over the 98,000 incarcerated in 1954, the year of the landmark *Brown v. Board of Education* decision.[131] As Michelle Alexander observes, "huge segments of ghetto communities [have been] permanently relegated to a second class status, disenfranchised, and subjected to perpetual surveillance and monitoring by law enforcement agencies."[132]

Poor people, whose primary line of legal defense against prison terms lies in the hands of overtaxed public defenders, are pressured to "plead guilty to crimes they did not commit because of fear of mandatory sentences."[133] Penalties for felony drug convictions extend well beyond the walls of prison and keep ex-offenders locked in a cycle of indebtedness; frequently saddled with heavy fines and court costs, they confront "'one strike' housing policies that make it difficult to obtain and remain in public housing" and they are rendered ineligible for educational "grants, loan or work assistance." In many states, moreover, they are "permanently bar[red]...from receiving federal cash assistance and food stamps during their life time."[134]

A 1999 report by Amnesty International cited widespread "violations of the internationally recognized human rights of women incarcerated in *prisons* and *jails* in the United States of America." Violations cited in the report include "rape and other forms of sexual abuse; the cruel and inhuman and degrading use of restraints on incarcerated women who are pregnant or seriously ill; inadequate access to treatment for physical and mental health needs; and confinement in isolation for prolonged periods in conditions of reduced sensory stimulation."[135] Long after their release, both Roxane and Elizabeth continue to contend with traumas they experienced in prison. Roxane continues to suffer from the health effects of medical neglect at the Washington Corrections Center for Women (WCCW), also commonly referred to as 'Purdy.' Following the death of prisoner Gertrude Barrow, for a "ruptured peptic ulcer," in 1993, prisoners at WCCW filed a class action lawsuit, *Hallett v. Payne*, that cited a "litany of health care horror stories." WCCW "settled the case immediately."[136]

Standing for Douglas
Dawson and Tonya "Sonshine" Smith

In July 2006, I attended my first Women in Black vigil, which marked the death of a fifty-year-old amputee named Douglas Dawson. On June 23 2006, Dawson had been sleeping outside in his wheelchair on the streets of Spokane when he was deliberately set on fire. He died a few days later at Harborview Hospital in Seattle. Dawson's murder earned more media attention than most who die on the streets; it was the focus of a few articles in the *Seattle Times* and the *Post-Intelligencer* (PI). PI columnist Robert L. Jamieson reported, "When emergency dispatchers first sent word to fire crews, they had no idea a human being was even involved. The airwaves initially mentioned a trash fire." Dawson, wrote Jamieson, had been "lit up like a human candle." "'Trash' fire turns out to be a man,'" read the headline.[137]

Mona, who was homeless at the time, choked back tears of rage when I interviewed her following the vigil. "This man only had one leg and they set him on fire. This is what society has become. If that man had had housing, more than likely he would be alive today..." Of her involvement in Women in Black, she felt compelled to observe, "Just because I'm a homeless person doesn't mean that I can't be involved or that I don't want to change things or help people. That's just a natural part of me, that protecting and wanting to make their lives easier for them if I can. That comes from love. I mean, you love your neighbor, you know? Why do people hate homeless people? Why?"

A couple of days later I was back home in Portland when I got a call from Michele Marchand. Women in Black was gearing up for another vigil. A forty two-year-old woman named Tonya Smith, known as "Sonshine" to the women of Mary's Place, had been stabbed and left to die in the "hobo jungle" just outside the International District.[138] She'd dragged herself from the blood-spattered cardboard that had been her bed for the night, out of the brush, the blackberries and the brambles, and onto the sidewalk, where she died and where the garbage collectors found her body just before dawn. I'd seen Sonshine a number of times at Mary's Place, but we had never spoken. I knew who she was by the description of the bruise that ran down one of her cheeks from a recent beating. She was a regular at Mary's Place and she'd stopped by the Women's Empowerment Center a day or two before she was murdered. She told the women of WHEEL that all the shelter beds in the city were full and that the thought of spending the night on the street terrified her. And she asked about the progress of the city's Ten Year Plan to End Homelessness.

At the memorial service before the Women in Black vigil in Tonya's memory, women line the fraying couches of Mary's Place that are tilted to face the choir and the makeshift altar. Women around the room are leaning against each other, literally crying on each other's shoulders. Rev. McLaughlin, "Marcia" to the women, invites anyone who wishes to come forward to say a few words about Tonya and light a candle in her memory. As the women file to the front of the room to speak, grief and outrage come together in the women's voices. Mona inveighs the women to join in the Women in Black vigils. "If it wasn't for the Women in Black, who would stand and weep when we're gone? We beg the Mayor for a visit with him," says Mona, choking back sobs and raising her quavering voice to rally the women. "It's time we quit crying. It's time that the jungle no longer exists. It's time we're no longer treated as animals. How would you feel if this was your mother? How would you feel if this was your sister?"

Then "Flower" steps forward to speak. I'd already interviewed Flower a couple of times. Abandoned along with her older sister in early childhood, and prostituted by her foster parents from the age of eight, Flower had recounted her life to me with a mix of pain and detachment, but without any hint of bitterness. My next interview with Flower would be in a rehabilitation facility in 2007, where, at the age of forty-seven, she would be recovering from her second stroke, suffered on her way to an appointment at the Seattle Housing Authority. The day I visited her, she interrupted the interview to marvel at the flowers that another visitor had brought by, and then asked that I refer to her in the book as "Flower."

Coming forward during the memorial service to light a candle in Tonya's memory, "Flower" had this to say to the women of Mary's Place: "I feel like all you women that's come into my life, you're all sisters to me, and I have a deep affection for all of you. I really know the Creator is listening, and I know Sonshine had a lot of beauty in her and I know the Creator would want to know that... I just hope we all make it..."

In the evening, after the vigil across from City Hall, Women in Black gather at a bus stop under the freeway overpass at Eighth and Jackson, Flower dressed in her Sunday best, Mona cradling a bouquet of flowers, a mix of sunflowers, mums and daisies donated by one of the vendors at Pike Place Market, and Anitra lugging along a couple of gallons of water. When everyone is assembled, the women make their way across a parking lot edged with weeds and broken glass to the corner of Tenth and Weller and on down to the encampment at the bottom of the hill, where they take turns dipping a leaf into a wooden bowl and scattering drops of water like tiny lights across the grass and the garbage and into the thicket where Tonya crawled on the last night of her life, looking for shelter.

Methodology: the Nuts and Bolt of Interviewing and Editing

I chose to focus these interviews on women in particular because I have spent far more time in the company of homeless women than homeless men. I did not want to limit interviews to tracing events or factors that led women to be homeless, or to assume that homelessness had been a defining experience in their lives. Rather I wanted to provide narrators an opportunity to listen to the women's accounts of their lives in their own words.

Even before I began consciously seeking out women involved in organizing, my selection of subjects was not random. From the beginning, I sought out women who seemed particularly interested in speaking about their lives and experiences. Among the early interviews conducted in the 1990s, I specifically sought out interviews with both Pam and Anna Tailfeathers, whom I remembered from my time at the LCC. Debra Martinson and Elizabeth Thatcher were identified by LCC staff as women they thought would be willing to speak about their lives and experiences.

While Mary's Place started out as merely a convenient place to interview women involved in WHEEL, I was quickly drawn to the community of women who congregated there and some of the women with whom I struck up conversations, and whose interviews I included here, turned out to also be involved in *Real Change*, and/or WHEEL, and most had participated at various points in the Women in Black vigils. At Mary's Place, like at LCC, I was formally introduced to the women at house meetings, and on some occasions, staff and regulars introduced me to women they thought might be interested in being interviewed. Other women, including "Flower," Roxane, and Marlowe, I met sharing meals, participating in group discussions, and hanging out in the smoking area outside the center. In the cases of both Roxane and Marlowe, I wanted to interview them precisely because of the vocal social critiques they voiced when I first encountered them.

Early interviews were each conducted over the course of two days, sometimes separated by a week or two between interviews. I came at these early interviews without any set questions; rather I opened by sharing my own critique of narratives that objectify homeless people and reduce their stories to "case studies," and invited each woman to speak about memories, observations and insights she wanted to share with the public. I tried, as much as possible, to confine myself to follow-up questions to try to fill in details. I approached the book in this way in the hope that it would challenge stereotypes about "the homeless" as an identity category, enabling readers to recognize the obvious: that people who experience homelessness are first and foremost human. Their stories speak to common experiences of the working poor, the disabled, the elderly trying to survive on fixed incomes; they speak to the common experiences of women confronting sexism, racism, and classism, and struggling to overcome the trauma of sexual abuse and violence. Their struggles to make meaning of their lives and to create community have broader value, moreover, for anyone searching for meaning in an increasingly nihilistic consumer culture that views human life as a disposable commodity.

I have organized the interviews in rough chronological order beginning with interviews conducted in 1991, followed by interviews from 1996, and finally from the period between 2006 and 2008. Over the course of close to two decades, I interviewed more than thirty women. In some cases, I deemed that a narrator was incapable of giving informed consent. While all of the women whose interviews are included in the book have suffered traumas to varying degrees, I aborted interviews with women whose storytelling seemed in danger of triggering old traumas. In a number of cases, given the mobility of homeless people, I was unable to reconnect with narrators after conducting one or more interviews.

As much as I worried about preserving the confidentiality and anonymity of some of the women, I grappled with issues around authorship and attribution. All too often, those who study homeless and other disenfranchised and oppressed communities make paternalistic assumptions about "protecting" informants, without providing narrators with a choice in the matter. While the use of pseudonyms and unattributed accounts remain standard practice in studies of homelessness, many of the women I interviewed, particularly those who have repeatedly been interviewed in the media or spoken out publicly on homelessness, were strongly invested in claiming their own stories from the beginning. More stepped forward after they read through their own stories. I have honored the women's wishes here.

However much I tried to limit my own questions, confining them as much as possible to the work of mapping more intricately narrative trajectories chosen by the narrators themselves, my questions have to varying degrees shaped the women's stories as they appear here. In working with the transcripts, my practices as an editor reflect Michael Frisch's seemingly paradoxical assertion that "the integrity of a transcript is best protected, in documentary use, by an aggressive editorial approach that does not shrink from substantial manipulation of the text."[139] The majority of the women I interviewed were involved in the daily work of finding shelter or housing, meals, medical care, or food stamps; they were always running off to attend classes, support groups, to care for grandchildren, sick friends, or loved ones. Interviews were abruptly terminated and restarted. I lost contact with narrators, in some cases reconnecting after a year. Narrative threads were broken, sentences at times trailed off, and stories were revisited from multiple angles over the course of several interviews. Some of the interviews are condensed down from as many as 90 pages of transcripts. As is invariably the case in oral history interviews, narrators jump from topic to topic, theme to theme; their stories cross time and place. In most cases, I've imposed a measure of linear chronological order on the stories to make them more accessible to the reader.

I tried as much as possible to hone in on stories and observations that seemed most important to the women themselves, listening for repetition, expressions of outrage, grief, and humor, and moments when the women's voices seemed to erupt out of the realm of prose and into poetry. In every instance but one—in the case of "Sweet Pea," whom I have not spoken with since I interviewed her in 1996—the women were able to read through draft chapters—though rarely the final version— and suggest editorial changes. But that experience is quite different from working with the raw transcripts. Had the women themselves worked directly with the transcripts of the interviews, they would undoubtedly have made different editorial decisions than I have done here.

My own interventions as an interviewer and editor are, moreover, one more remove from the women's own editorial decisions in deciding which stories and observations to approach during the course of my interviews with them. These decisions were influenced, no doubt, by how they interpreted my motives as a white academic, and the brevity or longevity of my connections with them.[140] The later interviews in most cases reflect more long-standing connections with narrators, particularly those active with WHEEL, and with Women in Black, with whom my research was more participatory in nature. I stood with them through vigils for Tonya Smith and Doug Dawson, and videotaped events to assist them in the work of creating archival records of their annual women's empowerment luncheons in 2005, 2006, 2007, and 2009. And I arranged trips for them to present on their organizing work at conferences at Washington State University Vancouver, where I teach, and Portland State University across the river in Oregon.

History, whether based on archival records or oral narratives, is inherently subjective in nature, forged, in its simplest terms, in a conversation between the past and the present. As Alessandro Portelli has noted, oral memoirs, more frequently than written documents, including written memoirs, are more frequently seen as vulnerable to the "distortions of faulty memory."[141] As he notes, however, "While written memoirs of politicians or labor leaders are usually credited until proven to be in error, they are as distant from some aspects of the event which they relate as are many oral history interviews, and only hide their dependence on time by assuming the immutable form of a 'text.'"[142] And the social standing of narrators plays no small role in the authority and factual status conferred upon accounts, whether oral or written.

At the same time, however, as Portelli also notes, oral narratives may be "told over and over again, or discussed with members of the community," in ways that may help "preserve a textual version of an event."[143] Undoubtedly a number of the stories that women recounted to me had been told and retold, to friends, therapists, and confidantes, and in the communities they variously forged among other homeless women, in shelters and drop-in centers, in long waits in social service offices, and in more public settings through their work as political organizers. In some cases, while I might have heard the same stories from a woman two or three times over the course of interviews broken up by months or years, the stories remained nearly identical.

Particularly where the stories recounted here bear upon public institutions, or where clear documentary evidence exists to corroborate or complicate the narrators' accounts, I've made some attempts to frame the stories with references to those records. Some of the women whom I came to know best, most notably Roxane and Mona, readily offered documentation to corroborate their stories. Roxane encouraged me to access court records and undertake phone interviews that would help substantiate her story. However, because people who are homeless—particularly for protracted periods of time—routinely encounter skepticism and invasive forms of inquiry, for the most part I chose not to seek corroboration for stories or probe apparent inconsistencies, which were frequently addressed or resolved when a more complete narrative emerged.

The skepticism that chronically homeless people, in particular, frequently encounter from social service providers, health care providers, police, and the broader public, is due, at least in part, to the fact that they are rarely afforded the opportunity to tell their stories in detail. Even those who are well steeped in the literature on homelessness, in structural, statistical and ethnographic analyses, can remain largely unaware of the multiple traumas that chronically homeless people often confront in the course of a lifetime—both prior to and in the course of homelessness itself. Anyone who has worked closely with homeless people for any length of time has heard war stories. But like medics in a warzone, they are not about to stop and take pictures, and like so many homeless people, they're too exhausted at the end of the day to write about the suffering they've witnessed.

Some of the narrators whose stories appear in these pages, and who expressly rejected the use of pseudonyms to mask their identity, accuse family members of sexually assaulting them. Particularly where accusations relate to events that are separated from the present by decades, and where no physical evidence or eye witness accounts can be mustered to support the accusers' claims, criminal prosecution or civil redress is notoriously difficult and rests on sorting through multiple and conflicting memories and accounts. To my knowledge, none of the women whose stories are recorded here have attempted to bring criminal charges against their assailants, but I have let these accusations stand in what may be for some one more step toward pursuing future legal channels for redressing these claims.

As Sandy Polishuk observes in framing her oral history of radical organizer Julia Ruutila, "Everyone, consciously or unconsciously, creates a persona to present to the world, a face that may be different depending on the context and the audience."[144] The women whose stories are collected here are no exception. At times stories that we tell about our lives that foreground defiance, resistance, and fighting back, whether metaphorically or literally, may be attempts to reframe the story to compensate for moments of vulnerability and trauma. Depending on how we imagine our stories, we may variously foreground socially transgressive acts or minimize or gloss over incriminating details. Again the women here are no exceptions. At times, in the interest of informed consent, I voiced reservations about including details that seemed to me potentially incriminating. While a handful of the women clearly reveled at times in these details, framing themselves as outlaws and rebels, others were committed to including them in the interest of honesty. In this respect, their narratives are far afield from the silences and self-serving omissions and gaps in memoirs of so many public figures, who minimize their histories of serial marriage and divorce, marital infidelity, and domestic violence, and write out altogether their struggles with drug and alcohol abuse.

Many of us will never know the strength and determination it takes to get through a night of homelessness, let alone the years, if not lifetimes of struggle that these narrators have endured. Storytelling is, as Portelli says of memory, "an active process of creation of meanings."[145] These women's stories testify to their persistent struggle to assert the value of their own lives and experiences in the face of a social order that, for all its sentimental rhetoric, treats their lives as disposable commodities. I'm grateful to every one of them for sharing their stories and for allowing me to join in some small measure in their struggle.

CHAPTER 2

"Mama Pam"

Pam was one of hundreds of women whose stories I heard in the mid-1980s as a counselor at Lutheran Compass Center. When I embarked on the book, the staff agreed to locate her for me, and she readily agreed to be interviewed. When I first met Pam in the 1980s, she was the process of recovering from one of many strokes she suffered beginning in her late twenties. It was clearly work for her to maintain a grip on her cane, let alone make her way across a room. A raconteur with a Texas twang, Pam embraced storytelling as her preferred form of physical and occupational therapy. If many of her stories dealt with growing up in small-town America in the 1950s and 1960s, the experiences they touched on seemed about as far from Lake Wobegon as you could possibly get. It was clear that Pam had begun honing her gift for storytelling and for standup comedy as survival strategies that enabled her to subvert, survive, make light, and make meaning of physical and emotional violence dating back to her early childhood.

Like so many children in military families, Pam's family moved frequently—from Missouri to London to Texas, and in Texas from city to city and town to town—so that whatever consolation or order Pam found in school was always short-lived. Pam was raised Catholic, and came of age in the late 1960s, prior to the 1973 Roe v. Wade *decision legalizing abortion. Having no access to sex education or birth control either at home or at school, Pam became pregnant for the first time at 17.[1] She reports that she was coerced into signing adoption papers while she was still under the effects of the sedation she had received during labor.*

If Pam's job options as a working-class woman were limited, they became more so, when she became pregnant again two years later and was expelled from nursing school on a morals clause. Small wonder, then, that Pam saw marriage as the only option that would enable her to keep and raise her child. Like her mother before her, financial dependence played no small role in keeping Pam in a marriage in which she endured years of battering. When she was raising children in the 1950s, Pam's mother did not, in fact, have the option of going to a battered women's shelter. In the United States, the earliest battered women's shelters did not emerge, along with "consciousness raising" about battering, until the women's movement of the late 1960s.[2]

In 1999, I ran into Pam at Rose Haven, a drop in center for homeless and low-income women in Portland, that she visited periodically to pass the time and get out of her Section 8 apartment. I was able to share with her what was then a lengthier version of her story, but the chapter would go through considerable changes before I would talk with her again in 2009 by phone. She moved again shortly after we spoke and it would be December of 2010 before I was able to locate her again to enable her to review the final version.

"I've always said there was a little gypsy in my soul. I don't like being in one spot too long."

I was physically and sexually abused by my father and then emotionally and mentally abused by my mother. I think I'm a fairly well-adjusted person. Considering what I've been through, it's a wonder I'm not in Western State [Hospital]. We moved around a lot when I was a kid, 'cause Dad was in the service. I always said there was a little gypsy in my soul. I don't like being in one spot too long.

I became homeless in Florida. I've been on the streets of St. Petersburg, Florida. I've been on the streets in Dallas, Texas. I've been on the streets in Phoenix, Arizona; in Tucson, Arizona; in Virginia, and Seattle. I guess that about covers it. I've hitch-hiked all over the country. It started with running away from an abusive husband and just continued. And I tend to repeat this pattern of getting involved with abusive men—alcoholic abusive men. And they always have to be run away from.

My mother was complaining once about my last husband—she said, "Well, your father never put me on the street." I said, "Well, Mother, that's only cause you didn't have enough sense to leave him." She said, "I never had to stay in a shelter." I said, "If you'd had any sense and self respect, Mother, you would have left him more than once. And stayed."

I can understand why Mom didn't leave—up to a point. First of all, she wasn't aware of the options. People are more aware especially of domestic violence since movies like *The Burning Bed* and the like. And second, she had seven kids. And like she once told me, "How am I going to raise you all by myself?" You know? Back then a woman without a partner was nothing—wasn't even a human being hardly. A woman was just *part* of a partnership. My identity has always been linked either to my husband to my children or to my parents.

It's really terrible, the shame they make you feel when you're homeless, especially if you're battered and abused. You're really made to feel shame and guilt. "After all, you must like it, or you wouldn't stick around for it." Which is a bunch of bullshit!—in plain English. "*Well*, if you didn't like it, why didn't you leave a long time ago?" Well sometimes you can't leave.

My sister S., she's been married twice. She's been divorced from her first husband three times. She met him through my father. He was a work buddy of my dad's. They were both machinists. Dad brought him home to introduce him to S. They got married, and on their wedding night, W. beat the *living daylights* out of her. She ran and locked herself in the bathroom, and he put his fist through the bathroom door and pulled the towel rack off the wall and beat her with that. She came home on her wedding night with a broken nose, and a black eye and a split lip and teeth knocked out. And our daddy said, "You married him, you go back to him." That's all there was to it. "He's your husband, you go with him. You're not staying here." *And she went back!* What choice did she have? He wouldn't let her stay there.

I've been in several abusive relationships. The worst one I left him nineteen times in eighteen months, and he found me eighteen times out of nineteen. Well, the nineteenth time I ran *him* off with a butcher knife. I finally came down to it: "Well, we're going to have to fight violence with violence here." He was beating on my head with a wooden cutting board, but he screwed up when he cornered me in my own kitchen, 'cause I reached over the sink, and I picked up the first thing my hand hit, and it was a butcher knife that was about a *foot* long and *brand* new. And I put the point to his belly and I said, "Come on chicken shit, hit me again!" I said, "Well *what's* the matter—you don't want to hit me no more?" I said, "You hit me again you're going to end up pinned to the wall behind you." I said, "Come on, 'cause I'm fixing to cut your liver out. And I just might take your heart with it." I had gotten to the point where I just was not going to take it anymore. If I had to kill him to put a stop to it, I was going to kill him. I had been with him nearly two years. He was a preacher when I met him.

"He was in uniform, holding the suitcase and the six pack of beer, and I just stood there at the door with my mouth open."

I was thirteen when my father came back from Vietnam. He was in a special unit—in communications. So he didn't really see action. He was in a combat zone, but he didn't have to carry a gun or anything like that. So I can't blame it on 'Nam. There's no way to blame it on 'Nam. He wasn't over there but maybe a year—eighteen months.

It was on a Saturday morning. We were cleaning house, getting it ready for him to come home. The front door was propped open, and the screen was closed and locked. There was this knock on the door. He was in uniform, holding the suitcase and the six-pack of beer, and I just stood there at the door with my mouth open. My mother looked at me and said, "Who is it?" And I just looked at her, and she come running over, and he said, "Well is somebody going to let me in?" So we let him in, and him and Mom sat down on the sofa.

I was wearing my typical blue jeans and white tee shirt. He's sitting there with a can of beer in his hand, and I walk across the room, and he says, "Well, it's about time we put a bra on that girl." And she says, "Well she's been wearing one for a year." He says, "Well it *looks* like it." It was very embarrassing for *me* for my father to notice my developing body. It was embarrassing.

Daddy was a *binge* alcoholic. On Friday—on payday—he'd disappear. Take the car, the checkbook and his paycheck, and he'd be *gone*. Sometimes for a night or two, sometimes for a *week* or two.

I saw my father put his fist in my mother's face when I was fourteen years old. That was the first time I'd seen him hit her. When I confront her with it, she still tries to deny it. I said, "You all woke me up with your yelling and screaming and fighting in the middle of the night. I got up to go to the bathroom, and just as I walked past your bedroom door, I saw him plant his fist in *your* mouth. So I *know* what I saw." I'd be under the covers. I'd bury my head so I didn't have to listen to the yelling, and the punching, and the crying, and the screaming, and the carrying on. Sometimes I'd go in the back bedroom with the little kids and hide back there with them. I'd just hold them while they cried. And we'd just all sit and cry together. You know, what else could we do?

Mom had seven kids to take care of, and she didn't feel she could do it by herself, so she put up with whatever the hell she had to put up with it in order to keep her family together. Which sucked. *Two* unhappy people *cannot possibly* raise happy children. The kids are left with a sense of guilt: "Well Daddy's doing this to Mama and Mama's letting him do it because of us." It became our guilt, our fault.

The sexual abuse started when I was thirteen. I guess I should have been old enough to handle it by then. My mother, she was working nights at the post office, which was really convenient for Daddy. At fourteen, I was raising five of his kids, keeping his house, cooking his meals. No wonder he thought I was supposed to fuck him too. I mean, shit, I did everything else a wife did except that. A couple of months before my seventeenth birthday, I went to Mom, and I said, "Will you *please* keep Daddy out of my bed?" She said, "What do you expect me to do about it?" She said, "I can't raise you kids by myself," and she turned around and walked off. I blame it as much on her as I do on him. He was sick—he had a problem. But it was within her power to force him to get help.

But she was a busy woman. She had an alcoholic husband and seven kids. She was one of eight children herself. And her attitude toward sex, that's a whole other story. You know, she was never told anything about it by her mother, so she didn't feel that she needed to tell *us* anything about it. My sisters and I learned by trial and error. I had a baby, gave it up for adoption and was *still* six months pregnant when I got married. It was lack of information. Bad girls don't get pregnant. It's the uninformed girls—the ones that don't know about contraception or anything else that get pregnant.

My mother always told me how ugly I was. So my father's sexual advances let me know that maybe I wasn't *quite* as ugly as Mama always told me I was. I still believe I'm ugly. It's a fact of my life. My first husband—every time I'd start to put on my make up, he'd start laughing and say, "Pam, forget it. The only hope for your face is to blast and start over from scratch." It was sort of an unspoken fact in our family that if you're pretty you can have anything you want. All you gotta do is catch the right man ...

"They sent a *psychiatrist* in to talk to me, and this shrink sits there, and he says, 'Now tell me,' he says, 'Why did a pretty young girl like you try to kill herself?'"

We were in [a Texas town] for nine years, longer than anyplace else. I was happier there than anywhere else. I had friends that were *friends*. The guys liked me and didn't just want to get in my pants. That's why I hated to leave there so much. Senior year, that's a *really* hard year to switch schools, to switch towns, and switch schools.

I've always been a friendly person, because moving around as much as we did, if you didn't make friends fast, you didn't make friends at all. I learned real quick how to get dates, how to get asked out. You want to go out, you put out. It's as simple as that. Up until then I was an uninformed, innocent, naive little virgin. My senior year all that changed—drastically.

The thing is, I'd go to bed with almost anybody. As long as I didn't care about him. Because the boys that I *liked*, I wanted them to respect me. One of them raped me. It was a date rape. He said, "You've been giving it to everybody else, and damn it, you're going give it to me!" And I ended up getting pregnant. Then while I was stashed in the home for unwed mothers in Dallas, my mom and dad had him—and they knew who it was—and his new girlfriend over to the house for Sunday dinner...

The first baby I had *was* a premie. She only weighed four pounds eight ounces. They took her away from me—in the delivery room. I never saw her in the delivery room and never saw her again. They told me she had red hair, and I wished they hadn't told me that even, you know. But I have a penchant for red hair now. When I die my hair to cover up my gray hair, I always dye it red. I've got a thing about red hair.

Back then, for most girls their only option was get married and leave home. You didn't find too many runaways back then or too many girls getting a job and moving out on their own. So I figured some day some man would come along sooner or later and rescue me. And carry me off on his white charger. And then I'd have my own house.

I've OD'd six times. The first time I was six months pregnant. I OD'd on feornal capsules with codeine. I had it for my headaches. I had migraines since I was four, which they figure now were probably caused by the aneurism. I overdosed to try to get away from the house and almost made it that time. I had felt the baby move for the first time that night, and I knew they were going take her away from me. At the hospital, they gave me a dose of epicac. *Finally* they decided they were going have to pump my stomach, you know—do a little gastric lavage. So they proceeded to stick that damn tube down my throat, and I pulled it out four times before they decided to tie my hands behind my back underneath the table. And during all this, I am screaming and crying. "Leave us alone and let us die! No one wants me *or* my baby!" And my mother hoping the earth would just open up and just swallow her, because after all the trouble she'd gone to hide my pregnancy, here I am broadcasting it. And this was her biggest concern—was her embarrassment over my pregnancy, and the fact that I wasn't married, you know?

They sent a *psychiatrist* in to talk to me, and this shrink sits there, and he says, "Now tell me," he says, "Why did a pretty young girl like you try to kill herself?" I said, "Well"—smart ass that I am—I said, "Well Doctor, I'll give you a little bit of case history and see if you can't figure it out *all by yourself.*" I said, "I'm nineteen years old, I'm not now, never have been, married. I'm pregnant for the second time. My parents forced me to give the first baby up for adoption. They're trying to take this one away from me, and I'm not going to let them. I'm afraid to go to sleep at night because my father won't keep his hands off of me. Do you have enough information yet or shall I continue?" He said, "No I think I can figure it out." I said, "Oh how very astute of *you.*" I mean, you know, it doesn't take a *genius* does it?

I had gotten kicked out of nurses' training because of my pregnancy. They couldn't get away with it nowadays, but back in the 60s they could. I was a "bad influence." They kicked me out on a morals clause, which now seems silly, but it was a *very* real fact of life back then. I just didn't feel like I could support my child and provide for my child alone. So I married the wrong guy.

A few years after we got married, he got out of the service, and we moved to New York, so I've always lived far away from my family ever since then. I started working as a nurses' aide when I was sixteen. I'm a licensed LPN with a lot of experience as a charge nurse in nursing homes.

I was twenty-six when I had the first stroke—from a cerebral aneurism. Well, they assume it was congenital. They don't know if it was from a blow on the head or what. After my stroke, the people I was working for when I got sick promised me that when I got well, I would have a job there. The administrator said, "Well, we promised her a job when she got well, and now you're going hire her back." The director of nursing still called me into her office after a week and said, "Pam, we can't have a nurse here that carries a cane." I said, "Hell, I don't care if I'm carrying ten canes—*as long as I'm doing my job.* What's your problem?" And she said, "Pam, pack your stuff and go home. Get out." So I was fired. After my first stroke, I applied for social security benefits, and I got turned down. So I just took the first denial and accepted it. I didn't even appeal it. I didn't know the ins and outs of what you could do then.

I was with my husband *sixteen* years. One of his girlfriends called me up here from Florida, and said, "Pam, was J. violent with you?" I said, "Do you mean did he ever hit me? You're going to have to define 'violent.'" She said, "Yeah, did he ever hit you?" I said, "D., well, I've got to tell you this: In sixteen years, he tried to choke me three times, and he tried to run me over with a car once, but no, he never hit me." You know, I mean, how violent do we have to get here? You know, is choking okay or does it have to be hittin'?

I made plans to leave, but usually I'd become self-destructive. I'd OD to get away from the situation, end up in a hospital, in the psych unit. After the sixth stroke— the hairy one—I had brain surgery. My husband divorced me, and he got custody of the kids because I was in a wheelchair. They gave me a choice: "Either go back to

Texas with your mother, or go to a nursing home." So I went to Texas. *Bad* decision. That was in '80. It was a bad move to go back to my mother's in Texas. I would have been better off in a nursing home.

"The preacher thought my head was a wrecking ball, and when the cops got there, he was trying to knock a concrete wall down with it."

I worked a year and a half to get out of the wheelchair, and then I went to Florida. I was thirty-five. I just wanted to get away from my ex-husband and that scene. He wouldn't let me see my kids. I met the preacher at a mission in Florida. He was working there. The pastor who ran the mission threw me out and fired him, so we ended up out on the street in St Petersburg, Florida.

Now you talk about *abusive*. That preacher fellow was *abusive*. I took beatings in the head with crescent wrenches. He broke a broomstick across my back once. He knocked me down, and then he kicked me with those steel-toed construction boots—in the belly and the solar plexus. I have had some beatings. He came after me with a knife in a motel room. I held a pillow up in front of me to keep him from cutting me, and he sliced up the pillow and almost got me too. He reminded me of my father for some reason.

Believe it or not, the preacher put me on the street. And if I came back without enough money, he'd give me a black eye and send me back out. And if I came home the second time without enough money, he'd give me another black eye. Now honey, a whore with two black eyes makes even less money than a whore with one black eye. He liked to dog me—he liked to watch me. And you can't pick up a trick with a man following you.

The first time I went out, the guy turned into a regular. He was a *nice* guy. He used to take me over to Tampa—take me out to nice places for dinner. He tried to talk me into leaving my old man, and I should have listened to him. I should have run then, but I didn't have enough sense to do that. It was too new in the relationship—it hadn't gotten bad enough yet to run. It's got to get bad enough before you run. You keep thinking that you can work it out. There's that old saying that there's a little bit of bad in the best of us and a little bit of good in the worst of us. I thought, "Well, he's the worst of us. There's got to be a little bit of good in there somewhere. All I've got to do is stick around long enough to find it." But I don't know that there was any good in him *at* all. What he did to me—I've got brain damage. They don't know if the brain damage is from the strokes or from the beatings. I forget things. I can remember what happened yesterday, last week, or last month or last year, or even ten years ago. But I have a really difficult time remembering five minutes ago.

Down in Florida, I called the cops. The preacher thought my head was a wrecking ball and when the cops got there, he was trying to knock a concrete wall down with it. They came out, and they said, "Lady if you don't quit screaming, we're going take you to jail." The only way I got away that time was I took my false teeth out and threw them in the street. A car ran over them. I've had new teeth made since then. But I got a chip in my bottom plate, and everybody'd say, "How'd you get that chip in your bottom plate?" And I'd say, "That's where a car ran over it." "Well how did a car run over it?" And I'd say, "Cause it was in the middle of the street." "How'd it get in the middle of the street?" "I threw them there." "Well that wasn't a real smart thing to do," my brother said. *Well*, I thought it was *real* smart—when I took my teeth out and threw them in the middle of the street, he quit hitting me and went after my teeth. My teeth were chipped, but my head was in one piece. I thought it was a real smart thing to do. I thought I was doing real well.

"Everybody thinks that all carnies are dirty, nasty thieving..."

I traveled for the carnival for years. I was a ride jockey on kiddie rides. I also worked as an agent in some of the games. I don't like working the games—it's too much like stealing. You've got to hustle too much. You've got to con people. And I don't like it. I'd rather run a ride. People go in. They lay their money down for a ticket. They know what they're getting. And they get what they pay for.

Everybody thinks that all carnies are dirty, nasty thieving—whatever—and it's not true. They are *hard* working people trying to make a living just like everybody else. And it's long hard hours and not too much money. I used to put in fourteen-hour days for ten dollars a day. That ain't very much—you got to love what you're doing to do that.

I was the oldest female on the show at that time. I was thirty-six. So all the boys, all the young ride jocks, always called me "Mom." They also called me "the Nicotine Queen," cause when I was in the ticket box selling ride tickets, you could see the smoke signals coming out of the ticket box. Everybody's got their nicknames. There was "Shakey" and "Blackjack" and "Dog." And we used to get into it.

They had a certain amount of respect for me, because *I did not* have to tear down and rack the rides, being a woman. The boss had called a meeting on the merry-go-round one day for all the kiddie land ride jocks. There were about four of us women in the outfit; the rest were guys. And he said, "Okay, you ladies don't slough." "Slough" is tearing down rides and getting ready to move. After the meeting, I walked up to him. I said, "Wait a minute—are you paying the guys more than you're paying me?" He said, "No, matter of fact, you're making about ten dollars a night more than they are." I said, "*Then I'll do the same damn work they do.*" I said, "I ain't a lady—I'm a jock. *And jock's slough.*" I said, "I can't lift that heavy equipment, but I can unscrew a light bulb and wrap poles as well as any man. I'm making the money. I'll do the work."

When I was traveling around the country, I used to make some damn good money at truck stops. The truckers call them "coin-operated beaver." I had money in my pocket. I stayed fed. I had clothes to wear. I had cigarettes to smoke. I was fine. It was survival. It makes absolutely no sense whatsoever to sit on a gold mine with an empty belly. No sense whatsoever. Back then AIDS wasn't an issue. Gonorrhea and syphilis. I have had gonorrhea once, thanks to my first husband. Ain't that a kick in the head?

"See, the guy that raped me was dumping his own shame and guilt on me, and I refuse to accept it."

Do you realize as of today I've been sober for three thousand four hundred and nine days? I like big numbers. I haven't had a drink since May fifteenth of '82. I go to an AA meeting and bake a birthday cake for myself and take it to a meeting. And brag about it. I like the meetings up at the Morrison best. They're not a bunch of refined ladies and gentlemen up there—they're just a bunch of street drunks.

Not a day goes by that I don't think about drinking. But you know, giving an alcoholic who's been sober a couple of years an award for staying sober for one more day is like giving a cowboy with a boil on his butt an award for not getting on his horse. He don't get on his horse 'cause he knows it's going to hurt. I don't take a drink 'cause I know that if I take one drink—just one—I am going to die somewhere in an alley, drunk, with a bottle in my hand.

My father was an alcoholic, which is why right now the smell of beer just turns my stomach and makes my blood run cold. So when these guys come up wanting to kiss and hug on me and smell like beer, I just say, "Get away!" I mean it's an immediate turn off. The most abusive one that I ran off with the butcher knife was an alcoholic. I refused to drink with him, and he beat me with a metal studded belt until I went into a convulsion. Then he dragged me by the ankles, and he locked me in the closet for three days. So I have gone to the line for my sobriety, and I don't allow anything or anybody to threaten my sobriety.

Two years ago this coming January, I was raped in my own apartment at the Morrison. Well I don't shower everyday anymore. I'm sorry, I *don't*. I get a little ripe sometimes. And I don't comb my hair, and I don't wear make up. It's kind of like I make myself as unattractive as possible. Which is silly—because rape doesn't have anything to do with attractiveness or sex.

He took a lot more from me than just a piece of ass—he took my self-confidence, my freedom to go where I want and do what I want when I want. He robbed me of that. Primarily he robbed me of my self-confidence in being able to take care of myself. But what can you do? The guy that raped me was dumping his own shame and guilt on me, and I refuse to accept it. He can pack his own shame and guilt. Just like my mother was dumping her own shame and guilt on *me*.

There's *a lot* of education needs to be done out there about rape. Rape is about violence and control and power and domination. That's the only purpose sex serves in rape—is to humiliate and degrade you. When I finally called rape relief after he left and told them the entire story from beginning to end, the counselor that I had gotten a hold of asked me if I'd ever had a course in or gone to a seminar in survival—in rape survival. I said, "No, why?" She said, "Cause you used every survival technique we've ever taught." I said, "Well I guess I'm just instinctively a survivor."

CHAPTER 3

Annamarie Tailfeathers

I met Annamarie when she was a resident of the Lutheran Compass Center, where she was known as something of a hell-raiser. The staff at Lutheran Compass Center contacted Anna at my request. It had been several years since I'd last seen her or spoken with her when I sat down to interview her at her apartment in 1991, where signs posting rules governing the use of the phone provided evidence of Annamarie's practice of providing shelter to friends who were still on the street.

The search for community, acceptance, and love emerged as central themes in my interview with Annamarie. For Annamarie, the nuclear family was a nightmare of abuse and a setup for abandonment. If she found some connection with other children in institutions where she was placed following her parents' divorce and her mother's remarriage, it was among the homeless teens and adults in L.A. in the 1970s, where she migrated after either aging out or running away from the "home" in her mid to late teens that she first found community and acceptance.

Far more than any other woman that I interviewed for the book, Annamarie had spent substantial time sleeping outside and explicitly self-identified as a "street person," even though she was housed when I interviewed her. In refusing to repudiate her identification with "street people," despite her housed status, Anna was insisting on her common humanity with the most stigmatized members of society. Linked by the common experience of abuse and abandonment by their families or its surrogates in social services, they had been deemed deviant, damaged beyond repair, and thus disposable. For Anna, the label "street person" marked her seemingly permanent separation from and rejection of mainstream myths about family and "civil" society in the United States. In 1991 Anna represented substance abuse among "street people" as symptomatic of their internalization of abuse and oppression.

While there are undoubtedly police who do their best, within the parameters of their jobs, to look out for the security and well-being of homeless people on their beats, referring them to shelters, treatment, and other social services, Anna's account of a Seattle police officer beating a man to death is an extreme example of the kind of brutality that homeless people frequently witness—and experience—at the hands of police. The police shooting of John T. Williams on August 30, 2010, serves as a recent example. Indian Country Today *reported that Williams, who was "hobbled" by arthritis and nearly deaf in one ear, was "shot in the span of a minute," when he didn't immediately respond to a police order to drop the three-inch carving knife he carried along with a block of wood.*[1] *A "long time Seattle resident and a Ditidaht member of the Nuu-chah-nulth First Nations of Canada's Vancouver Island," Williams "was a seventh generation master carver" who was well known in downtown Seattle, and routinely "carried his carving tools with him, and carved in public."*[2] *In Portland in September 2006, Portland police officers beat to death James Chasse, a 42-year-old man who suffered from schizophrenia and whose disheveled appearance identified him as possibly homeless, though he was not. Chasse suffered "16 broken ribs, a broken shoulder and sternum, and massive internal injuries" when Portland Police, suspecting him of the crime of public urination, chased him down, tackled, beat, and kicked him before a crowd of witnesses.*[3]

Anna's account of having a Seattle Police officer ask her if she "enjoyed" being raped speaks to the kinds of struggles that many homeless women—and particularly women who are visibly so and known to the police—may encounter in reporting sexual assaults against them. Anna's story of subsequently meting out an ostensibly life-threatening beating to one of her assailants demonstrated her resistance to being categorized as a victim and her defiance of normative gender roles.

Annamarie also touched briefly on her involvement in Operation Homestead, a grassroots campaign in the late 1980s that helped organize the unhoused and their housed allies in a multipronged campaign that coupled legal challenges with sustained building occupations to preserve SROs slated for demolition and conversion. In a phone interview, John Fox, an activist and organizer with Operation Homestead in the 1980s and now executive director of the Seattle Displacement Coalition, informed me that the first building occupation on New Year's Day of 1987 immediately followed the Lutheran Compass Center's annual memorial service for those who died homeless on the streets of Seattle.[4] *Whether it was through her involvement in organized resistance to the demolition of low-income housing, in confronting police abuse, or in nursing other victims of assault on the street, Anna took pride in asserting the humanity and basic human rights of other "street people."*

"The reason why homeless people give up is people don't listen to very reasonable, quiet talk. They'd be willing to talk quietly if people would listen...."

My name is Anna. Known as A.T. to the people of the big wide world known as the streets. A city within a city in any city. Isn't it a pity? We are a community within a community, a city within a city, a culture within a culture, several cultures within a culture. There's thousands of us.

There's three levels to a pie: the lower crust, the filling, which can be sweet, and the upper crust, which keeps it moist. Well, it's the same way with society. There's your street level, or the bottom of the crust, which is still useful. Then there's your upper crust, like the president, the Congress, the senators and all your people that have the bucks to keep things rolling. And then there's the middle class, which is sickeningly sweet, because they're in the middle. Their hands are tied because the upper crust has basically the political pull.

I feel that just like all the levels of the pie make a whole pie, street people are just as useful as the upper crust or the middle of it. You've got your day laborers or people who work at the market. Have you ever gone down to the market, seen people sitting there with their booths, painting, doing their pottery, and sharing culturally what they have? Some of them are homeless. I mean anybody can become homeless.

But they don't listen to us. We don't have the money. Street people could put our vote in on a subject, for example, that thing about the McKay apartments a while back. Street people wanted to renovate it, to make it low-income housing. The city voted it out, and it's now leveled. Totally a waste. We have the ideas. We have the courage. The only thing we don't have is the pocketbook.

I agree with some of the beliefs of the people involved in Operation Homestead. But the protesting part is not the way to go about it. What you do is get a petition—a silent petition. Take it to the governor's office, or the mayor, and you get about 8,000 to 10,000 signatures. *Somebody* has to listen.

Once, at one of the protests, I had an egg thrown out of a car window at me, and a can of beer. I turned around and flipped him off. I pulled my pants down, and he saw my behind, and I said, "Guess what? This one's for you, and it's not a Budweiser." I mooned him right there on Pike Street and almost caused a traffic jam. At that time I weighed 300 pounds and had quite a big behind. I was mad because they threw that beer bottle at me. I didn't mind the egg so much—it was hard-boiled. I laughed it off, but when he threw a beer bottle, that could have hurt somebody. That's when I pulled down my pants, and said, "Kiss my ass." I said, "This one's for you, and it ain't a Budweiser," and I gave him the middle finger. I flipped him off. People rolled down the window and said, "Fuck you! Get a job!" "Give me one! Show me where to work! Pay my wages! Otherwise fuck off!"

The reason why homeless people give up is people don't listen to very reasonable, quiet talk. They'd be willing to talk quietly if people would listen, but they don't. The McKay was knocked down, and just like the Puget Hotel down here, which has 140 rooms, it could be renovated. It might take time, but I'm sure people could team together, instead of paying for the politicians to go off in their Lear jets. And they bitch about the homeless! Why not put some of that money where it belongs? Where it would do the most good for people. Have people be able to speak their mind. Have a good advocate for us. We don't have an advocate and it's shit.

"A lot of my friends are still on the streets. These are people that I'll never forget because they've taught me how to stay alive."

People are afraid to speak up. They're afraid of the police beating the shit out of them. I've been harassed by the cops so many times it's sickening. And you know what? I look at 'em like, "Yeah, I might be poor, but fuck you, I have rights!"

I've seen the way the police beat people. They beat women. They beat a partner of mine to death not too long ago—about three years ago, right in front of me. There wasn't a damn thing I could do about it. We were in the park. They accused him of being drunk. He was not drunk. The man had had a seizure. And they kept grabbing him and pulling him, and grabbing him and pulling him. Me being an epileptic, I know what that's like. When people pull you, it freaks you out. 'Cause when you come out of a seizure, you don't really know what's happening. And then all these people just pulling you, poking you, pulling you, it's gonna piss you off. Well, he reacted. And they beat him.

I told the cops, I said, "I seen what happened." They said, "You didn't see nothing." I said, "Fuck you, I ain't lying. If somebody asks me, I'm gonna tell them you killed him." The family's still around and I don't know that they'd want me to mention his name, but he was a Native American. He was a Sioux Indian. And not a damn thing was done about it because he was a street person. He was homeless. They didn't give a damn. According to them, it was just another gutter person, you know?

I've seen people who were upper crust in the 60s and 70s standing in soup lines today because they just couldn't make it. I was in the gutter. In fact, I've got one foot in and one foot out now—I'm kind of straddling the fence. I'm trying to get both feet on the better side, because maybe I'm just tired of being in the gutter. A lot of people haven't had the courage—they're afraid of not being accepted by their old friends. I'm trying to break that cycle. I'm sober. I quit drinking, and if I can quit, by gosh they can. I'm a street person. People got to set an example because some of these people have never had an example—they've never had an example of somebody who really gives a damn. That's why they're street people now. And it's like it's a community within a community because they stick together.

A lot of my friends are still on the streets. These are people that I'll never forget because they've taught me how to stay alive. Without them, I probably would have died. Some revert back to the alcohol and drugs. But some really do make it. Some become so pious and proud that they forget they ever saw a day on skid row.

I met one at an A.A. meeting—no names because A.A. has a privacy policy. Last time I saw him, he was hanging on to me for dear life in an alley. This was back in 1978 when we met in Los Angeles. He was covered in sores and lice. I got him some Kwell and some Neosporin for his open sores from my panhandling money. I cleansed his sores with hydrogen peroxide, put gauze on them. And the man, now he denies even knowing me. He's like, "Oh, I'm sober now for ten years. I don't hang out with bums." And I said, "Hey Laughing Boy! Remember me from Los Angeles? In MacArthur Park—when you collapsed in my lap because you took a little too much of that stuff?" He turned red, said, "I'd rather not talk about that part of my life. Why don't you leave me the hell alone?" I said, "No, because you're downing people, and you're living a lie. I can't allow you to go around denying what you really are." I said, "I came up above it, became a human being, and it's something to be proud of."

I am a street person, but I am not a dirty person. I am a human being who could give you love. Show me how to grow, and I'll grow like a weed. Plant me in good soil and I'll grow, man. That's what people need. They need encouragement. Sometimes you've got to be rough, but it's not about closing the parks so nobody has a place to sit. It's not kicking people in the behind because they're an alcoholic, and it's not babying them. It's telling them the truth. It's telling them, "Look, there is another way. If I can do it, you can do it. I'm no better than you, and if I can do it, by god, you can too."

"My mother asked me, 'Do you want to live here?' I says, 'Hell no. I don't want nothing to do with this house and its memories or nothing.'"

I was seventeen when I hit skid row. I think the reason that I left home to begin with was because I really was not understood, was being shuffled around from a very early age, from about six years old. I left home trying to find myself. I had a dream. Like Martin Luther King says, "I have a dream." I had a dream—I still have a dream. And you know what that is? I am really somebody. I can be somebody. Because Anna has the right to live just like anyone else. I am important because I am a living, breathing person.

Growing up, I felt like I was abnormal. Brain-damaged. Retarded. Sick. Stupid. They labeled me mentally disturbed because I retaliated, because I got tired of being made fun of, taunted. "Crazy Anna! Crazy Anna!" Do you know what her father is like?" Well, my name is not "Crazy Anna." My name is Anna.

My mom, she had come from a bad environment, too. Her parents were alcoholics and she was codependent. They abused her so badly that this woman didn't know if she was coming or going. She married an abusive man—my father—after getting out of an abusive marriage. My mother was Catholic. She became a Jehovah's witness when I was eleven, but when she was a Catholic, she used to take drinks at night of Wild Irish Rose wine in the privacy of her bedroom. But it was, "Oh, I'm not an alcoholic. I don't have a drinking problem." She smoked those Pall Mall bare backs. I'd hear the sound of the coffee cup in the morning, and the smell of the cigarette, and I knew mother was up. At night, I'd smell the wine on her breath, and I knew it was bedtime. And I vamoosed.

She grew up in the depression era—the 20s and 30s. They were raised different than my generation, which I can understand. She's beautiful person—don't get me wrong—in her own way, she is a wonderful woman. I tried to show her that just because I'm my father's daughter doesn't mean I am my father. We're different as night and day.

My father was known as a punk. Everybody knew the schmuck! My father was a rebel, a rebellious person, a very domineering type. If a woman didn't listen to him, she got the living daylights beat out of her. I had no right to express myself. My father never allowed dancing or rock and roll in the house. I had this dance routine, and he'd flip out on me, starting screaming and swearing at me, telling me I was a whore like my mother. I didn't think my mother was a whore, personally. I mean [*laughs*] she didn't bring anybody home. He was jealous because she had three sons from a previous marriage, and I was the only child that she could produce for him. I turned out female.

If he got mad at my mother, he kicked my behind. If my mother tried to stop him, she got beat up worse. I can remember the time he tried to put a hot iron to her. She took all this for thirteen and a half years. My mother couldn't take it. She was sitting out on the lawn chairs a week later, and she just disappeared. She took off to her sister's. After she left, I remember I was in my room, and he tells me, "You clean up this f-ing mess." I says, "No problem." I did what I was told. "Go in the kitchen and do the dishes." "Yes Daddy. No problem." "Don't talk back to me! You punk ass kid. You're a whore just like your mother." And then he took off his belt, and that's when I really got it. He hit me with the belt, the buckle, you know, anything.

When my mother came back, I was ticked at her: "Benedict Arnold! You left me to deal with this big marine with a bad temper, you jellyfish." But I never told her that because I didn't want to hurt her. One day when I was eight years old, I begged her, I said, "I want him out of here. I want him out of our lives. I'm tired of the beatings. I'm tired of the verbal abuse. I want this jerk out of my life." He had gotten the house on a GI loan, and he said, "Well, this is gonna always be your home, and if I die, this will be yours." My mother asked me, "Do you want to live here?" I says, "Hell no. I don't want nothing to do with this house and its memories or nothing."

Then my mother got a place to live with this lady, Ruth Ann, who was trying to start a business where they groomed dogs and stuff. I always had babysitters, because my mother had to work. She got a job as a cocktail waitress, then she was a nurse's assistant for a while with retarded children. She didn't have it easy. Her health was bad. She married a man that had an income—he was a truck driver, made good money—and she didn't want me in her life. She was willing to accept his kid from a previous marriage, but she put her boyfriend above the responsibilities of being a mother to me.

> ## "And then they wonder why there's women that are prostitutes to get money to sleep somewhere or women go home with a man just so they don't have to be on these damn streets."

She put me in an institution-like setting. It was one of those deals that went on in the 50s and 60s that have become obsolete since. They no longer do this to kids, thank god. They've outlawed it. Because they used forced medication and restraints. There was a lot of physical abuse, sexual abuse.

The first time I was assaulted I was young. I wasn't even in the first grade. I was molested by my mother's brother, who is now deceased. It's not nice to talk about the dead. When I reported it to my mother, she treated me like I was a liar, and when I told her about this later on, I said, "You never did believe me." She tried to deny it. I said, "If you'd a believed me, you wouldn't have turned on me and told the family I was a troublemaker—not to believe anything I said." And I caught this attitude towards her: "Well, fuck you. You don't care about me." You know, "I don't want somebody whose gonna abuse me. There's other things in life besides the bullshit." And I had to learn that, and I did learn that once I hit the streets. I didn't become bitter. I became better. And it was me meeting up with my current fiancé that helped me become better.

I've known him since I was little. We met in school. He had emotional behavior problems just like me. We were both rowdy, but around each other, we were very calm. We talked. Then he ended up at the home with me. We were both labeled incorrigible kids who were emotionally disturbed. Even when I ran away and I hopped freights and stuff, I always looked for this man. It was the secret that I never told my mother about. She would try to take apart my relationships by telling people, "You can never believe things she says. She's a habitual liar. She fantasizes a lot."

When I met up again with my fiancé, at a shelter, I didn't even want a relationship. I was afraid. He tried to hug me, and I cringed, because I was afraid he was going to hit me. I was in an eight-year marriage of hell. If I didn't know better, I'd swear my ex-husband was kinfolk to Satan himself. I'm epileptic because of the beatings. He beat me in the head. I laid in a coma for six months. The day I told him we were getting a divorce, he put a gun to my head and forced me to have sex. Which was traumatic. Back at that time, they didn't have the rape law like they do now, where you can put the sucker in jail. I didn't report it, but I carry the emotional scars. Now if a man hurts me, I'm going to punch him. I will punch him.

The first time I got raped, I went to the police about it and they made fun of me. You know what they asked me? "Did you enjoy it?" "How long did you know the person?" Hey! Yo! Nobody enjoys rape. It's an act of violence. They asked me if I enjoyed it. I says, "Fuck you! If this was your mother or sister, you wouldn't be saying that. It's 'cause I'm a street person. You kiss my ass." The cops didn't do jack shit, and the guy's still running free.

The same thing happened in '87. I was sleeping in a place that I thought was safe, and I got attacked. They took me in an ambulance, 'cause I was bleeding—I was bloodied up pretty bad. They beat me. I have a scar above my eye. See this? And in here and here and here. I got stabbed in the gut and left for dead. I seen one of the people that did that to me in '87, and he's scared of me, 'cause I took a dog choke chain, and I wrapped it upside his head. I put him in the hospital. It took me two years to catch him. I caught him behind the market. I stuck a padlock on the end of a chain, and I beat his ass. I beat him damn near to death. I haven't seen him around since. I told him, "Get the hell out of town, or I'm going to kill you."

I got assaulted again this year. My cousin was down here at the time, and I stayed with him in low-income housing, taking care of him as a chore worker—cleaning, cooking, stuff like that. And I ended up jacked around, messed over by him. I went to a mission to ask for help. The worker said, "I'm saving this room for someone else." And then she goes, "Well, um, I heard from the church members that your temperament—I don't think you'd fit in here." So I go, "Look, if I don't get some help, I'm gonna end up either back on drugs, assaulted or dead." I said, "Where am I gonna go?" And then they wonder why there's women that are prostitutes to get money to sleep somewhere or women go home with a man just so they don't have to be on these damn streets.

I was sleeping behind the Public Market in a secluded place. I thought I was safe but they found me. Not singular-plural! Plural! Plural! I had a broken rib. I'm damn lucky I didn't have a disease, you know. This is the 90s. I'm lucky. I've tested. I waited three months, and then I went to the doctor's. It takes three months for anything to show up. I do not have AIDS. I'm lucky, lucky, lucky, lucky.

"A street person is a person who has taken refuge in the streets to escape another environment."

I lost my kids because I was in an abusive environment. I lost every last one of them, and that broke my heart. [*Anna lists the names of her eight children.*] They were split up. They were split up. They were split up. I was afraid of becoming violent with them. I mean, if I can get mad at a grown person and put them in the hospital, I don't want to take a chance on *ever* even *saying* something cruel to hurt my children's minds or emotions. They don't deserve it. I want them to have better than I had. I want them to feel important from the beginning. Because they are.

There's only one that I know where they're at, and that's my ten-year-old. My ten-year-old is with one of my best friends, a lady who took care of me during my pregnancy. She knows I'm her mother. It's not like my mom. My mom just kind of stuck me in the home, turned her back and said, "Oh to hell with her. She's nothing but trouble anyway." I never did that to mine.

My daughter doesn't know I'm a street person. I'm not too rich or too proud to say that yeah, I'm a street person. I'm just a sheltered street person at the moment. I just happen to be paying for a place to live. A street person is a person who has taken refuge in the streets to escape another environment. To me the streets were a refuge. To some people they're a nightmare, but to me the streets were a sanctuary where I couldn't be messed with. Where I could really be me. They've helped me find a way to come above the "Poor-pitiful-little-victim-me." Because I am not any less fortunate than another person. In fact, I feel I'm a richer one. I've learned how to love. I can understand a person when they come to me with a situation. My heart can feel deep for them. I want to help them to come above their hurts. I came above mine. I feel they can in their own way, in their own time, do the same.

I even tried suicide twice. I laid in a coma twice because of it. One time I overdosed. Another time I slit my wrists. And I drank so much alcohol that I darn near died of alcohol poisoning. That's been over eleven years. They asked me why I did it, and I just told them, "I'm despondent over my children." I had lost custody of my kids at that point, and it was like, "Oh shit, now I'm a failure. I'm a fuck up. I'm nobody. I'm a piece of shit." Right away—with the pounding when I was a kid. I had to learn how to overcome that and say, "I'm not a piece of shit! Maybe this wasn't the way to go about this." I had to think. I had to learn. God gave me a brain—use it.

I talked to my mother on the phone not too long ago, and I told her for the first time, since I was a kid that I really wanted to get to know her now that we're adults. She asked me if I hated her for all the things she did, like putting me away, like rejecting me. I say, "No." That's cause I've made up for it by becoming a street person. And I've found my dream. To find someone who would really love me, not for what I could do for them all the time, how good I was in bed—or how bad I was in bed—whether I could cook, how much physical, sexual, mental, spiritual abuse I could put up with before I blow up.

"When we were born, we weren't born addicts. We weren't born drunk. We were conditioned to become that by abuse."

I believe in the Christian God, but some people conceive him as Buddha, Vishnu, Jehovah, you know, whatever he is to you. God almighty, Jesus Christ—it's still the Great Spirit. It's still one god. What really hurts me as a woman is seeing other Indian female people—American Indian or Native Americans, Human Beings, "The People"—sleeping around, not respecting their bodies, their spirits. When we were born, we weren't born addicts. We weren't born drunk. We were conditioned to become that by abuse. The abuse continues within ourselves. It's like self-hate. Whether you are Caucasian, whether you are Black, whether you are Asian American, whether you are Native American, whether you are mixed, biracial, triracial, or however, people have a tendency to hate when they are on the street, and it's a shame, because we all have something to offer in life.

I've been sober since December 12, 1986. I begged to be arrested, and they wouldn't even do that. The cop says, "You have to go through detox." Detox says, "I don't like your attitude. You get out of here." I ended up in jail, because I got into a fistfight. During my stay at jail, I was put on medication, which still acted in my body like a drug. It still got me stoned. There's more drugs in than out—at that time there was, but not any more. They've stopped practically all that bullshit. They've cleaned up quite a bit. But I got out of jail, I says, "Fuck jail" [*laughs*]. I said, "I ain't never going back." And I won't. When I got out, I went over to Georgetown,[5] to a friend's of mine, and I was withdrawing in this apartment.

There should be more treatment available. There's not shit available. Not good programs. They're like, "Oh yeah, we'll sober them up for a little while," then they cut them loose, back on the street, instead of looking at what the roots of the problem is, where the abuse began, how they can come above that to realize that they are a good person, they are worth something, and life is worth living. You can do it sober. You don't need a fucking crutch. And you have to have guts to look in the mirror. What taught me that was realizing it wasn't the other people's fault all the time. That maybe Anna was doing something that Anna really shouldn't do.

I realized that when me and my present fiancé had to separate because we were both fighting for sobriety. He was an addict—I was an addict. We were deeply in love with each other, but my attitude was so bad that he couldn't deal with me. I wasn't violent to him, but every time his back was turned, I was beating the heck out of somebody. He says, "Anna, you're a wonderful person, but your damn temper—your attitude stinks." I've heard this all my life. I could hear it from him because I really loved him and he loved me in return and didn't think of me as: (a) a piece of ass; (b) somebody that could make money for him; or (c) a place to stay. It took a lot of love and patience from my fiancé to start helping me to heal up. 'Cause for a long time, I lived by the rule of "Don't hurt me, and I won't hurt you. You hurt me and I'm going to fight you."

When I would fight, I would just completely blank out. Usually when a person fights, they have sense enough to know they're hitting someone. When I get that angry, I don't have any sense. I've come to and found that I've literally laid a person out. That's why I no longer drink. They said it comes from emotional and physical abuse. I've had counselors tell me there's only one cure for that. And that's to be in a loving environment with low stress. So therefore I do not put myself in those predicaments. When I was a kid, I didn't have a choice. I can choose now. I have a choice. No one chooses for me anymore.

CHAPTER 4

Elizabeth Thatcher

I interviewed Elizabeth at the suggestion of the staff of Lutheran Compass Center (LCC). She had spoken at a number of fundraisers for LCC and was clearly open to speaking about her life story. Elizabeth was 52 when I interviewed her in 1996. She was born in Butte, Montana, where her father worked as a miner. He died of black lung when she was an infant, and her mother and two siblings relocated to Seattle. By her own account, Elizabeth been incarcerated for some twenty years of her life, beginning in childhood. Her long history in the criminal justice system is traceable to the traumatic and destabilizing effects of the state's considerable power to police normative gender roles, and to suspend or revoke the custodial rights of poor and working class women deemed by the state to be "promiscuous" and hence "unfit mothers." In this case, the perception of Elizabeth's mother as "unfit" was likely exacerbated by the fact that she worked in a succession of nontraditional jobs, from airplane assembly during World War II to bus driver.

Though Elizabeth reports that she never had any run-ins at school or at home—"I was the perfect child, who didn't get into any trouble"—as the child of an "unfit" mother, on the brink of puberty, Elizabeth was taken out of her mother's care and placed at the Martha Washington School for Girls located close to her family's home in the Seward Park neighborhood of Seattle. Elizabeth reports having run away "eighteen to twenty times," returning each time to be with her mother and siblings. After participating in "a riot," with 12- and 13-year-olds, she was court-ordered to the Home of the Good Shepherd in Seattle at the age of twelve. Throughout its operation, from 1907 to 1973, alongside "orphans" and students who were "voluntarily" placed at the facility, were court-ordered girls who were deemed "wayward" or "penitent[s]."[1] The mission of the Order of the Good Shepherd Sisters was to "purify and strengthen the souls of girls living in poverty and in environments considered immoral."[2] Though the facility opened in 1907, the first home visits weren't instituted until 1942 and contact with the outside world was severely constrained:[3] "To prevent residents from seeing the outside world and leaving the Home, locked doors and opaque glass were used in the earlier years. A little later, barred windows, barbed wire fences, then window alarms were installed.[4]

In my 1996 interview with her, Elizabeth offered a laconic history of the event that led to her being transferred to Maple Lane School for Girls, a much more hard-core juvenile detention center. "I beat up a nun," she told me. I reconnected with her on Facebook in 2009 and pressed her for more details about the incident. Elizabeth told that she had hit the nun "between the shoulder blades" and the nun had fallen to the floor. Asked if there was any immediate catalyst to the incident, she recalled, "I was angry at everyone and I acted out. I felt like no one wanted me or loved me and that's why I did it. Just to get any kind of reaction, to get someone to stop and look at me and acknowledge my existence. Because it seemed like no one even knew I was around most of the time."

Had Elizabeth been sentenced to Maple Lane a decade earlier, she might have been among the hundreds of individuals who were forcibly sterilized in prisons, juvenile detention facilities, and mental hospitals under the 1921 Washington State Eugenics Law. The law extended to those who were deemed "habitual criminals, moral degenerates, sexual perverts," and having "inferior hereditary potentialities."[5] After her release from juvenile detention, Elizabeth tried to stave off her childhood trauma by self-medicating. Her heroin addiction and years of "training" at Maple Lane laid the groundwork for future felony convictions.

"I don't think she was ever as promiscuous as they say she was. I think she just was ahead of her time."

I think I'm luckier than the average person. I've had a real weird life and still have a really good attitude. I've seen a lot of people real bitter with no hope for ever becoming any different. I keep that hope. I guess if I didn't have that I'd be a shambles.

I don't remember a lot of my growing up years. I guess as a child, I can remember the house that we lived in. That was the happiest for me. After that, I don't ever consider any place I ever lived a home. The houses that we lived in with the kids, I can't even picture them. Even with my kids, it was never a home.

I guess my basic thing is that nothing ever stays the same: that all things change. I had grandparents and a mom, but I don't have any memory of that. My sister and brother, they're like strangers. I don't have any childhood memories of them at all.

I was locked up when I was twelve. They declared my mother an unfit mother. My mom was pretty promiscuous. But she worked, and she took care of us kids, and no one ever battered us or beat us. We always ate and had good clothes.

I still picture her, she'd be asleep putting her hair up, 'cause she was always either putting her hair up or going to work. She would fall asleep. I would come home from school, I would walk in, and she'd be sitting on the couch asleep with her hands up in the air going to put a roller in. That's my memory of her. She was a really nice person, a wonderful person. Her problem was she liked men. I've always been under the impression that I wasn't really my father's kid. My parents got divorced six months after I was born, and I never seen my dad, so I don't know.

She married my stepfather, and they were married I don't know how many years. I remember vaguely he was a bus driver. They both drove Seattle metro buses. He was a big deacon in the church. *He* was a religious fanatic. We would go to church every Sunday and Wednesday and Bible school in the summer. We lived across the street from the church. But I don't much remember him being around, or being mean, or being nice, or being much of anything.

I don't think she was ever as promiscuous as they say she was. I think she just was ahead of her time. She drove *trucks* before women did. She built airplane*s* before other women did. She drove a *cab*. She did things way ahead of her time. She tinkered. I guess I got that from her. I take things and make things. I can make sweaters and crochet doilies and do all those things. She loved to do crafts and things with her hands.

One of the reasons they declared her an unfit mother was because she had an illegitimate baby. She put the baby up for adoption so she wouldn't lose me, and she lost me anyway. I was the baby of the family. My sister and brother had both been in reform school, so they were going to try and save *me* by locking me up, which didn't make a lot of sense. I didn't do anything. But they didn't want me to go to reform school [*laughs*], so they sent me to Martha Washington School, out on Lake Washington.

I wouldn't *stay*. I kept on running away, going home. I think I was there a year, and I ran away something like twenty times—to my mom. Every time. The only thing I was thinking was getting home to my mom. And they'd be waiting for me. Or they'd eventually find me. She always kept me. She never turned me back in. But I don't remember her ever coming to visit any place. I'm *sure* she must have, but I don't remember her ever visiting me.

"My biggest nightmare has always been being buried alive."

Eventually I was in a riot. They had to close the school down. We tore the school apart. So they put me in a Catholic girls' school, the Convent of the Good Shepherd in Seattle. I beat up a nun. They decided I was "incorrigible," and they put me in Maple Lane, which was a state training school for "incorrigible" girls. My mom never came to see me. It was like I was deserted, abandoned, left there. No one really cared about me.

It was a tough girls' school. Right across the hill was Green Hill, which was the tough boys' school. I remember being in a lot of fights. I've always been small, and there was a lot of Black girls—a lot of big girls anyway—and you had to fight to prove that you could survive. I was always afraid. And I was little, so when I had to fight, it was always bigger people, and I always lost. We had male and female houseparents, and I was always afraid of them, 'cause I knew they had control over my life. No matter *what* I did or said, it was their decisions.

The biggest memory I have, my sister was coming to see me, and they were going to lock me up—probably for fighting. There were all these little cottages in Maple Lane, and they put me in the cells underneath the cottages. They'd come in and feed you, and that was it. I was in there for like six months. I was fourteen—thirteen or fourteen. I can still remember the smell, the slimey walls, and all the bugs, and how dark it was. There was no window. They had that sheet metal with the little holes in it, and that was our ventilation and our windows. Solid wood doors. Spending all that time in the dungeons. I remember being really afraid and alone and determined not to let them know I was any of those things. I think my biggest nightmare has always been being buried alive, and I'm sure it has to do with that. Being in those dungeons and being in the dark and not being able to breathe.

"Someone asked me one time what it felt like to shoot dope. It was like I was in a little glass bell, a crystal glass bell."

I was at Maple Lane for like five years. I got out when I was seventeen. I came out really bitter. I came out real belligerent. I hated my mother. For years and years and years I hated her. I didn't need anybody, didn't need anything, and I was like that for years. I got out and started on heroin. I was a virgin—I sold my cherry. From the time I was seventeen years old when I shot my first heroin, that's all I wanted. I didn't want *anything*. I didn't want any*body*. I wasn't with *anybody*. I worked the *streets*. I didn't have a pimp. All I had was my dope.

Someone asked me one time what it felt like to shoot dope. It was like I was in a little glass bell, a crystal glass bell. I was inside of it, and no one could get inside if I didn't want them to. I could see them, and they could see me, but this bell was around me. I was warm and comfortable and happy. No one could touch me, and I couldn't touch anyone. No one could get close to me. I could take care of myself.

When I was using dope, it was like where ever I happened to land, if I was lucky enough to be able spend the night, I did. A lot of times I just stayed with whoever let me stay on the floor. A lot of times, if I didn't have that, I'd sleep standing up in a phone booth with a phone cradled in my ear, if I didn't have anything else. I was perfectly content just to live in shooting galleries and with cockroaches. I *didn't care* so long as I had heroin.

"When I first went to Walla Walla, I was nineteen…I was scared to death."

I was out I think six months, and I was back in jail for like eighteen months in the old, old, *old* King County Jail. I was about eighteen years old. Then I got out and the first time I got arrested for a felony. I had a shoot out with the police. That was real exciting [*laughs*].

The day I got married in 1968, my ex-husband and I, they came to arrest us, and we had a shootout with the police. It was just Bonnie and Clyde style. The shotgun blast picked up the TV and shattered it across the wall. I beat the case. I went back to court, but we did two and a half years in prison before we ever got together.

After I had the shootout, I had nightmares for a good year. For probably the first six months, I remember dreaming about being in a room with no way out and it filling up with blood, and I couldn't get out, and I was going to drown, and I would wake up screaming—just soaking wet. I had that one for a *long,* long time. And I still have that one every so often. My nightmares are about being buried alive. Being someplace I can't get out of. Going down a tunnel and not being able to find the end of it.

We went to Idaho prison first, and then they closed the Idaho prison down, and then they sent me to Nevada prison. So I've been in prison like six times. I made them all. I was in Walla Walla. I think maybe we had 200 women there—it was a real hard-core penitentiary. The doors clanged shut. The guards didn't touch you. They didn't put their hands on you, because the inmates didn't have nothing to lose. They were going to die anyway, and they just didn't care. You couldn't stand up in the dining room, because they would *shoot* you because that was considered escape or a riot. So you had to sit there until you were told to stand up. And you shuffled like in the prison movies—you shuffled in and sat down and ate, and you *shuffled* out for an hour in the yard.

When I first went to Walla Walla, I was nineteen. I was scared to death. They had an emergency bell on the wall so if you fell or something happened and someone else was getting hurt, you could push the emergency bell and the matrons would come. I had no clue what was expected of me, and I rang the bell. And god, they put me in the hole because I rang it for no reason. The hole there was not as bad as the one at reform school. It was just a boarded up room with no bars or nothing, and they slid your tray in. I was only in there for maybe a month or so. It wasn't so bad...

They pulled all my teeth. I mean, my teeth were bad, 'cause I was using drugs, but they didn't have to do that.[6] They pulled all my teeth and gave me dentures. And nothing but aspirin. No drugs. Absolutely no drugs for the first six years I was there. The second time I went back, the doctor was a little more lenient, and he would give me sleeping pills and dexedrines, uppers and stuff. The third time I went in, he said, "What do you want?" So I had all the drugs I could possibly want.

I got real cocky. I mean, I'd been in reform school. I was cool. And I was a junkie. My sister came to see me, and she said, "Where do they put the murderers?" and I said, "*They're everywhere.*" [*laughs*] "They don't segregate us according to crimes." There was a real scholarly lady there, and my sister asked what she was in for. She was in for double murder. She looked very professional. And she *was.* She was a schoolteacher, and she came home and found her husband in bed with another woman, and she took a shotgun and blew both their brains out. They called it premeditated because she reached into the closet to get the gun. She was doing twenty-six years.

I remember a lot of the people I did time with. There was one girl, she used to snitch on everybody, and we used to take turns beating her up. I mean she was on *massive* doses of thorazine, which is a real heavy-duty tranquilizer they'd give almost everybody in prison to keep them numb. Like sinequan—or haledol or whatever they got now. They'd give massive doses to everyone—trying to keep us all quiet.

"For eight years, I was the perfect mother. I did Tupperware parties, and crystal parties and backyard barbecues…"

When I got out, I was clean for like eight years. My mother-in law, when she first met me, I had just gotten out of prison, and she thought I was the *greatest* thing that ever happened to her son. She didn't know I was an ex-convict. She just knew that I was going to school, never been married. Twenty-four years old. Intelligent. She thought I was just great. He took me home to meet her, and she said, "Well, if you guys are hungry, you can go into the kitchen and fix something to eat." And I went in there, and I just stood there crying [*laughs*]. Ted came in, and he said, "What's wrong?" And I said, *"I don't know how to cook. I've been locked up my whole life! I've been served on a metal tray. I don't know how to boil a hotdog!"* Then she found out I was an ex-convict and a junkie. When the kids were born, we didn't use, and she grew to really love me. And I love *her.* I've got a great mother-in law. She adores my kids.

Growing up I wanted to have a big backyard with trees and a big house and stuff. I think I probably always wanted to have a family and security and a big home. I know I always wanted kids. We were there for almost two years, and I got pregnant. For eight years, I was the perfect mother. I did Tupperware parties, and crystal parties and backyard barbecues, and all the kids played in my yard. I had all the swing sets, and we went to church every Sunday. I *loved* it. I had a wonderful time. I took my daughter to work with me 'til she was two years old. We lived with my in-laws when the kids were little. We either lived with them or across the street from them or down the block from them.

We didn't use for eight years. Somebody walked in one day with some cocaine and said, "Try this." As soon as I shot that dope, I actually started crying. My husband said, "Why are you crying," and I said, "I just stuck my kids in my arm." And he said, "Aw, that's just dope talking." Six months later I was back in prison. When we went to prison it was just natural that my in-laws took the kids. My kids came to see me there a couple of times, and I just decided that I didn't want my kids visiting me there.

My ex-husband, who I'd been with for almost twenty years, divorced me while I was in Purdy. He met another woman in California and wrote and told me that he fell in love with her and wanted a divorce. When I got out, I was in work release for a long time, and so I couldn't take care of the kids—I *still* can't. Besides my drinking part of it, I don't make enough money to take care of them. And if I'm working, I don't have time for the kids. They're both teenagers now. I really wouldn't want to leave them alone.

"I couldn't stand to watch her die. After hating her for so long, then I felt guilty for hating her for so long."

My mother came to see me once when I was in Walla Walla, and I wouldn't visit her. It took me until my daughter was born to forgive her. She had a trailer out in the south end of Seattle, and when I got out of Purdy, I went and stayed with her. She had lung cancer. By the time they discovered it, it had already gone to her brain.

I remember them calling me and my sister and my brother to come up to the hospital, to decide on her treatment plan. I would go in the morning and give her a bath and breakfast. 'Cause when the cancer went to her brain, she lost her memory, she'd forget things real easily. I'd go in the morning and give her a bath and dress her and feed her and fix her a lunch. She lived with her dogs, and she was perfectly happy. My sister would go over after work, and she'd feed her and get her ready for bed. We had a real routine going.

Then my sister took over her *complete* care and moved her in with her. I couldn't go out there very often. I couldn't stand to watch her die. I felt guilty for hating her for so long. When she died, they called me at work and told me she was dead, and I cried for two or three days. And I didn't think I could do that. I don't cry very often. I just lost it. I was *really* furious with her. I thought, "All these years I'd built up this immunity to caring about you, and then you die on me." I was furious for the longest time.

"Ray had more control over me than anybody. I still haven't figured out why I let him do that."

I met Ray as soon as I got out of Purdy, so that's been seven or eight years. He's not a junkie—he's the first man I've been with who's not a junkie. He's an alcoholic— who likes to beat women. Ray had more control over me than *anybody*. I still haven't figured out why I let him do that. It was like I was *completely* captivated by him. It was like I was brainwashed. He said I wasn't capable of doing anything, but I was the only one that did anything. He said I couldn't make a decent wage, but he *didn't work*! I couldn't pay the rent on time, but *he didn't pay the rent at all*. But *I* was the bad guy, and I believed it.

So I took eight years of getting whipped almost every day. I still don't know why I went through it, because I'm not a stupid person. I went to LCC two or three times because of it.

I don't have a problem with drugs—I have a problem with alcohol now. One time I just checked into LCC, and I decided to quit drinking. And I didn't drink for a year. I went back to him, and he was still drinking. When he doesn't drink he doesn't beat me, but there's the verbal, mental abuse thing that keeps me in check, under his thumb.

I left him for good August of last year. I made *him* move out. Before, I would go to shelters and pay the rent and let him stay there. I mean real stupid stuff. So I made him leave a year ago, and he's found me twice since then. He comes to my job, and I get fired or I quit my job. I was working at [a Seattle hospital] in January, and he came in there as a patient. They discovered he had cancer, and they took out part of his lung, and I felt real bad for him. I didn't go back to him, but I tried to help him, and he took that as meaning we were back together, and so he started *beating* on me again. So I moved from my apartment, quit my job at the hospital, changed my phone number, got invisible—I thought. And then he found me again.

He came here about a month and a half ago and hid in the hall. I didn't know he was here. Somebody let him in the building. When I opened my door, he tried to come in. So I called the police. I just decided I'd had enough, and I went down and got a restraining order so he can't come to my job. He can't come here. He can't call me. But he still does. The first of the month, he called me. As soon as he gets drunk, he forgets, or he doesn't care. That's another reason I want a new job, maybe start all over again.

"I guess most of my life I've just felt like I was on my own."

I guess most of my life I've just felt like I was on my own. I had no one I could rely on. My sister says that she thinks I don't figure anybody loves me. I know people *love* me, but when I get depressed, nothing—no one cares. But I don't do that very often. Once a year I get real depressed like that and go off on a binge and go straight down the tubes and lose everything and then start all over again.

I don't have any really close friends. The closest friend I have is Ruby. She's twenty-seven. She's just a real sweet kid. Right now I feel obligated to Ruby, because she's pregnant. I have met none of her family, but they all think of me as sort of her protector, so I watch over her. She makes more money than I do, but she's trying to save up for the baby, and she's taking her vitamins and eating healthy and stuff and tries to get me to do that. Tomorrow I'll spend a lot of time trying to take care of whatever she needs me to do. I wouldn't abandon her.

But when I didn't have any place to stay, I went and found it. No one found me some place. If I didn't know a resource, I found a resource. I made sure that I never slept under a bridge. I *admire* those people who do that—I couldn't do that. I would rob a store first [*laughs*]. Most people would rather sleep under a bridge than commit a crime. I'd rather commit a crime than sleep with bugs. I don't think I could do it. I mean I could if that was all there was, and I'd survive that too. And come out probably with a good sense of humor. Make a joke about it . . .

I did the AIDS walk on Sunday. I don't want my kids to get it, and I don't want my grand kids to get it. I'm lucky I don't have it. I'm *really* lucky. I was a junkie for twenty years—twenty-five years I was a junkie. Used dope after everybody. Slept with everybody. Didn't care. Didn't use rubbers. It never occurred to me. I never got anything—I never had syphilis. The worst I ever had was crabs. I'm *really* a lucky person. I should have had *all* of those things. I never had anything, and I don't want my kids to have it.

In the last six months, I have turned myself into detox three times and been turned down [*laughs*]. They won't take me. I'm going, "What else have I got to do?" You know? It's a lot easier to quit through detox. I will quit. I mean I'm getting tired of it again. At the AIDS walk, I saw a lot of people that were really bad off—I mean *really* bad off—*walking*. They just won't give up. I think that's why I'm lucky. Because I won't give up either...

"I can't imagine spending the rest of my life staring at that brick wall."

There's got to be more to life than this. People look at my apartment and think I don't have much. Those windows look into a brick wall. It's just sort of like jail. I've been so depressed that I thought there's no end to it, but I always keep telling myself when I get that depressed, "Go to sleep. When you wake up it'll be better. If you make it through the night, then you can make it through the next day. If you give it up now, then you don't have another chance." So I mean I've considered suicide, but, I have to put that out of my head and do something else.

I'm going to speak tonight at a fundraiser for Lutheran Compass. I don't know what I'm going to say. I'm just going to go in there and look sharp and tell them, "You don't have to live here—you don't have to stay here. You can get out if you want to." But for the grace of God, I mean any minute I could be there.

I keep seeing the *light* at the end of the tunnel. You know, I keep trying to *pull* myself up out of the tunnel. Cause I *know* it's got to get better, and then things fall apart again. I'm almost fifty years old. I'm too old to do all this scuffling. But I don't give it up.

When I first moved in here, I lived her for about a month by myself before anybody came to see me. I would go to work and come home, and I would sit here and think, "Is *this* all there is to life? I can't imagine spending the rest of my life staring at that brick wall." And then I got the plants and got my grow light and started getting flowers. They're kind of dead right now. But I'm trying to add things to make it mine, and it became more comfortable. But I don't want to spend the rest of my life in this room. And so in order to get out of it, I have to do something different.

I want to start my own business, and I don't have any credit to do it, and so I want to do word processing at home. I want a computer, because I know computers are "tomorrow," and, you know, I'd like to leave my daughter something and my son. So I started taking an international correspondence school that Sally Struthers advertises on TV. You get a computer. You have to do school work and make payments for like six months, and then they'll send you a computer, and then you finish paying it off. It's fifteen hundred dollars for the whole thing. I'm doing the schoolwork and making the payments. I know a lot of church people, and I'm real good at looking for agencies and stuff. What I want to do is print their flyers, keep a job and do that at home and pretty soon get my own business going so that so I can just be my own boss, my own person.

I think it will be real exciting to do the word processing thing at home. I'll meet more people, and I have enough connections, and I know enough people. It may not be a *Bill Gates* Microsoft kind of thing, and I may not make a lot of money, but it'll be fun because it'll be mine.

CHAPTER 5

"Sweet Pea"

I met "Sweet Pea" in 1996 when she was a resident of the Lutheran Compass Center Women's Program. We struck up a conversation in the shelter kitchen and she readily agreed to be interviewed. A white woman in her early twenties, with three children recently placed voluntarily in foster care, she looked young enough to be in her late teens. Sweet Pea was the youngest woman I interviewed by about a decade, and despite having already suffered a succession of traumas in her life, she seemed upbeat and optimistic about her future. The moment in the interview when she seemed most distressed and vulnerable was when she spoke of reading The Diary of Anne Frank *as a child.*

While I have no doubt that Sweet Pea had been involved in drug trafficking during the several years that she spent with the Crips, given the relatively brief time that she lived in Seattle, it seems likely to me that her account of her central role in the gang was likely exaggerated to enhance her status.[1] When I interviewed her in on the single occasion in 1996, Sweet Pea had just secured a job as a motel maid. But in 1996 as today, given fair market rents in Seattle, even with a maximum of three months emergency shelter at the Compass Center, Sweet Pea would be hard-pressed to scrape together enough money for a security deposit, first and last months rent for herself in Seattle, let alone for her three children as well. In the absence of any viable social safety net, when her early enthusiasm for going straight might begin to wane, Sweet Pea would be faced with strong incentives to return to prostitution or drug trafficking, or to take her chances in yet another relationship with a man who might be able to help support her and her children.

"In a way it's rewarding...to be square and to do things the right way...not to have to worry about somebody coming and shooting me because I'm wearing the wrong colors."

I'm not a drug addict. I'm definitely not a drug addict—alcoholic—anything like that. Man, I was nice. Normal. I got married when I was nineteen, but I got with my husband when I was sixteen. Got three babies: a five-year-old girl and four-year-old twin girls. Just a plain old nice, normal housewife. My husband was abusive, though. He still is. He's been stalking me lately.

He started smoking crack and stuff when we moved up here. So I said, "Hey, what a neat idea to make some money." So I started slinging. After a couple of months they raided my house, and I got in big trouble. There was a big gunfight in my house and they ended up boarding up the house 'cause of me. When they raided the house, they found some AK's and Mac-10s and a couple of nines. Popo, the police, got mad, 'cause I wouldn't snitch out nobody.

I had the biggest crack house in the hood. I was making four or five grand a day. During the day, we served through the window. Nobody ever came in the house until after the kids were asleep. I was very careful to protect them from that, and I never let them hear us talking about it, or see us talking about it. I did show them the guns and let them know that they were not to touch them. I had the guns up over top of the stove in the cabinet, where I had to be on a chair to get them. So I mean there was no chance that they could have gotten them. Those were the guns for the hood. They were our gang guns.

CPS [Child Protective Services], they took my kids, they took them automatically when I went to jail. But I only stayed in jail for like two weeks, Then they let me out. "Personal Recognizance" and all that because I had no previous adult record or anything. When I got out of jail, they gave the kids back, but then I gave 'em up voluntarily. I figured I was going to go to jail for that for a while. But I had a really, really, really good lawyer, so I got off with probation. But CPS lied—they lied. They don't give the kids back. I mean, they will eventually, but they just put you through so much.

I'm supposed to see the kids every week, but I missed two visits because of court dates. And [the caseworker's] saying "Well, it's not stable. The kids get their hopes up, and then they can't see you." So she cut visitation back to every two weeks. *When I voluntarily put them into foster care.*

When I got out of jail, I started hoeing. I was making pretty good money—never had a pimp or anything like that. To me it's stupid for a female to have a pimp. Why would she got out there and sell her body and give her money to a man? So I hoed for a while, and then, I met this really, really nice guy who I'm going with now. He's neat. I mean, he's treated me like no other man ever, ever treated me in my life. He's just so sweet. I'm really stuck on him. But he's totally square. Got a job, car, lives a nice, normal, square life. He's taught me a lot about being square.

It's kind of fun being good. That's why I'm in the situation I'm in now. I stopped hoeing, I stopped selling drugs, I stopped stealing, I stopped doing all of that stuff, and so I had no income. So I'm homeless. But I just got a job today, and you know, things are coming together. It's going slow, but in a way it's rewarding to be square and to do things the right way, not to have to worry about somebody coming and shooting me because I'm wearing the wrong colors. Not having somebody trying to jack me 'cause I got dope, and I got money. No po-po trying to chase me down. It's nice just being able to relax—no warrants out on me or nothing. So I'm doing things the right way.

"Before my mom started doing things— before I got my first taste of freedom—I was totally square and I was quite happy being square."

I grew up in [a city on the east coast]. My mom was a really good mom—to most people she may not have been—but she gave me the good moral foundation that I have. There's always been some lines I haven't crossed and some lines I never will cross because of that moral foundation she instilled in me. Like when I was gangbanging, I mean, there are a lot of killings, and I could never do that. The only way I could ever do that was if it was me or them. Even when I was hoeing, I wouldn't rob the tricks like a lot of girls do. A lot of my homies would sell dope to pregnant girls or kids. I mean kids, man! I could never do that. I'll pass up the money before I'll do that. Regardless of the things I've done, I'm a good person. I was a good person—I was just doing bad things.

Growing up, I lived in a fairly decent neighborhood. It was mixed and middle class. I was totally square and I was quite happy being square. When my friends were off stealing candy from the store, I wouldn't even go in with them. I didn't lie. I cried if somebody hurt my feelings. I cried. *In front of people!* It didn't occur to me to do wrong. I just wanted to make my mom proud of me, you know. She always made me feel good when I did good.

I was smart. I got skipped up. I skipped second grade; I skipped third grade; I skipped fourth grade. I was in gifted and talented programs. I liked school. My mother started teaching me to read when I was two and a half or three years old. I got my own library card when I was four. But I wasn't allowed to go to the library myself until I was seven. I've always read. When I read, the words stop being words that I'm reading. It's like my eyes see it, and I'm just there. I love to read more than I love to watch TV or anything else. When I was a kid—six, seven years old—I liked the Hardy Boys and Nancy Drew. I liked the Great Brain books by John D. Fitzgerald. The Great Brain was a really smart kid and told about his life and the little swindles he used to pull on everybody. I liked the Encyclopedia Brown books, and I always figured out how he figured everything out, but they made me think.

I read *The Diary of Anne Frank* when I was ten. I thought it was pretty screwed up how one person could make such a horrible thing happen to all those people, and I felt really sorry for Anne Frank, that she had to spend her childhood in this little secret compartment. She had to be afraid of living and dying just because she was Jewish. She was probably lonely and didn't have any friends. Couldn't make any noise. Couldn't go to school. Couldn't do anything. And she had that creepy older man liking her. And then what she had to go through in the concentration camps. My mom didn't think I should have read it. It just bothered me that that kind of thing did actually happen, that there were probably a lot of other children like Anne Frank.

I love Stephen King. I love Dean Koontz. And I like trashy romance novels too. You just wish you could find somebody like that, that life could be like that, romantic and in love. I like Sidney Sheldon. I read *The Outsiders* by S.E. Hinton when I was about eight or nine. I've read it over a hundred times, I'm sure. It's about gangs. It's just so sad. But it's so much like real life. But back then I was totally square. But I kind of wanted to be on the other side. I wanted an exciting life. My life was boring to me, you know. But I also enjoyed being square, I enjoyed my mother's approval. I was always told I'm very intelligent, that I must live up to my potential.

"I'd find a Seagram's 7 bottle in my room with an ashtray full of her butts, like she was in there thinking about me."

The one my mom says is my dad, he left when I was two, then when I got eleven and twelve, that's when my stepfather left. She still tried to make it and live in the same type of area, but she couldn't, so we lived with the po' white trash. After the divorce from my stepfather, my mother started out snorting cocaine as recreation with her little yuppie friends. She says she has an addictive personality. She says it runs in the family—that I'd have to be really careful because I could easily get hooked on something. Her father was an alcoholic.

My mother started using cocaine and all kinds of drugs. Me and my boyfriend at the time were taking care of her. She was hoeing. I was twelve, and I remember a couple of times she was strung out, and she tried to make me turn a trick for her to get money for drugs. But no, I never did that when I was a child. I know that wasn't her—it was the drugs—but I had to get a lock on my door. And I had to have a pistol. I hated her at one time. We'd get in a fight and I'd leave. When I would come home, I'd find a Seagram's 7 bottle in my room with an ashtray full of her butts, like she was in there thinking about me. So I know it hurt her really bad when I left.

A couple of times, she called the police on me. I remember one time, man! Oh she pissed me off. She made me go to a mental hospital. She was high. I was selling dope for my boyfriend, and I wouldn't give her any. She got really mad, and she had a gun, and she said she was going to kill herself. I said, "Okay, if you're going to kill yourself, I'm going to kill myself." So I went and got a razor blade. So she's holding a gun to her head, and I cut my hand right here in the palm of my hand, and then I let the blood run. But she cocked the gun back, so I called 911. I said, "My mom's trying to kill herself. You all gotta do something, she's trying to kill herself." She stands at the phone saying, "No, no, my daughter's trying to kill herself." So Po-po came and they saw the cut on my hand, so I went to a mental institution.

I was thirteen. It was supposed to be for a thirty-day evaluation. I was not a danger to myself or others, and I knew my rights. But they put me there as an uncontrollable child. I hadn't actually done any crimes to be locked up. But no foster home would want me because of how rebellious I was. They had me on some antidepressants. I learned their games real quick. They just want to drug you up. You would not believe how many kids are in these mental institutions just because of their behavioral problems. Some of them, I think, really do have problems, but for the most part, they were just kids. Their moms didn't care, so they just went out and acted stupid. They did no real crimes. They weren't a threat to themselves or others. They weren't crazy. So they just call them depressed and dope them up.

I always questioned authority, you know. My mom gave me that right when I was a kid. I could say my feelings as long as I was respectful about it. I got to voice my opinion, and I've been like that ever since. You're not supposed to go in seclusion unless you're a danger to yourself or ones around you, but when you holler, cuss them out or anything, they'll put you in seclusion in a strait-jacket. So I questioned the hospital, "I'm not a danger to myself. Why am I being put in seclusion? My right are being violated." And they weren't used to a kid being able to voice an opinion like that and they just got pissed.

"I hitchhiked across country with truckers. I mean, I've been in to every state except for nine of them. I wanted to set foot in every state."

I saw my father maybe one or two times until I was about fourteen. I was supposed to graduate when I was fourteen, but the state they shipped me to my dad for a month. I stayed with him for about a month, with my three half-brothers. When I stayed with him, he was working like two jobs, and he didn't really care about me anyway, much less the other three. That's when I started being bad, running with gangs.

I lost my virginity that month that I stayed at my dad's. I slept with one of my brother's friends. I was drunk, but I wish I'd never done that, because it didn't mean anything. I didn't want to be the only virgin. I wanted it to be done and over with so I could say, "Yeah, I did it." But I wish I'd saved it and it had meant something.

Then I ran. I hitchhiked across country with truckers. I mean, I've been in to every state except for nine of them. Whatever state we stopped in, I had to get out and set foot. It makes me crazy to think about what could have happened. But it didn't. I never had a bad experience with the truckers. Most of them never came on to me. I guess they could see I was real young or something. A lot of them got me high. I experimented with a lot of drugs when I was on the road. Truckers are really good people for the most part. They'll pick up a hitchhiker, they'll feed you. I've had them give me coats, give me clothes, just take me out, and show me a good time. I guess 'cause they're really lonely.

I saw a lot of different people, a lot of different ways they talk, a lot of different things they did. I liked the ride. I didn't have to think about anything. I was just totally free. I was doing what I wanted to do. I sent my mom stuff from different states I had been to. When I came here, I sent her some apples. When I was in Georgia, I'd pick up stuff from the swamp, like pieces of weeping willow trees. I mean, I sent her this great big old grasshopper. She still has all that stuff.

"I don't know if it's God or fate or karma. There's a reason for everything, and I think at that point in my life, I needed him."

I got in a gang when I was back east. It was just kids I grew up with. They were just my homies. East Coast is not as bad as the West Coast. And there weren't all these big Bloods and Crips. It was little neighborhood cliques. Well, we all got beat in. The whole set beats you in, and you gotta stand on your feet long as you can and fight back. You can't cry or nothing like that, 'kay. You know they don't want no punks in the set. Nowadays, a lot of females get sexed in, but they get no respect, because they're just hood rats. But yeah, I got in the Piru Crips for life. In Florida, I was a plain old normal housewife. Then when I got to San Diego, I got beat in. Up here, I got beat in. Every time you gotta get beat in by twelve, fifteen people.

I was young when I met Jimmy. Fifteen. Two months later I was pregnant. It was like instant love, man. Instant. I think there's a reason for everything that happens. I don't know if it's God or fate or karma. I think at that point in my life, I needed him. Maybe it should have been over after those two years, before things went bad. But at that time in my life, I needed him, so that's what I got.

We struggled: he was working, I was working. I was manager of [a fast food chain]. I'd worked there maybe a year. I was a cashier, but then I worked my way up to manager. So I was making good money for a fifteen-year-old. When I was about eight months pregnant, I stopped working, and I never went back to work again.

I was stupid. Oh god, I was stupid. I just followed that man everywhere. First we stayed with his aunt and uncle, who raised him for most of his childhood until he was a teenager. From what he told me, he was abused. And I think that's where a lot of his abusiveness came from.

"Because when I was growing up, I wanted this nice, normal, baking-cookies-taking-your-kids-to-school-PTA-mom. That's why I married him."

We got married when I was nineteen, which we shouldn't have did because things had already started going bad. I had three kids for him. I didn't want to be one of these women that ran around having kids for every man and end up with a gang of kids by the time she's twenty-five and never been married. I wanted to have a nice normal life—the picket fence, the kids, the dog. I've had that dream since I can remember. Because when I was growing up, I wanted this nice, normal, baking-cookies-taking-your-kids-to-school-PTA-mom. That's why I married him.

I treated Jimmy really good. He would come home from work, he had bath water ready. He had his clothes laid out. As soon as he got out of the tub, I'd lotion him down and massage him. That's the way I think you should treat a man. I did it because I enjoyed spoiling him. But Jimmy, see, I was his property, He still considers me his property, and I don't feel that's what marriage is. It's an equal partnership.

We hadn't been getting along good for a while, and then he started smoking crack, and it was really, *really* bad. He would leave. One of the times he left, he left for a whole month, and I thought he was gone for good. And then I made a lot of friends. He didn't allow me to do a lot of things, and I made a lot of friends while he was gone. You know, I was trying to move on. He was really jealous, and he came back one night, and there was another guy there. There were a couple of people there, but the one guy he was really jealous of. He thought I was doing something, but the whole time we were married, I never cheated on him. He cheated on me all the time, but I never cheated on him. And he just swore I was doing something with the guy, so he starts fighting him. Then some of my friends beat him up really bad.

A couple days later he came back, and he kicked in my door, and he started hollering and cussing at me. So I got a knife and I told him I was going to kill him if he bothered me again. I forgot my oldest daughter had been sleeping with me in my room, so I ran in, and he kicked that door in on both of us. He cut my neck with the cleaver. He messed my back up pretty good, because I was trying to cover her. I was laying on top of her.

The neighbor's son called 911. What gets me mad, they had him for attempted murder and assault with a deadly weapon. He took a plea bargain. They dropped the weapon charge. They dropped the attempted murder charge. He got a felony assault. He got six months, and he did four. Now he'd a did this to somebody on the streets, he'd still be in prison. That's what gets me. He called up here and was threatening my life and threatening the kids. And [Child Protective Services] is still letting him visit with my kids Thursday.

Splitting from Jimmy was really hard for me 'cause I was just so used to him. Even though he did the things to me that he did, I was still secure there. I knew he was my husband. I was still with the father of my kids. I was still trying to have that little perfect square life. Even after all the abuse and the things he did, I still loved him. He was my first true love. He's my husband. And to me, marriage is meant to be forever. I've seen my mom go through five of them, and to me, marriage is meant to be forever. I wanted to marry one man and be with that man for the rest of my life.

"But just like in the books…[t]here's always ups and downs, and one of them acts like they don't want the other one, when they really do…"

I think I've found that man now. But he's confused. He's the most sensitive man I have ever met, and he don't care if anybody sees that. His marriage messed him up pretty bad. He told me he loves me, and I believe him. I've been seeing him since the end of April, and then he says, "Life's getting too intense. Let's just be friends a while." So we're still friends, but we make love still. It's weird. He has all these feelings and he's scared of them, and he's trying to run. And he's lucky I'm not the type of person you can push away too easily. See, I know he needs me. And I know he wants me. And I'm not going to just let him fuck off his happiness. I know life can't be like one of those books, but just like in the books, there's never a straight through romantic thing so that they immediately fall in love. There's always ups and downs, and one of them acts like they don't want the other one when they really do…

Up until Ted, I never had anybody make love to me. Even when I was married. I'm not saying certain acts weren't done. It's just the way it was done and the feelings that were put behind it. When I was hoeing, I met some hell of crazy people. Really. I don't think they were mentally ill, but they were sick people. Now, I read *The Happy Hooker*. You ever read that? I think I read it when I was about eleven or twelve. And I just couldn't believe some of the stuff she wrote about. And then when I started hoeing, *really, what she was writing about—that's true!*

I had this one dude take me to a hotel, and he said, "I want to kiss you all over. I want to lick your feet." He wasn't into sadism or anything like that, but he wanted to be punished like he was a bad boy. I could never do that sadism thing. I could never get pleasure out of deliberately hurting somebody else. And then there's guys that act like they want to pick up a date, like they want to have sex, but they don't. All they really want to do is talk, because maybe they're not able to talk to their wives like that, or they don't have anybody close.

Ted's treated me better than anybody's treated me. I was settling for less than what I deserved. And now, even if it never works out between me and him, I will never ever be able to have sex for money again. I will never ever be able to just "get my fuck on" as I call it when I fuck just for fucking. There's a big difference between fucking and making love. And I will never ever be able to do that again.

"When they see me, people think I'm a thug. People said I looked young and innocent—a long time ago."

I'm not stressing on Ted. If something's meant to be, it's going to be. That's why I'm not scared of dying. I'm not worrying. Even when I was gang banging, maybe it was a dangerous lifestyle, but it wasn't my time to go. I think there's a time and a place for everything and everything happens for a reason. And that's why I'm not scared. I feel like if you're a good person, good things will come back to you. When I tend to do evil things, evil things tend to happen to me. When I do good things, something always comes along or somebody always comes along. Maybe it's just a kind word that you need at that moment that makes you feel really good. That's my philosophy on life.

I've had a lot of good times. I think that's why I'm pretty calm now. It's easy for me not to run the streets like I used to and do those things I used to do because I've had total freedom. Total. I guess I'm lucky. I never used any drug addictively. I drank a lot when I was a teenager, but it's just something that I outgrew. And then I went back, and I finished school.

I have a lot to look forward to. I'm young and everything, but once you get past, like twenty-five, headed toward thirty, there's this image you must uphold in order for anyone to have any respect for you. When they see me, people think I'm a thug. People said I looked young and innocent—a long time ago. So I guess maybe I made myself look mean. Now people don't look at me the same way.

I look forward to being financially stable, and doing it the right way and being able to go where I want to go and learn everything I want to learn. When you stop learning, you might as well be dead. I want to know everything there is to know about everything. I want to travel to Europe and Asia. I don't want to just go and stay a couple days and be gone. I want to stay and find out about the people and their cultures. I want to know. I want to see. That's all. That's just how I am.

CHAPTER 6

Debra Martinson

Debra was a resident at Lutheran Compass Center (LCC) in November 1996, when the shelter staff informed me that she was willing to be interviewed. Debra had recently relocated to Seattle and only months before, in January of 1996, when she was still living in Chicago, she had launched "Secret Shame," the first website directed toward people who engage in what is now termed "non-suicidal self-injury," following it up in April of that year with a list serve and web board, both known as "BUS," an acronym for "Bodies Under Siege" after psychiatrist Armando Favazza's influential 1987 book Bodies Under Siege: Self-Mutilation in Culture and Psychiatry. *Favazza's book challenged dominant theories that saw behaviors like cutting and burning as evidence of suicidal intent and as symptomatic of "borderline personality disorder," which was itself deemed singularly resistant to treatment.[1] The website "Secret Shame" includes links to articles positing theories about underlying causes and strategies for coping with the urge to self-harm, along with chat rooms to enable sufferers and survivors to critique prevailing theories and support each other in their shared struggles.*

When I interviewed her at Lutheran Compass Center, Deb was in the process of applying for SSI and waiting for space to open up in a transitional housing facility. But even homeless, Deb continued to operate and find comfort and support in the virtual community she'd played a central role in creating. I lost touch with Deb shortly after the two interviews I conducted with her in 1996, and it would be another fifteen years before we reconnected.

"I mean, it's like, this isn't supposed to be my life. There's an REM song somewhere that has a line over and over again: 'It's not supposed to be like this.'"

This is the first time that I've been officially "a homeless person." Always before I would manage something. But, but after my major suicide attempt last April, it just became clear to me that I had to get away from Chicago, so I moved here. In part because I wanted to go to grad school at the University of Washington, which I still want to do. When I first moved here, and I had a job that hadn't started yet, I had friends on the Internet who were sending me money, but there was a time when I didn't have any money, and I had to spend two nights in shelters, and that was pretty scary. It was a bad scene. And I was also very ashamed of myself at the time for having fallen that far.

There's an REM song somewhere that has a line over and over again: "It's not supposed to be like this," and that's how I feel. It's not supposed to be like this. I had the total expectation that I was going to have a completely different life than what I've had. I lost my job due to depression, not being on meds, all kinds of things happening together, and I ended up in Three Mental Health (3MH).[2] While I was there, I was evicted from my apartment. The thing that really pissed me off was that I had a wonderful therapist at 3MH, but she only saw in-patients. The way that the whole mental health system is set up now is "Get 'em in, ship 'em out." They don't really care what happens to you once you leave. I got out, [and] I didn't have anywhere to live.

I had a voucher for a week in a fleabag downtown, and my time was running out. I was starting to get pretty stressed, so I burned myself rather severely, ended up back at Harborview in the burn unit and then got put into the involuntary unit. They restrain you—three-point restraints: one ankle, around your middle, and a wrist. And then they put a table by your bed, with a bedpan on it, and some toilet paper and a glass of water. And that's pretty much it. They couldn't restrain my left wrist because that's where the burns were, and I was still on oxycodone for pain for the bums, because they were chemical burns, and they were quite painful. I still have massive scars that itch a lot.

After the seventy-two-hour hold, I was transferred to Northwest Evaluation and Treatment Center and put on a fourteen-day hold. And I mean there was nothing there. There was nothing to do. My symptoms were nowhere near severe enough to justify two weeks. And finally we all agreed on this, and I got out a few days early, but I never got to meet with the social worker, so I had nowhere to go. I had no idea where I was going to live—what I was going to do. I had been planning to pick up my GAU check and food stamps, but the check wasn't available, because they didn't mail them until after they knew I was out of the hospital. I'm sitting here in the middle of Seattle, lugging around a ton of stuff. I don't have money to leave it anywhere, and it was kind of embarrassing to be carrying around a bunch of stuff and not have anywhere to go or anything to do.

"I was walking, and it was raining, kind of drizzling down, walking over that big bridge on Pine, over the freeway, and thinking that I could just jump off of it if I wanted to."

So I went down to the Speakeasy, which is a cyber cafe, and logged on. They closed at midnight, so I got on the Number Seven bus and went up to Twice Told Tales on John Street. I had a couple of dollars so I could buy a couple of books, because that's what I do when I'm not happy is I buy books. I either eat, or I buy books. I was up at John and Broadway, and it was like maybe one-thirty in the morning. I went to the Jack in the Box to get a Diet Coke. By then the buses weren't running anymore, so I walked all the way down from there to Seneca and Third. I was walking, and it was drizzling. I walked over that big bridge on Pine, over the freeway, and I thought that I could just jump over it if I wanted to. And how silly it was to have it be there.

I went to Third and Seneca and sat there for a while at the bus stop and this guy came up on his bike and started talking to this girl and it became really obvious really fast that this fifteen-year-old, sixteen-year-old kid was a major crack dealer who was facing trial and was riding a stolen bicycle and was looking to go see if he could score some more crack. And some chick rode up on a bicycle, and they were comparing where they'd stolen their bicycles from. And it was a strange feeling, a very eerie feeling.

And they finally left, and the bus tunnel opened, and I went over to the eastside, then came back, went to the library, started calling around and found an opening here. Even though it was only one night, I felt like I had been wandering in the wilderness, and now I had found a place where it was safe, just to be and to have my stuff and lie down and let it go.

"When I was a kid, when I was little, before my dad remarried, he used to tell me that I was smart enough to be anything I wanted to be, even though I was a girl."

It's kind of hard being here, because I'm educated. But I've had a lot of stereotypes shattered here. Like Sweet Pea, okay, she's a thug, you know, but when you get to talking to her, she speaks French and Latin. She was an honor student. She and I were roommates when she first got here, and we hated each other's guts. And now we're friends. She's been hurt a lot. She's been disappointed a lot, and she wants somebody to make it all better. But I think that's what we all really want, and, I finally resigned myself to the fact that it's just not going to happen.

When I was little, before my dad remarried, he used to tell me that I was smart enough to be anything I wanted to be, even though I was a girl. I could be anything I wanted to be when I grew up. He really gave me that feeling. And years of abuse just eroded that feeling and left me feeling like I would just drift through life waiting to see what's going to happen next. In some ways I feel like, how much lower can I get? Am I going to be sleeping in doorways? Being homeless is, to me, embarrassing and a mark of failure. If I'd done it right—if I'd been a better person—then I wouldn't be here.

I was five and six when my dad was in Vietnam. There were four kids. My mom was overwhelmed, I think, and so she really never had a lot of time for me. My brother had epilepsy and something wrong with his legs and something wrong with his kidneys so he had to go to the doctor. We were living in Western Massachusetts, but the only Air Force hospital was Chelsea, which is outside of Boston. My little sister, she was extremely pigeon-toed, so for a while she was in one of those night braces where they turn your feet outward, and those weren't working, so they put casts on both her legs. And I wet the bed. So, my mom was dealing with all of this.

After my father got back from Vietnam, my mom died. She was diagnosed in mid-August and died September 4. She had leukemia, and she died of pneumonia caused by the leukemia, and it was a shock to everybody. We were good little children, and we didn't get upset. We didn't cry. My dad was single; he took a second job, though he didn't need to. He was in the military, and the military paid for my mom's medical and funeral expenses. But I think he just couldn't stand to be around the house without her. I think he really did love her, and he took her death really hard. Then my father remarried, and the abuse started.

I remember right after they got married, she put all my stuffed animals into a trash bag, and then gave it to my brother to use to collect the dog shit out of the back yard. These were stuffed animals that I had had for as long as I could remember, and they were incredibly important to me. And they were all gone. I've gotten to the place now where I have totally inured myself to losses, because I have lost so many things in my life. I just start over. Within a month she had convinced my dad to throw my older sister out in the street. She was sixteen, but she and I were close. We weren't allowed to mention her name anymore. I didn't see her again for eight years. She was just gone. She didn't exist.

I lived for seven years in an atmosphere of total violence and terror and control. I just remember she would beat me and throw me around, and then I would come back and stand in my room and clench my fists and say that it was never going to happen again. I would never let her see me cry. And it just never ended.

Everybody in school picked on me. I was the scapegoat and I got beaten up a lot, but I was also the class brain, doing really well as an honor student and being recognized as a gifted writer. And then I would go home and get beaten up. My little sister remembers a lot of things that happened that I don't. I have a lot of holes in my memory. She remembers me fighting back and yelling at my step-monster, and she remembers thinking, "Oh god, she's going to get killed this time." I don't remember any incidents like that. She remembers usually me defending her. I protected her as much as I could. I couldn't protect her when the step-monster would get out her gun and say, "I'm going to come and shoot you in your sleep at night."

My father wasn't around, and so we kind of ran wild. We used to go to bed early, but kids would come over and hang out at our window and we'd talk and goof off and do kid things. The boy next door was fifteen, and sexually molested me. I know I was nine, and I didn't know what it was, but I still feel deeply ashamed about it.

When I was in twelfth grade, the final semester, I got into journalism. By the time that the district championships in high-school journalism rolled around, I won district. I went to state, and I won first in editorials and second in features at South Texas Press Day. And it was like the first time anybody from our school had ever won anything. I went off to Baylor on [a] National Merit [Scholarship] and was the first freshman on the newspaper staff. I had to leave after a year because of depression and a lot of other things, but I won two awards for writing while I was there.[3]

In 1982, after I went off to school, my little sister ran away. I told her before I left, "You're not going to last six months," and she didn't believe me. She didn't last six months. They put her in a fundamentalist children's home. She ran away to a friend's house in another city, and the friend didn't want to take her in. Her friend's pastor took her in and presented my parents with a list of children's homes, because he wasn't going to let them have her back. They chose one in Mississippi. And so she was sent there.

Then I got a letter from my stepmother saying my sister ran away, and they weren't going to look for her. I spent thirty-six hours straight on the phone looking for her. I finally found her. I tried to get her into [another church-affiliated children's home in Texas] somehow, but I was just her sister; I was seventeen, and I didn't have any power. There was nothing I could do. I felt so guilty. I was put in the student health center for two weeks because they were afraid I was going to hurt myself. It was the beginning of the second semester, and I sank into a major depression and failed all my classes except for journalism and English. Those are the only ones I went to anymore.

"The things that I've lost, they're in my past and they haunt me, but I just don't think about them."

There's just so much stuff that is painful, and sometimes I think it's never going to stop hurting. I was raped twice. My house was broken into four times. When I was in Chicago, I was living in an apartment. I moved part of my stuff, and then I went into the hospital again and wasn't able to move the rest of it right away, and the landlord said he would hold it for me. But I never was able to get hold of him again, and so I just basically lost it all. The things that I've lost, they're in my past and they haunt me, but I just don't think about them. If I thought about them, I'd cry, and I'd never stop. I guess that's one of the things about being homeless is that you worry a lot about losing things. And so I've gotten to a point where I don't get very attached, because if I do, I can't deal with it.

My brother died in 1987. He was twenty-six. He was an epileptic; he had petit mal seizures. And after my dad remarried, my stepmother convinced my father that my brother was faking. I remember sometimes, if he had a seizure while he was doing dishes, they would shove his head into the dirty dishwater and slap him around. There were holes in the sheet rock from where they hit his head against the wall. They hit him hard enough to break his glasses.

He left home at sixteen and drifted. He was pretty much a drifter, in and out of a state hospital all of his life. Then his epilepsy got worse, and eventually, before his death, he was having grand mal seizures. I saw him a year and a half before his death, and he was just so proud that I was his sister. He called me about a year later. He wanted to know if he could come and live with me, but I was in the middle of just utter chaos in my life, and I couldn't take on responsibility for him, so I told him no.

But before he died, he had just gotten an apartment of his own. He had a job as a janitor. He was making friends. And then, in '87, he was taking a shower, and he had a seizure, and it killed him. The cause of death on the death certificate was "seizure disorder." I borrowed the money from my in-laws to have him cremated, because I didn't want to give his body to the state. There was a memorial service, and some friends of his came up to us afterwards, and they told us about how they had gotten together a house warming, how they'd given him a bunch of apartment stuff, because he didn't have any. He took half of it, and he went out and found somebody with less stuff than he had, and he gave it away. And I felt so unworthy to be alive at that moment. So incredibly unworthy of living. I buy things for different residents at the shelter or give them money if they need it, and if I've got it. When I do things like that, I'm doing it in honor of him. Because I feel like I should have been the one to die, not him. He was just such a forgiving person, such an open person. I spend approximately 10 percent of my GAU check on other people, and it's in his memory. He was a better person than I am. He deserved to be alive.

As far as I'm concerned my parents killed him. And they didn't even bother to come to the memorial service or the funeral. My stepmother died in 1992 of cirrhosis of the liver. With any luck it was a long and painful death. She bled to death internally. My dad left for work during the morning and came back, and she was dead.

Last night I was at Safeway. I was walking past the produce department, and I saw mushrooms, bulk rate white mushrooms. And I wanted to cry, because I could remember that period of my life. I was living in my little studio apartment with my cat, and there were cat toys in all the doorways. I bought cookware, and I bought kitchen things, and I bought little electrical appliances, and I would go out shopping and buy mushrooms and buy things and make my own dinners. And every payday I would stop at Woolworths on the way home, or the pet store and buy cat toys. And I would come home from work and relax. And for some reason seeing mushrooms last night made me think of that.

"They couldn't see me with the camera. So she came in and found me in the bathroom, and before I knew it, I'd been stripped down, put in a hospital gown, thrown on the bed and in five-point restraints."

One night I called my grandmother, and somebody answered, and they said she was too sick, and they said call back tomorrow. And I said, "Okay, and by the way are you somebody I should know? Are you a relative?" And he said, "I'm your father." My grandmother turned out to have had breast cancer that had spread to her stomach and her groin and her brain. My father kept in touch while my grandmother was dying, and then after she died, he disowned us again. That whole incident totally just destroyed me. I ended up losing my job not long after that. I overdosed shortly after I got back from there. I was hospitalized, then I went back to work, but I couldn't deal, so they fired me. I was hospitalized immediately, taken from there to the emergency room, [and then] to a mental hospital. Which was a hellish place.

There was a nurse there who didn't like me, and one night I was playing solitaire and waiting for the meds line to go down. I could see it from where I was. The line was almost through, so she stuck her head in the room and said, "If you haven't taken you meds go get 'em." And I said, "Okay, cool. I was waiting for the line to get small." And she said, "After you take your meds, you have to go the Quiet Room for fifteen minutes." And I'm like, "Why?" And she said, "Don't question me." So I went and got my meds and took them and went back to my solitaire game. And she came in, and she said it again: "Go to the Quiet Room." And I said, "I don't see what I did wrong." And she said, "You just do what I tell you." And she got these two big thuggy attendants, and they dragged me off down the hall to the Quiet Room, and they threw me in there. I was crying. There's a bathroom in there, and I went in the bathroom to blow my nose, to try and stop crying. They couldn't see me with the camera. So she came in and found me in the bathroom, and before I knew it, I'd been stripped down, put in a hospital gown, thrown on the bed and in five-point restraints.

That was around five or six o'clock at night. There's a rule that when you're in restraints, somebody's supposed to come in at periods of time and put you through a range of motion exercises and to make sure that you don't need anything to drink, that you don't need to go to the bathroom. That's the rule. And they didn't do that. Somebody came in right after I was put in restraints, took my vital signs and gave me a sip of water. Somebody came in at nine and gave me my meds. And somebody came in a couple of hours after that to see if I needed to go to the bathroom, but I'd already wet the bed. So he just left in disgust. Finally, at three in the morning, I was released from restraints. I was completely soaked in urine. Some had gotten into my hair. I mean, it was dripping when I walked down the hallway. I was in that hospital for three weeks, and then my friend Allen took care of me for a couple of months. And since then I've been in a depressive episode, and I haven't been able to get it together long enough to keep a job for more than two or three weeks.

If there's anything, anyone that I really love in this world it's my best friend Allen in Chicago, and my cat, Eve. One of the things that's really bothering me right now is what am I going to do with Eve. I've had him for two years now. Pets are a luxury. You can't have one if you're homeless. I don't know what I'll do if I have to get rid of Eve. And I can't bear the thought of him going somewhere and getting killed.

"They can talk about wanting to cut. They can talk about wanting to bleed. But they can also celebrate victories."

During one of my hospitalizations, I broke a light bulb and started cutting myself with the glass. That was like opening a door and making it okay to cut. Since then I've cut and burned myself several times. My left arm looks like a battleground. And, I don't know why I do it exactly. It makes me feel better, in some way that I can't explain exactly.

I was on a mailing list for depressives, and other people were talking about cutting, and I thought, "I could write and ask questions, document about cutting." And so I set out to figure out what I could find out. And that was back in January or so. At first I didn't do a whole lot of research. I just wrote up what I had from what books I had around and what I could find in books like *Women Who Hurt Themselves* and *Trauma and Recovery*.[4] Then I mailed out a questionnaire for people who cut themselves, and I quoted some of those. I've thought about expanding the website even more. It's won awards from the Mental Health Net. It won a three star award of excellence.

When I was feeling suicidal once, somebody posted this [Anne Sexton] poem for me, which is just beautiful. It's the first stanza of "Wanting to Die": "Since you ask, most days I cannot remember./I walk in my clothing unmarked by that voyage. / Then the almost unnamable lust returns." That describes how most of the people I know who do this feel about it. It's an addiction. It's a lust.

I also run an e-mail support group, for people who cut themselves. It's a place where people can speak the unspeakable. They can say things that would horrify other people in their lives. They can talk about wanting to cut. They can talk about wanting to bleed. But they can also celebrate victories. One man who was sexually abused by his grandfather, he beats himself, and he was thinking he was going to have to hurt himself that night. He was putting his kids to bed, and he started talking about how they have Cat Town, the kingdom of the cats, and they go on adventures and they make up stories about the adventures that the princess and the tomcat go on. And I almost cried because it was just so beautiful to me that this man, who had been hurt so badly, could overcome his own demons and just be there with his children. I mean, these people are tough. These people are survivors.

There should be places where people who are homeless...who have been damaged, can stay, like wildlife sanctuaries, where you take the birds with the broken wings..."

I don't think I'm your typical homeless person. But I don't know what a typical homeless person is anymore. Any stereotypes I have have been shattered. I mean, it's not at all like what I thought. I still think that the government needs to be doing more. There should be places where people who are homeless, who have been damaged can stay and pick up the pieces and get treatment, and get what they need, and get respite. Like wildlife sanctuaries, where you take the birds with the broken wings and take care of them for five or six months and then let them go. Especially if you've been homeless a long time, you're out of the mainstream, and you don't know how to live in it. And this would be a place where you could learn—to quote Wallace Stevens—"How to live, what to do." Learn how to get a job. You could learn social skills. You would learn how to love yourself.

The shelters can't do it by themselves. They don't have the money. People have been tricked by—let's get political here—by the Reagan-Bush era, into thinking that homeless people want to be homeless. I'm damned lucky that I have a bed here. People think it's all taken care of by the nice shelters and the nice charities. Somebody's sleeping in a doorway, they must be a wino or a bum, or whatever. I spent a night walking around Seattle because I was scared to sleep in a doorway. But there's not enough [shelters] out there. And it's not right—it's not right that this should be entirely done by private means.

One of the things that influenced me to go ahead and go on SSI is that I'm viewing it as the government's investing in me—helping me to get well. And they will be more than paid back by the tax dollars that I earn once I'm able to get the kind of job I'm capable of doing. And, people don't see that. They look at the short term. They don't look at it as investing in people, because we all know that all homeless people are lazy and slobs and degenerate drug users. Millions of people are being written off as useless, and it makes me very, very angry.

I think it came out of the whole 80s, "I got mine, you get yours" attitude. What people don't realize is that I got mine and you got yours because you had a lot of help and a lot of advantages and a lot of luck. Just being born white is an advantage. Being born a white male is a huge advantage. And people don't notice. They want to think that they did it all by themselves on their own virtue. And I'm not ashamed to say that half the reason I'm alive today is because of lucky breaks and things people have done for me. I've done a lot of it myself, and I'm proud of that, but I wouldn't have made it without other people.

I get so angry at the way this country views homeless people. I was reading an article in the *New Republic* about how the Republicans were trying to get the Pentagon to request more money for their budget. Going to each branch and saying, "Here. Give us a list of like three billion dollars more stuff you want…" What you could do with three billion dollars distributed among the shelters in this country! It's just little things, like the hot plate died, and we can't replace it. But they don't want to see it that way. They'd rather buy big mean metal things to kill people with than take care of people. And I don't even know what it's like in family shelters. I would shudder to think what it's like being a kid growing up like this. These kids could be so much, they could contribute, and the government isn't willing to do a fucking thing.

And then the whole incredibly, incredibly, incredibly hypocritical thing about looking down on alcohol and drug users. I mean the most addictive drug used in this country is nicotine, for god's sake. And these people sit there with their cigars talking about how if you use money for the homeless they'll just go out and get drunk—while they 're swilling down a scotch and water. Shit, I mean if I were out living out on the streets, I'd want to be drunk or stoned. I wouldn't want to have to be there. If you never learned how to dissociate, you'd sure as hell have to get some chemical help to do it.

If you'd asked me ten years ago, I would have said this will never happen to me. This is not my life. It's not supposed to be like this. You go from being a capable adult running your own life to being almost completely dependent upon the mercy of other people, and a lot of the times your fate is not decided on merit. It's whether you're in the right place at the right time.

But I've always been lucky that way—falling on my feet. Things have never been as bad as they could be. Whenever I feel like I am desperate, something happens. Like I was pretty desperate, and a place here opened up. That was just utter, complete serendipity. Sometimes it makes me think maybe there is a god. But if there is a god, why in the hell does he put me through all of this? Your religious people would say, "Well, you're tempered by fire." I didn't ask to be tempered, thank you. I would have been quite happy being weak. But I'm strong, one of the strongest people I know.

CHAPTER 7

Anitra Freeman

Figure 2 Anitra Freeman at a Women in Black cleansing

I was introduced to Anitra in 2006 by organizer Michele Marchand, and I interviewed Anitra on several occasions between 2006 and 2008 and again in June 2010, when I met with her to discuss the penultimate draft of this chapter. Anitra is among the most visible of Seattle's homeless or formerly homeless activists working to end homelessness. For the past fifteen years, she has contributed countless hours of work to grassroots organizations in

Seattle that share a common commitment to empowering homeless people. My interviews with Anitra had to be squeezed in around her organizing commitments at various sites around town, including Mary's Place before and after Women in Black vigils, in the offices of Real Change, *the WHEEL Women's Empowerment Center, a Portland restaurant during the annual conference of the North American Street Newspapers Association, and in the apartment that she shared with* Real Change *columnist Wes Browning, whom she married in 2010.*

Anitra was raised by middle-class parents whose economic struggles were exacerbated by untreated mental health issues, but who instilled in their children a concern for civil rights and social justice, a love of literature, and a commitment to independent thinking and critical analysis. Anitra's activism is as wide-ranging as her analysis of the root causes of homelessness and its consequences. An Air Force Veteran and the child of a Korean War veteran whose post-traumatic stress disorder (PTSD) went undiagnosed and untreated for decades, Anitra's work with other area peace organizations, including Veterans for Peace, the Fellowship of Reconciliation (FOR),[1] and the Seattle Raging Grannies,[2] speaks to the economic and human costs of war both locally and globally.

"Personal problems don't dig the hole in the sidewalk; they just influence who is going to fall into it. It's systemic factors that create the hole."

I have said often that people have personal problems, of course, but personal problems don't cause homelessness. Personal problems don't dig the hole in the sidewalk; they just influence who is going to fall into it. It's systemic factors that create the hole. I might have had the same personal problems if there was social justice, economic justice, environmental justice, and everything the peace and justice community is struggling for. But would I have become homeless even with the same personal problems? I would have had more teeth left because I could have gotten dental care even during the times when I had no money. My physical health would have been better, and I would probably live longer. I probably would have still spent the rest of my life as a poster child for codependence, but I wouldn't have parts of my body that will never relax again, because when you're homeless you're scared all the time—you're scared while you're asleep. If we had social and economic justice, I wouldn't be in chronic pain all the time.

If we had peace and justice in the world, my father would not have returned from Korea with five bullet holes in him and something that they didn't know to call PTSD back then. There are some things that economic justice in the world, housing for everybody, the necessities of life for everybody, won't fix for everybody. But there's a chance that if we had a real community health system, and if we had an economic system that hadn't driven my parents from place to place so rapidly, fleeing from creditors, or looking for a new job, my mother might have been diagnosed earlier as bipolar and gotten treatment earlier and not self-medicated with alcohol, and I might not have memories of mom naked and screaming at three o'clock in the morning throwing coffee cups at the wall because the demons were coming through. And maybe I would have been in one place with one doctor for long enough that someone would have realized that *I* have bipolar disorder and that I have attention-deficit disorder (ADD), and maybe it would have been identified and treated if I had been able to get medical help when I needed it.

And I would have had a place of my own, even a standing room only apartment with bare walls, even during the times when I was in the great gray fog of depression and couldn't do a damn thing. I wouldn't have been wandering around dependent on the kindness of strangers, going home with whoever would give me a place to sleep at night. And I wouldn't have been couch surfing until I ran out of couches.

Bipolar disorder II is hard for anybody to diagnose, and when you don't see someone consistently over a lengthy period of time, it's even harder. At the times when I was at the stage of manic when you really are smarter than everybody, and you really do work harder than anybody, I was an employer's dream. I would work ninety-hour weeks. First the hypomanic, the competent manic is running, then the mania goes hyper, and you think you can fly, but it's your judgment that's gone flying. Then comes the fast drop off from the way too manic down to depression when it would take me four hours to put a letter in an envelope and get a stamp on it and get it in the mailbox. As I got older and older, this erratic work history made it harder and harder to get a job. The manic highs became less and less, and the depressive periods got longer and longer, and in 1995, when I was forty-five years old, I went through the longest depression in my life, and I ran out of couches to sleep on. After eight months of sleeping on my friend's couch, I spent the last money I had on the YWCA for a couple of nights. And then I was officially homeless.

"The day after I became homeless I looked around Third and James and I said, 'Where did all these people come from?'"

Before I became homeless, I was either at work or I was at home or I was on the road in-between and in my own car in-between. There's a lot of stuff you're insulated from in the middle-class cocoon. The day after I became homeless I looked around Third and James, and I said, "Where did all these people come from?" There are a lot of things that just don't register because they aren't part of your reality, and you literally don't see them.

I spent one night out at the airport. There were three or four older Black men in the airport lounge, and three or so older white men, and a woman and her adult daughter. All of them had that gray pavement look on their faces, and they were all sitting there for hours and hours, not going anywhere. So I sat there, and eventually I lay down and eventually went to sleep. At four o'clock in the morning, the airport security came through, and they rousted the Black guys. They didn't ask any of the rest of us any questions. So I knew that civil rights, the end to racism that my mother and I had marched for together in the 60s, hadn't completely taken yet. And that was just one of the ways in which my country slowly radicalized me every single day from the time I became homeless.

When I was homeless, I was afraid all the time. As a working woman making $48,000 a year as a computer programmer, a wife and mother with a house of my own, I might have been tense about a lot of things including the bills, but I wasn't scared. I wasn't scared as a middle-class woman walking down the sidewalk, but walking down the same sidewalk as a homeless woman at the same time of day I was scared. It's not the same place; it's not the same world. You're surrounded by different forces; you're subject—you're susceptible—to different risks.

One of my most vivid physical memories of being homeless is standing on a street corner at Third and James at three o'clock in the morning in the rain and going, "I have no place to go." And one of those nights when it was raining, I went up to my friend's place up on Beacon Hill to try to see if he could let me use the couch for just one night. He was out of town, and the place was locked up, so I slept underneath his back porch. During the night, when I had to pee, I peed into an empty can, and during the night when I went to sleep, that knocked over. That was the low point— the absolutely low point for me.

Another memory that I keep with me is what it felt like to sit among people who were eating their lunch in the plaza and drinking their espressos and eating their braised sandwiches and pretending that I wasn't hungry and wistfully hoping that the woman that I'm chatting with will ask me if I want something. But it would really embarrass me to ask her.

One night when I had been walking all over Capitol Hill, looking in windows, daydreaming about seeing a sign that says, "Wanted: one manic-depressive computer programmer who will live in the office. Food provided," and I didn't find it. I stood on a street corner, and I said, "Okay, this is it. I'm forty-five years old. I'm manic depressive." I had been to a clinic and gotten diagnosed. I had a prescription for lithium, but I didn't have any money to get it filled. I knew I had bronchitis, I was physically sick; I have bad teeth; my hair's a mess. I'm overweight, and my tits hang down to my navel, and I'm homeless, and I have no place to go. I'm out of work, and I'm broke, and I've been through everything. And I just said, "Okay, that's the way it is."

It was a moment of self-acceptance. I could literally hear all my defense systems crashing on the pavement. And weeks later, I finally realized that this self-esteem thing that everybody kept talking about all my life, I had it now. I had it now because I totally accepted myself. I did not have to deny or defend anything about me because I wasn't ashamed of anything about me, so I was in the middle of the biggest growth period of my life.

As soon as I had that moment, I recalled that I had passed a subsidized apartment building, and I walked back there, and I walked in, and I said, "I'm homeless, and I've got no place to go. I'm out of work; I'm broke; I'm sick. I'm manic-depressive. I need help." And they sent me down to Angeline's, which at that time was the only day center for homeless women in Seattle. I walked into Angeline's, and God bless them, they gave me a stack of material about everything that I'd ever think of—every housing program, every clinic program, every food bank. Everything that existed was there. I was just coming out of depression, and they gave me this stack of material, and they pointed to the [free] phone. I went and made two phone calls, and I got voice mail at both places, so I just left a message, and I went over and sat down on the couch for the rest of the day.

"I was one of the shuffling figures, who went in, head down, and just meekly got the mat."

At the end of the day, Angeline's had one of the other homeless women walk me down to Noel House, because everybody knew it was two blocks away, and in the state I was in, I'd get lost. Thankfully, I walked into Noel House on the night of the week that a mental health outreach worker happened to be there, and I was at the point where I was ready to talk to her. She was able to get me my lithium, and she was able to be a continuous counselor for me. She was able to get me onto state disability pretty quickly, and eventually get me into housing.

At Noel House, there was a meal for everybody, and the first forty women on that list had beds there at Noel House. The rest, you have your meal, and then around seven o'clock, seven-thirty, the vans start coming by, and each van takes a few women—half a dozen—to one of this whole network of overflow shelters in church basements. So that night, I caught a van out to the shelter, and I was doing the "homeless shuffle." I was one of the shuffling figures who went in, head down, and just meekly got the mat. The volunteers, these caring women, pointed me to the mat. I'm not sure whether it was that night or a subsequent night when the women beside me was a sixty-eight-year-old woman with arthritis. It took her about five minutes to get down on that mat and another five minutes to get back up. And that cut into me. Even through the fog, I thought: to have that life, to have that happening to that sixty eight year old woman sleeping on that little rubber mat, that concrete floor . . .

The next day Debbie handed me my prescription for lithium and I began to perk up a bit, and I could see the color on the wall, and I could taste my food, but I was still pretty much limping along. A volunteer at Noel House came in to make Halloween cards, and for my Halloween card, I cut a rectangle of dark brown paper and put it onto a rectangle of orange paper, and I wrote a two line poem which was the first poem I'd written in six months: "Now all threatening shadows open into warmth and light."

And it was only a few days later, when I perked up a little bit more, and I realized I could not stand *one more day* of coming into Noel House and having my food served to me by these people and being given little plastic forks and spoons to eat with that I couldn't hurt myself with [*laughs*]. I noticed a poster up on one of the walls for self-managed shelter, so the next day or the day after that, I went to the offices of SHARE and WHEEL, and I screened for one of those shelters.

"Out of limbo I come to find myself/scattered across the pavement,/ creating from found objects a life."

It was in the cafeteria of Catholic Community Services, and when I first started going up there, it was an achievement to use my bus ticket and get up there all by myself. I could help bring out the mats and the blankets, and I could help set up the tables, and I could do some chores because we all did something. We had a weekly meeting of the shelter where we discussed any problems and helped solve problems among ourselves, and after a while I could actually participate in that. Every week, the shelter needed to send one or two people to "the Power Lunch," a meeting of all of SHARE and WHEEL shelters, where we'd all learned what was going on in the group at large. So I started going.

I was still going down to Noel House to get my dinner and check in with all my friends, and I was passing this place on the corner called the Street Life Art Gallery, which had been started by one of the guys in SHARE. It had grown out of the very first tent city at the same time as the shelter network, but it was run independently. It was a self-managed place for homeless and low-income artists to do and also to display and sell their art and get the proceeds. So I walked in and this very nice gentleman named Wes Browning introduced himself as the president of the art gallery. And I began palling around with him. One day I went to the library and checked out some books on very inexpensive ways to make your own handmade paper, and walking back to the gallery, I composed the second poem: "Out of limbo I come to find myself/scattered across the pavement,/ creating from found objects a life." I eventually became one of the coordinators of the gallery.

Tim Harris from *Real Change* came down to the gallery one day. Wes introduced him to me, and they both said, "We need you on the editorial committee." Very quickly I saw a lot of the stuff that was being submitted from vendors and other homeless people and low-income people from the housing projects around here had real spark and passion to it. Most of them needed polish before they were ready for publication.

I was born into a family of "bookaholics" and "wordaholics"—I never stood a chance. Reading and writing were considered normal human activities. I had been doing it since I was five. In the mid-80s, after my divorce, I was working full time at Boeing, but every Tuesday night there was an open mike at the End of Time Café in Tacoma and I would go there. I'd read poetry at the Folk Music Open Mike. I had a poetry mentor at the time, and I went to regular workshops and he told me, "Anitra, you write a lot of junk. You write a lot of really lousy stuff, but every now and then..."

So I began helping people one on one, including one of the women who was staying in my shelter, who had a folder of scraps, of bits and pieces of things scribbled on torn pieces of typing paper, torn pieces of napkins. One of them was a piece of a paper bag. And I helped her compile one short essay out of all of that. I'd been lucky enough to be involved in a lot of really good workshops, where everybody is an equal, and everybody helps each other. And I decided that that would be a lot more empowering model than my trying to teach every homeless person in Seattle how to write. And so I started a workshop I call StreetWrites, and *Real Change* gave me space and resources.

So that grew and grew and grew. I'm very proud of StreetWrites, and it's all the same model, SHARE and WHEEL and StreetWrites. It's gotta be people doing it for themselves. The place of the organizer is to help the people—help them be the leaders. Because it was egalitarian—everybody was helping everybody—we ended up doing a lot more projects than I could ever have done. We hung out there at least three nights a week and most of Sunday, but eventually I would get tired, and I'd have to go home to my apartment, to my bed, and know that some of my friends were going out to sleep in the bushes or in the doorway down by Bethel Temple or in some shelter or tent city if they were lucky. And I could go home and have a shower and eat something and go to bed, because the whole idea is to increase everybody's well-being. You do not do that by bringing yourself down; you do it keeping yourself up there and bringing other people up. So it's good to enjoy life. And it's great for the people who have problems to have a place to think and enjoy life. Not only will I not come to the revolution if I can't dance, if you aren't dancing, you aren't having a revolution.

I say often that I am convinced that if I had not gotten involved with the whole network of people and had all these projects to pull me out of my apartment once I got up there, I would have sat there isolated, withdrawn, gone back into depression, stopped taking my meds, stopped seeing my doctors, stopped doing my paperwork, dropped off of disability, gone back, lost my apartment, gone back on the street. And I would have been wandering around in the great, gray fog until something killed me.

"You need community. Human beings need other human beings."

There are four things that got me out of homelessness and that keep me out of homelessness. One is a source of income. For me it's now Social Security. I am now officially retired early on disability. I've worked enough in my life that I get close to a $1,000 a month, and I can live on that. Then there's subsidized housing, because there is no place in this country where a person who doesn't have something like $60,000 a year, or a person living on any Social Security or minimum wage or other limited income can rent a market rate apartment. I need health care. I need to have that mental health care available; I need to have dental health care available; I need glasses occasionally, and I need regular medical health including—at my age—mammograms. And community. You need community. Human beings need other human beings.

The thing is—and this is a permanent part of how I deal with people now—ultimately the change a person has to make is inside, and nobody knows when it's going to come, and nobody knows how it ultimately happens, and all that the rest of us can do is either make it harder for them to fix themselves, or we can make it easier to fix themselves. Don't push them or they're going to go in the other direction.

That inner moment for me had a lot to do with my whole lifetime of being very mystical and spiritual. Alice Miller, she once said that the key difference in the life of a child who grows up abused and grows up into an abuser, and a child who grows up abused and doesn't abuse—who's a healer—is that one of them had somebody else who knew and one of them didn't. Even if they can't do anything, to know that there's an adult who knows what is happening and knows it's wrong, who knows you don't deserve this. For me, my enlightened witness was God. When I was growing up, God was my witness. God wasn't there to rescue me; God wasn't there to magically supply me with everything I ever asked for. God was there to be my witness and to strengthen me and to help me to be good in spite of everything, to help me live by my standards instead of the standards of everybody else. To treat other people the way people ought to be treated and not the way I was being treated, that was what God and being Christian meant to me then, and that's what it still means to me now. And because that was my path all my life, it was at that moment on Capitol Hill that it eventually sunk into me that God loved me, God totally accepted me. So that's what I try to extend to other people. I know from my own experience that being accepted, accepting someone just as they are and not trying to fix them, is the best thing you can do to help them fix themselves.

But faith does not cure diabetes; you still have to take your insulin. And faith does not cure bipolar depression; you still have to take your lithium. For some people nothing works. I was one of the lucky ones; I had no side effects from lithium and within half an hour of taking my first lithium, I was like "Oh, my God, that's what they mean by reality" [*laughing*].

"A lot of people are homeless because they don't fit in the pattern of corporate America."

But I have to watch myself. I have to pace. I have a lot of support in the volunteer work. If I start to get manic, people know what's going on, and they settle me down or send me home to lie down. And if I get depressed people understand and give me some time to go home and rest. This would be impossible in the kind of work I used to do—in a data processing department. You have deadlines all the time, deadlines that are impossible for a human being to meet, and you meet them anyway, and any failure of judgment can doom you. It's an unrelenting, unmerciful, stressful environment. I could not handle it anymore.

A lot of people are homeless because they don't fit in the pattern of corporate America. There are lots of people out there doing very necessary work that helps the general community. They're doing it on a volunteer basis. They clean up the church after coffee hour, or they keep the shelters going. They're taking care of disabled friends and family and not getting paid for that; they're taking care of kids and not getting paid for that, or they're working in an environment where they can do what they're capable of with a lot of support around them.

If somebody sees me on an up day when I'm absolutely engaged in something, they might say, "Okay, here's a capable woman. Why isn't she working?" One of my friends, he was a very capable guy, but one night there was a fight, and we had to call 911. He just went white. He was standing up; his eyes were open, and nobody was there. He scared us all to death. I found out that my friend had been born with severe epilepsy. He'd had six operations on his head and skull before he was a year old, and nobody just looking at him knows that. They see a capable guy who's doing a whole bunch of work. So why isn't he at a job? Well, you know, he's not at a job because he never knows when an emergency or a stressful time will trigger one of these states. He needs to be in a supportive environment where, if that happens, people are going to take care of him until he comes out of it. You just don't know looking at people.

"Was George Bush ever homeless while he was using cocaine and alcohol? Are his daughters homeless? There are lots and lots of addicts and alcoholics who are in housing…"

The basic reason for homelessness is that there's not enough affordable housing for the people who need it. And you keep the price up by having fewer resources than you have demands. But when you're dealing with living necessities—water, food, housing, and medical care and education—that means that there are people who live without. It's the old people who have many problems—the people who don't fit in, the people who have special needs—those are the people who are left out. You have the hole in the economy, and the people who have the problems are the ones who fall into the hole. Was George Bush ever homeless while he was using cocaine and alcohol? Are his daughters homeless? There are lots and lots of addicts and alcoholics who are in housing because they have resources and a family and the family connections to keep them out of trouble. It's not drugs and alcohol themselves that cause homelessness. It's not even mental illness itself that causes homelessness, because there are lots and lots of crazy rich people [*laughing*]. It really isn't a matter of how many problems you have or how few resources you have. It's a matter of the ratio. If you have more resources than you have problems, then you're helped; if you have more problems than you have resources then you are not.

You can measure the amount of value that a human society places on human dignity by how low we will allow anybody to fall and accept it. You cannot walk right by somebody lying sick on the sidewalk—shabby, unwashed, teeth falling out of their head—you cannot walk right past somebody you've allowed to fall three miles below human dignity and not turn a hair, and then turn around and say that you want that person to have civility. You just can't have it both ways.

"[T]here was such negativity that I literally had visions of people breaking in and burning down the tents."

When we set up Tent City Four over in Bothell, there had been the most organized negative response we've had anywhere. Such a spewing of hate. I have been joking ever since that a bunch of us should have t-shirts that say, "I survived the Bothell Community Meeting." There was this whole big church packed with people who were saying some of the most incredibly hateful stuff: "There are elderly women in this neighborhood who won't be safe because there are sex perverts and criminals." This was the tone, that our children and our widows and our families are not going to be safe because these homeless people are coming in, and these filthy, criminal, drug addict, drunken, sexually perverted homeless people are going to eat our dogs and rape our children and [drop] needles under our rose bushes.

The day we moved the tent city to Bothell, I'm riding in a van with Leo Rhodes, being driven by a couple of community volunteers, friends, and we see the sidewalks just lined with people, this whole crowd of people around the church, and we're going "*Oh, my god.*" This is the biggest crowd that we'd ever run into. We pulled up, and we're going to defuse this if we can, so we hop out of the van and walk up to the crowd, and these people reach out their hands and say, "Welcome, we're here to help." They were all there in support. And all day long there were these floods of people coming with car loads and van loads, and truck loads of donations and just asking to help. One group brought in a barbeque set up and set it up there in the parking lot and was barbequing lunch for everybody. In Bothell, we experienced the most extreme hate we'd ever met anywhere, but the response to that was the most extreme love we'd ever met anywhere.

I've helped set up every tent city since 1998. I'd spend the first night, or maybe the first couple of nights, help set things up and spend a night or two, but this time, I stayed there for a whole week because there was such negativity that I literally had visions of people breaking in and burning down the tents. I was afraid that my friends were going to get hurt or killed out there, and I just wanted to stay until I was sure that everyone was going to be secure.

Especially with Tent City II, I did a lot of outreach up there on Beacon Hill, because I have lived up on Beacon Hill, and I knew a lot of people up there. Going to the neighborhood council meetings, that was fascinating. I had one of the few e-mail addresses publicly known, and I got a lot of e-mail correspondence. One of the things I learned out of it, all of the working class and small business owners, the more low-income residential folks, they were all just fine with the tent city, even supportive. All the opposition was coming from the more prosperous neighbors. None of them even lived around the tent city. They were all from miles away from where the tent city actually was.

Seattle has a very left-wing progressive faith community. Even the Southern Baptists in Seattle would be called left wing anywhere in the Bible Belt [*laughing*]. Three quarters of SHARE/WHEEL's major allies have got to be from the churches or associated with the churches. Lutheran Compass Center, the Archdiocese Housing Association,

Catholic Community Services, those are secular nonprofits but they're connected. There's the Church Council of Greater Seattle, Rich Lang down at Trinity United Methodist Church, Pat Simpson, and Dean Taylor up at the Episcopal Cathedral. He practically started what grew into Seattle's Committee to End Homelessness. Dean Taylor was active in the anti-apartheid movement in South Africa, that's where he comes from. He's very good friends with Desmond Tutu, who has been here a couple of times. Dean Taylor had the gravitas, the moral weight in this community, and he got the city and county, the social service people and business people to the table.

Last year when there was this big face off with the city over the funding of our shelters and the Safe Harbors' tracking program, when it came down to the eleventh hour, it was Dean Taylor who called a negotiation session and got mediation, got a solution to that. He got the mayor to come negotiate. A whole bunch of other social service providers objected to Safe Harbors, but they went along in order to not risk their funding, and then they just dragged their heels in implementing it.

"What part of inalienable rights don't you get?"

For SHARE/WHEEL, the principle was that your human rights are not conditional upon your economic status. There were a lot of people telling us that because we got money from the city, therefore the city had the right to invade our privacy, invade our dignity. I wanted to know, "Okay, you're driving on city roads, does that mean that you no longer have any privacy rights from the city of Seattle? That the state and the federal government has the right to put a bug on your car and track everywhere you go because you're driving on government-funded roads?" It seriously bothers me that there are so many people in the city who actually accept this argument that if you're poor and homeless, and you're living on the kindness of strangers, you don't have any rights. What part of "inalienable rights" don't you get? We really felt that we were standing up for much more than just ourselves. We were standing up for everybody; we were standing up for all homeless people, all poor people, and for all of the service providers who were too gutless to stand up for themselves.

In May, the Washington State Coalition for the Homeless paid my way to Yakima to give one of the keynote speeches. And I took the opportunity to rip the Ten-Year Plan and say, the real cause of homelessness is lack of affordable housing. The federal government has not put a penny into HUD since 1996 or so. It has been steadily cutting funding to it for the last thirty or forty years, and unless you reverse that, there's no way you're going to reverse homelessness. Livable wages and lack of health care and all of these things that are the real root causes of homelessness, there's nothing in the Ten-Year Plan about any of these things. The Ten-Year Plan is not about ending homelessness; you should call it what it is: "the Ten-Year Plan to Get Some of the Homeless People off of the Street in Ten Years" [*laughing*]. Afterwards, a lot of people came up to me and said, "Thank you. I'm glad somebody is telling the truth." Every single one of them I said, "What are you going to do about it?" Because the problems that are making your client on the other side of the desk homeless are the same problems that give you an ulcer when you go home and try to balance the check book and figure out how you're going to put dinner on the table and pay the rent and the heating bill and get dental care for the kids and send them to college. So, you are allies. It is to your interest—you know, you should be working together. I'll acknowledge there are some of the people, some service providers that do get that, and they are doing that, and that's the attitude that they work with people on, and I love them for it. The DESC people, the ones that I work with, the ones that manage the Union Hotel where I live, and the ones that work with the mental health outreach, almost all of them I like. Some of them are patient and respectful with people that I cannot be patient and respectful with [*laughing*]. But a majority of service providers don't get that, or they get it in theory, but they do not practice it on the job, that we are all in this together, trying to survive in a hellish system.

Homelessness is not going to change until you change the whole system. You have to change the way everybody does business, not just the Homeless Services Committee, and not just the homeless people themselves. You have to change the way that government does business; you have to change the way business does business; you have to change the economy; you have to change the criminal justice system, the criminal justice system which is run criminally.

You have to change everything, and in order to do that you have to get pretty confrontational. You have to be willing to step right up to conflict. That's very much a problem for the social service community, which tends to attract co-dependents, and it's a big problem in Seattle. Politeness is part of the culture, and it's almost terminal politeness. The people who help us don't help us out of politeness; they help us out of a courageous compassion that's ready to break through that politeness. The politeness of Seattle is not the kind of civility that grows out of actually respecting people, valuing people. It's the politeness of everybody's armed, so be nice. And we disturb that culture.

As the oldest of four children with two alcoholic parents, and everybody blew the ceiling off at the slightest drop of the hat, I was constantly making nice. Everybody's trying to paper over conflicts and trying to keep us going and keep it up with kindness. I don't do that anymore. After years and years of emotional recovery, I can see it. I can recognize it. This isn't real peace making. You have to be able to face conflict and deal with the conflict in order to have real politeness, real civility. Real civility does not allow people to be unhoused, unfed, uncared for. If you want civility in this town, then practice it. Get everybody housed, get everybody fed.

"No wonder people try to not think about other people as human like me, because it's almost too much."

The very first woman that we stood for, the very first person we stood for, was a woman named Debbie Cashio. She had been raped and murdered. She was homeless, she was sleeping out.[3]

If you're homeless, you're more vulnerable to anything, everything. If there's somebody out there killing women, you're on the streets 24/7, you have that many more times to be one of the women snatched. You're more likely to be hit by a car; you're more likely to be hit by a bus. If it's a bad pollution day, you're more likely to be one of the people that gets sick from the pollution. Heck, you're more likely to be hit by a meteor, lightning, whatever it is. Any risks that are out there, you're more susceptible to.

One of the things I'm hoping that Tonya's family gets out of the vigil for her today, I want them to come out of this hearing the people who loved Tonya and were not ashamed of Tonya and are not blaming her family for [her] being homeless. There are things that individuals can't deal with on their own; there are things that families can't deal with on their own, and they should not feel ashamed for that. It is shameful that people are homeless; it is shameful that people are on their own, but it is not shameful for them, or for their families. It's shameful for our whole country that we have gone from an era where a stranger could show up on your doorstep at midnight, and you would be obligated to take him in and feed him, to this. It's a shame that we let ourselves be cut off so much from each other.

There's something about grief and death that our psychological reaction is to withdraw, and we curl around our pain and go off somewhere. Maybe at one time this was a survival thing for the group: when you got infected and you got sick, you crawled off away from the group. But we need to grow out of that now. Sharing with, being at the vigil, being in the community has helped me bear this without going into a depression, going to the hospital. And I need to not wall off around that pain and be wordless. I need to use that pain, feeling that pain as a way of imagining how others feel. I am sitting here today remembering how scared I have been, how I've lived scared when I was homeless and how tight my muscles still are, and realizing these women are experiencing that now. No wonder people try to forget the homeless experience. No wonder people try to not think about other people as human like me, because it's almost too much. And yet, we have to if we're going to survive, if we're going to make it back out of this terrible, terrible society we've created. We need to make it back to a living body again. We've got to bear it, come out of the numbness and bear our pain, bear each other's pain.

CHAPTER 8

Roxane Roberts

Figure 3 Photograph of Roxane Roberts

*I met Roxane at Mary's Place in the summer of 2006 and interviewed her on three sepa-
rate occasions at Mary's Place, before she moved to San Francisco in the fall. I interviewed
her again when she returned to Seattle in 2008 to clear up a warrant that had resulted
in the suspension of her social security disability payments shortly after she'd settled into
her new life in San Francisco. I first noticed Roxane during a discussion of the film* The
Cotton Club *at Mary's Place. Once a week, on Friday afternoons, the couches would
be rearranged in rows in front of a standard-sized television, and a facilitated discussion*

followed. Roxane spoke out angrily about the ways in which the film's representations of racism in New York in the 1920s resonated with her own experiences in the present, particularly in dealing with police. Roxane agreed to be interviewed, but when I missed our first meeting and was unable to get a message to her, she read me the riot act, telling me that her time was every bit as precious as my own. It was a mistake I was not about to make twice. Many times over the next five years, Roxane would feel compelled to remind me of how my own position as a privileged white academic limited my ability to both grasp and adequately convey the brutality of the racism, poverty, and oppression she has experienced over the course of her life.

At times Roxane's rapid-fire speech made her story difficult to follow and posed a challenge to the transcriptionist. We kept contact by e-mail and phone as we worked to try to clear up areas of ambiguity in the transcripts, fill in historical gaps, and generally catch up on each other's lives. Roxane's narrative was precise and detailed, and her account of individual incidents varied little if at all. New and important aspects of Roxane's life history emerged in each follow-up interview, and it was only space and time constraints that ultimately forced a measure of arbitrary closure. Our ability to communicate by phone about the book was complicated when in December 2008 when Roxane's vocal cords were severely damaged during an emergency intubation at San Francisco General Hospital. E-mail became our primary means of communication, but in the fall of 2010, diagnosed with a brain tumor, Roxane began to suffer progressive loss of vision that further complicated our collaboration. I flew down to San Francisco a few days after Christmas of 2010 to go over the edited chapter with her.

Born two years before the historic 1954 Brown vs. the Board of Education *Supreme Court decision, Roxane recalls her mother Helyn Doris Walton as immersed throughout her childhood in the historic struggle against American apartheid in both Miami and Seattle. Roxane was seven the year that the family suddenly picked up roots in Miami and moved across country to Seattle. That same year, the Seattle branch of the Congress of Racial Equality (CORE) coordinated the city's first major campaign to challenge the employment discrimination that pervaded downtown businesses from the "Bon March, J.C. Penny, Nordstrom, Frederick and Nelson," grocery stores like the A&P.[1] Both locally and nationally, the movement picked up steam with the passage of the 1964 Civil Rights Act, which also established the Equal Opportunity Employment Commission to investigate allegations of ongoing discrimination, But it would be another four years before the 1968 Fair Housing Act would provide a legal basis to challenge systemic housing discrimination in the United States.[2] In 1969, the Defender Association was established with funding from the Model Cities Program to provide legal defense to low-income people,[3] and, as Walton's former supervisor, Jackie Rye, confirmed in a phone interview, Roxane's mother was one of the first of two Black women hired as private investigators. Rye recalls her as "strong-willed and fearless."[4] As Roxane also told me, in 1980, Walton was charged with the unarmed robbery of two Seattle-area banks. News reports indicated that she'd made away with barely enough to cover a month's bills for herself and Roxane's six-year-old half-sister, after her car was repossessed and the utilities were turned off.[5]*

When Roxane entered Garfield High School as a freshman in 1966, Garfield "was home to 75 percent of all Black high school students, who made up 52 percent of the entire school's student body… "[6] In 1966, the NAACP, CORE and the Central Area Civil Rights Committee (CACRC) launched a two-day boycott of area schools to challenge racial segregation in Seattle public schools.[7] In September 1967, at the age of 14, Roxane attempted suicide for the first time. She returned to Garfield to finish out the year, before moving in the fall of her junior year to Teaneck, New Jersey, where she lived with her father and stepmother for a few months. Roxane reports having been raped by her father on October 8, 1968. She returned to Seattle, to finish out her high school degree as one of only a handful of students of color at Roosevelt High School, while she simultaneously participated in the Upward Bound Program at the University of Washington.

The year that Roxane entered Upward Bound at the University of Washington, a program that rose out of Johnson's "War on Poverty," enrollment of Black students was at a record high of 465 students, up from 150 the previous fall.[8] The surge in enrollment was largely due to the work of the University of Washington Black Student Union (BSU), which over the course of a year of sit-ins, building occupations, and demand letters, significantly "transformed the University of Washington into a place that concretely addressed racial inequality."[9] The BSU's demands included the creation of a Black Studies Program, an Office of Minority Affairs and the Special Education Program (SEP), focused on "recruitment of new students, tutoring and advising services for students after enrollment."[10] In 1970, when Roxane formally matriculated as a freshman at the University of Washington, it was under the auspices of SEP, which was subsequently renamed the Educational Opportunity Program (EOP).[11]

"When we crossed the Florida State line in the middle of the night—I'll never forget these words—the last thing I remember was my mom saying, 'Goodbye, all you crackers.'"

I was born November of '52 and my brother Calvin was born November of '53, and I had to baby-sit him day in and day out. Because I was smart, my mom put too much on me at five and six, and then I blamed myself when I got raped when I was six in Miami.

Some guy my mother had stood up for a date previously, I remember seeing him at the swimming pool. I was crying because we were at recess, and we had to get out of the pool. Everybody was getting candy and a little Coca-Cola and balloons for a balloon fight. I was crying because I didn't have no money, and he said, "You want a quarter?" And I was all, "Oh a whole quarter!" In 1959, a quarter was a lot of money, so yeah, that's when it happened. 'Cause that's when she really got to drinking. For a long time I thought it was my fault and that led to me shooting myself when I was fourteen.

My mother—she was as smart as she was pretty, but she chose to live off her looks and to drink away the pain of losing my dad's fortune. She didn't qualify to marry my father. It was painful to be intelligent and *watch* Mom be a floozy. She was rich and beautiful, and she slept with big names, and she got to be associated with them. But money and a hotel room, that's just reinforcing that you ain't nothing but a pretty face. So she never lived up to her potential. She wasn't a lousy person. She just wanted instant gratification. It was childish, you know, because she knew she was pretty, she knew she was smart, she knew she cooked good. She wants a man in the house and the money and the bling-bling, and a car right now, and if you didn't give it to her, it was "I'll get it myself." So she worked, paid for a car, and the nice little house she owned, and never got the man to go along with it, because the great men she frequented, she'd give it to them immediately, because she thought that was the way to their heart and that was the way to have a nice evening. That was the way to her pain, but she didn't know no better. She didn't have anybody decent to pattern after. She did tell me something I never listened to: "Don't trust anyone." I never listened to it because I think trust is part of love.

When she did use her intelligence, she was a Black private investigator woman for the public defender's office here in Seattle when it was located in the Smith Tower. When Civil Rights got passed, my mom was the first Black hired by the State of Florida. She worked in the Employment Securities Office. She had a brilliance about her—someone that was going places. After she got the job, she moved us from Liberty City to a white neighborhood. Two blocks away was a beautiful all-white school. We didn't have nobody to play with. I wanted to go to a Black school. I was too young to be doing all this crap, but this is what she insisted on. "Well guess what, Mommy, you ain't going to get beat up every day after school, so why don't you let us go to a Black school?" And this is all the stuff she picked up working as a desk clerk at both the entertainment hotels for Blacks, the Carver Hotel and the Sir John Hotel. She met and knew all the entertainers in the years of segregation in Miami, from Dinah Washington to Sugar Ray Robinson, prior to our departure.

My mother thought I would stagnate as a straight A student in an all-Black school, and so she sent a letter to Kennedy. So Kennedy sent a three-man commission to the school in Miami to see why after integration was passed, we couldn't attend the schools.[12] At Douglas Elementary, I had been a straight A student, and they still said "no." After the commission, the school decided we should pass a test, and then they'd let us in the white school. I passed the test, but all of a sudden my mother woke us up like two–three in the morning and put us in the '52 Buick. She was literally throwing things in the back window of the car. She put our puppy in the back window, and I said, "Mommy, my toys!" She ran back in the house, and she threw our toys in the window. We drove through the Black area of Miami and picked up her boyfriend at the time. We drove all night. I remember driving past the Everglades, me and my brother looking out the window for alligators. When we crossed the Florida state line in the middle of the night—I'll never forget these words—the last thing I remember was my mom saying, "Goodbye, all you crackers." That was in late 1961, and she never in all my life told me why we left so suddenly. All my life I was afraid to ask her why. I never did. She died October 15, 1991. And that was the beginning of my demise.

We got here October '61. I was one of the first twenty-five colored kids voluntarily bussed to test integration. That was in 1964. My mother made me do it. We had to ride a bus up to Queen Anne Hill, and after three years, when Queen Anne Hill didn't burn down, they decided to integrate all these schools.

I didn't want to go integrate no more. In high school, I was going to school with the white kids so I couldn't hang with the kids at Garfield. I didn't fit in. At lunchtime, instead of dancing and singing and flirting and being hip and cool in the lunchroom, I hung out in the library. I loved the library any damn way. Why even today people say, "Yeah, you sure was pretty but you were a nerd." I didn't know the kids looked at me like that, but I guess that's why they didn't want me too much.

I couldn't hang out with the kids I went to school with after school 'cause we would park outside the tavern, and we'd sit in the car, and we'd do our homework out there. We'd sneak into the bar and they'd kick us out. And then she'd come out, and she'd attempt to drive home, talking and doing her thing, and we got to drive all the way to Capital Hill and pray we don't run into a telephone pole. I tried to tell teachers and counselors how bad the alcohol abuse was at home, and what did they do, but call and make an appointment to come. Well, what do you think? My mom's going to be sober, the house is going to be clean, she's not going to cuss. Until they leave. And we never do get taken out of our home and put somewhere good.

In 1964 Calvin and I flew by ourselves on the 727 to go to the World's Fair in New York and visit my father, and I wanted to go back the summer of '67 to be with my dad forever. I loved my daddy. He was white and Indian. My dad was rich. I'm probably the only person that wasn't gaga over what he had. I was there because I was his first born, and I admired him. I thought he was better than God. I liked New York. I liked being home. I liked the consistency in life. He wasn't drunk all the time. We had dinner on the table. My stepmother treated me like a queen 'cause I was just like him, and she was jealous of our closeness.

He could have any woman. In fact, he did have almost every woman. He had women all over New York, in their apartments with their allowances and their clothes and their cars and whatever they needed. And he'd see whoever he wanted whenever he wanted, and act however he did and do whatever he wanted. He sent me home after the summer was over, and I was just devastated.

"I shot myself with a thirty-eight special in 1967 at six in the morning."

My mom was always drunk. She was always gone. I was scared in the house all night, so I would sleep behind the chair with a BB Gun. We were too alienated, isolated in this big old house on Capital Hill. All the kids was rich white kids, and I just didn't know who to talk about my problems. We was still integrating the schools, and my mom was just always drunk, and she was embarrassing.

I had gotten confirmed down at St. Clement's Episcopal Church. I was leading the catechism class. I was proud of it. I thought, "I can pray," so I prayed to God to stop her from this drinking. But she come home drunk and burned the house up. Turned up the heat and passed out drunk. We tried to tell her the pipe was molten, and then it caught on fire. She ran with her boyfriend for two weeks, so we had to live with the priest, Father Kappas. We were there about two weeks. I had my own room.

I felt like I was laying on six mattresses—big old quilts and fluffy. We had a maid. Mommy never ever came by in two weeks to visit. She partied hardy.

I wanted to be an acolyte, and I was pissed off because they threw me in the choir. I didn't like the choir, because I can't sing, so Father Kappas saw me getting upset, and he sent me to camp at Gold Bar, a little east of Lake Washington, to placate me. Do you know, I went to St. Mark's a couple of years ago, when they were installing a gay pastor up at St. Mark's, and little girls were acolytes, with the incense, and I'm like, "See?" Here I was almost sixty, I'm still mad about that.

I shot myself with a thirty-eight special in 1967 at six in the morning. I was upset about my mom spending all her money on her boyfriends, not paying rent. She was cheating with somebody's husband, and they was arguing, and he slapped her on her birthday, and I went and got a BB gun and shot him. I don't know why I got to shoot everybody with a BB gun. It was terrible.

One of the days she's home, we're sitting on the floor just like Beaver and Wally, and she's on the couch, and we're watching Shirley Temple, and she said, "Shirley Temple bought her parents a swimming pool. What are you all going to do? If it wasn't for you all, I could live off of a cup of coffee a day." So later that night, I asked my mom, "How much would you get if I died?" "Twenty thousand dollars." God didn't think about me when I asked her that. I was confirmed that God wasn't answering my prayers. He wouldn't answer none of them. So it didn't matter about going to hell. I knew what I was going to do.

Every morning her boyfriend stopped by to put our lunch money on the TV and to talk to her. She had to leave thirty-five cents in two piles on top of the TV for us to take so we can catch the bus all the way up here to Queen Anne and integrate for her, and she was on the phone arguing with him about it. How are we going to integrate so well if we don't eat? And I just thought maybe she'd get twenty thousand dollars if I die, and that would get Calvin some clothes that she wouldn't buy 'cause she spent it all on her boyfriend. And that's what the note said: "Please buy Calvin some clothes with some of the money."

I took the note out and laid down in bed. I pulled the gun out. I had just read in the paper the day before that a guy got shot in the stomach in Miami, and he died. So, I figured that way if Calvin wakes up, my face wouldn't be all over, and I could calm him down while I went ahead and died. I figured I was going to fix all this stuff on earth before I go to hell, and that God ain't no good anyways if he wouldn't make her stop drinking. My father sent me away, and he's bigger than God, so what would I want with God? So I put the gun to my stomach and pulled the trigger and it came out my back, but I didn't know it at the time. It was a .38 snub nose special. I don't know nothing about hollow point bullets, but it went through me and out the wall next to the window, and into the front door of the apartment building across a parking lot from the house. The police had to find all of the bullets to make sure nobody shot me.

Hollywood is full is crap. You don't fall all back, and it don't hurt. You just get really thirsty. So I just lay down on the floor. I didn't know it was that loud, but my brother woke up. He goes upstairs, and I was lying there—'cause I sure couldn't do nothing else—and blood was everywhere. You just want people to quit making vibrations on the floor, and her boyfriend comes running upstairs, and he said, "You stupid girl, what are you playing with that gun for?" I said, "The note's on the bed." In other words, I wasn't playing with the damn thing.

I didn't want to scare Calvin. I was the one who raised him. And he isn't frightened as long as I'm in charge. So I told him to go get me some water 'cause I was really, really thirsty, and I wished that everything would get dark, so I can be done with this crap.

By the time the ambulance attendants got me downstairs, my mom pulls up. "Where are you taking her?" The ambulance guy said, "Well, it's an attempted suicide—so we have to take her to Harborview Hospital." So my mom said, "Don't take her to Harborview, Take her to Providence."[13] They took me to Harborview anyways. They rolled me in, and they prepped me for surgery. I didn't know what was going to happen. The bullet's out. What are you going to cut up? There were all these nurse's aides, and they was talking: "What'd you do this for? What are you— pregnant?" 'Cause I always had a potbelly. Some of these stupid gossip-mongers, they're trying to figure out why this beautiful little fourteen-year-old whose mother used to work on the nut ward shot herself.

I was fourteen and my birthday would have been in two months, but I'm sitting as they are asking questions. When you put a gun at yourself, sparks make this [pattern]. So they're getting ready to put IV s in there and suddenly there comes another nurse's aide: "Been popping a few huh?" I said, "What's popping a few?" You know, they took the time to describe skin-popping. I said, "No, I don't fool with drugs. I'm from Harlem." So I was arguing with those stupid nurses. I think that's why I lived to this day, just to argue. Then the doctor comes in, and then they all were quiet, and we had proper decorum in the room. And I know it's corny, but I said, "Doctor, why am I shivering? I'm not cold." He said, "You're in shock." Well, I didn't have to have him define that because, hell, yeah, I'm in shock. I'm shocked that I'm still alive, and you people are asking me stupid questions.

I was in surgery for about nine hours, and when I woke up, I had lost all kinds of weight. When she finally shows up after I came out of surgery, I just know I'm finally gonna get loving, and my mom walked into the room and said, "What did you pull this stupid trick for?" I couldn't believe what came out of her mouth. So, I didn't say nothing for two weeks.

When I could walk, I'd go around to other beds, and the nurses, they loved me. I knew all the pictures, and they knew my favorite songs. The nurse that worked at night, she wanted to take me home with her, and I thought she meant it. She said she did. I wanted to live with the nurse, because she wasn't like an uncaring mother, muttering about her job and looking good, and trying to blame me for everything. And I know the nurse didn't smell like alcohol.

The worst lesson, the hardest lesson, I ever had in life was when I checked out. I was supposed to come back and see the doctor in a week. When I went a week later—a lousy week—everything was different, everybody was gone. I went up to the floor and none of same staff was there. I expected all the same people would be in the same beds. I expected the same staff. I expected everything how I left it, and nothing was. None of the patients was there, and I was devastated. It was the saddest thing that happened in my life to this day, because I realized that had I died, life would have just went on. I was overwhelmed with my insignificance at that point, 'cause I was only fourteen. I didn't know anything at that time, but I thought the whole world stops when I die. I didn't talk for a couple of days. I kept asking myself, "Why did they make me live when it wouldn't have mattered if I had died?" It was my first really hard lesson.

"I'm in the middle of the San Juan strait, between Orcas and Lopez. I took a book that was very influential to me. It was called, *Manchild in the Promised Land*, by Claude Browne."

When I went back to Garfield, everybody thought I was pregnant, and that was why I was out of school for two weeks. They had cut me from here to here in the hospital, and the muscle hadn't healed, so my stomach poked out. In '67 you do not come to school with a poked out belly: *"Yeah, I knew she wasn't up in that library just study- ing."* Anything to taint somebody that they have placed above them. A couple of my friends told a few others what actually happened, but it was real distracting. And all I wanted to do was study. They gave me an I.Q. test, and it came out 137, and they said, "Maybe you need to be in a different school." I wanted to transfer because I was tired of the gossip and innuendoes. I especially hated people thinking I'm pregnant. I was a devout Episcopalian, and after what had happened to me at six, I didn't care if I never had sex, and I knew my mother's life had gotten messed up pursuing those baser pleasures. But those type of rumors in high school will kill you.

I started writing because I didn't like my life. I learned how to read when I was three, because I just loved words. I didn't know I was gay, but I was always the boy in my stories. I was always white, and I ended up being adopted and having two parents. In my stories, I was always going to be the leader; I always had this girl that loved me, and I always ended up dead or saving somebody and dying in the process. The ulti- mate codependent. I was a comedian, and class work was nothing. I'd sit in the back thinking up the next joke. And then pass the test with an A. Didn't even listen to the teacher. I got through school like that, and some people saw my potential.

My friend Robin—we were best friends since the eighth grade—her mom took me into her home when I was emancipated in January 1969 by King County Juvenile Court. I was the first Black person living in Laurelhurst. Her parents were really mucky muck. They had breakfast cooked when me and Robin got up, lunch ready and dinner. Everybody got to sit down, and this was kind of neat. Their house sat right by the ferry that arrives in Orcas Island. Robin took me up to Orcas Island every weekend because she felt sorry for me, and that's really when I started writing a lot.

Robin was proud of having a Black friend, and I was proud just having a friend period. We shared everything. We was tight, and then we got so close, pretty soon we were transparent. Wasn't no color. I could teach her how to dance, and she took a lot of B.S. from her upper class friends and family because she loved me. When we was on the ferry, I'd be writing poems. I was a teenager in love with my best friend, but oh, don't dare say it. So we hung out and I took all the love she wanted to give me. We'd go to dances and Robin kind of always looked out for me, because who wants to dance like a Black person on Orcas Island? She decided to stay there, and they teased her about me when she started the first quarter. They told her, "Well, it look like coon hunting began." And it devastated her, but she didn't hide that from me. We would talk about it. She really was the one that helped me write poetry by reading it and loving it—acting like I was really something. And it was something then to take me to a white only island and have my back and be proud to have me as a friend.

They had a little boat and one day I'm in the middle of the San Juan Strait, between Orcas and Lopez. I took a book that was very influential to me. It was called *Manchild in the Promised Land* by Claude Browne. I thought, "Wow, he was in Harlem like me, and it starts out with him being shot in the stomach. It was just amazing, the similarities. Not just the shooting, but Harlem and people giving up on you. The only thing was, he was a bad kid. I wasn't too bad. But his grasp of academics, and his pursuit of law, and how you can change your life, and he was good in spite of the lack. And that's what put in my head the notion to even consider college. I'm reading; I'm thinking, and all of a sudden I heard a "bammm," and this ferry is about to run me over, so I started the motor and got back and never got back in that boat.

Those are the people that probably have me so head strong right now, thinking I'm worthy to stand up to lying cops, and have me so idealistic, because without the virtues that people disdain me for now, I'd have never known great people like that. And now having to be called crazy because different people don't understand, and because I'm not in an academic environment. I'm too old for the academic environment; I'm too Black for the gay community; I'm too gay for the Black community. I don't fit in anywhere.

"When I started Upward Bound in '69, I really got a grasp on my writing and my potential. Oh, man I was just like a duck in a pond."

I started the University of Washington at sixteen, through the Upward Bound program, where I got credits which helped me graduate at seventeen from Roosevelt High School in January of '70. I got into the U. with an article I wrote about Harlem, and it got published in some Seattle publication. I read it to the class and got an A from the English teacher. My teacher used that as part of my application to Upward Bound, and I got accepted, which was great, because it gave me an opportunity to get out of a foster home I'd been in for two months. All of a sudden I kind of had my calling.

I took the publication to my mom. This was after I returned from New York because my father raped me. I took my mother to lunch. She was in her office, and she had never been proud of me before that or since, except when I got into law school.[14] But she said, "This is your calling," and I decided, yeah, it was, 'cause that was the only thing that made me happy, and it made me important, and it was purely me, and so I just kept going.

I was emancipated at sixteen, and I would have been released to the streets with nothing. They told me I could get the foster care money anytime I lived with an adult until I'm eighteen, but I was scared to ask people. There wasn't no such thing as homelessness, and I was afraid to disclose any weakness, which would mean I'd failed in my move to get away from my nefarious and inebriated mother. And if I stayed I'd be just like her. Her boyfriend was going to beat me up, or she was going to kill us in her damn car, making us ride everywhere with her.

After Upward Bound ended, I had nowhere to go, but my counselor at Upward Bound asked me did I want to live with her. She was just like a friend with me, and the foster care money helped her pay the rent. She was cool, and she thought the Black kid was cool, and ain't she cool because she's working with these inner city youth. And it worked out.

When I started Upward Bound in '69 I really got a grasp on my writing and my potential. Oh, man I was just like a duck in a pond. I took to reading and walking campus and being with myself and meeting people, and I found my niche. I was writing all the time, and people was rewarding me for things I said or questions I had or the way I understood a book or interpreted things. I wanted to be a lawyer or be a teacher or be a nurse or a prison counselor. I decided to be a prison counselor when I saw this movie called *My Three Convicts*. This guy was in there really changing some bad guys by caring about them, and giving them an education and giving them a life. That's why I majored in sociology.

I had the second highest grades in my Upward Bound class. My best friend, Jimmy, had the highest grades. He was the smartest kid in Upward Bound. We would have arguments together all the time, talking about political science, and he would show me the ropes in shooting pool. No one understood us. Me and Jimmy were just good friends, but that summer me and Tommy ended up moving in together.

I loved Tommy. He was my first boyfriend. He was handsome, and he understood that I didn't want no nookie, because it was still too fresh from what my daddy done. He was afraid of college. I was finishing up my semester at Roosevelt, and he called me one night, and he was scared to go give a speech in class, so he was going to kill himself. He took a whole bunch of pills. So we raced him over there to the hospital. The nurse said, "Don't let him go to sleep, whatever you do." One minute I'm mad at him, next minute I'm telling him a joke because I have to keep him awake, and he kept trying to go to sleep. This went on for about six hours and then he was out of the woods. I went and asked my foster mom, "Can Tommy come over here with us?" So Tommy moved in, and we moved up into the attic and had this room—a little summer place, you know. It had a roof with a V and a little window, and it was real sunshiney, and my bed was on the floor, and there was tie dye everywhere. Hell, it was 1970, and Chicago had just come out with that "Wake Up Sunshine" album. It was very romantic.

I had music and my own little typewriter, and we had a bedroom, and the sex wasn't terrible. The first time I said, "You've got to be kidding—this is what all the fuss is about?" When we moved up to the attic, the privacy made it a little bit more enjoyable. But he got to be too jealous and watched me so hard he wouldn't go to work. Tommy's brother Jimmy would come and see me. Jimmy was sixteen; Tommy was nineteen, and I was seventeen. The rent was one dollar more than the foster care check, and nobody was going to hire a seventeen-year-old trying to go to college. So, Calvin and Jimmy would go to the store and steal chicken and stuff for me to cook. They had quarts of beer and cigarettes, and we'd sit there and play chess all day.

I did four different courses at U.W. and got an A in a senior-level independent study in poetry, even though I had turned in a whole book of trite poetry. Mostly I wrote fiction and poetry, and now I can't write anything but nonfiction and poetry. But the week at the symposium, I read the poems that I had started writing when me and Robin used to take the ferry from Bellingham to Orcas every weekend.

It was the hippie days. We were experimenting with weed and having a ball. I never had anybody teach me money management, how to cook, but I sure knew how to cut to the chase as far as responsibility. I felt like I raised my mother and my brother. But I was scared, and I couldn't share that at all.

At the U.W., I started doing all kinds of "firsts" "only" and "youngest." I was the second Black and youngest dormitory advisor at Haggett Hall right after they built it. It was when Black people were allowed places, but people were so scared of them. I'm not fully a Black kid and not fully a white kid. At Haggett Hall, they were having racial tensions—mostly with the Indians—and I was the only one that would just walk up and say, "Hey, will you knock off the drumming? People got to go to school." 'Cause all the white people were afraid of being politically incorrect before we used that term. I went from Haggett Hall to work as at the Seattle Tutoring Agency for Youth (STAY).

I was assistant director at STAY. We taught and gave lectures and symposia to students to get them going to inner city schools and tutor[ing] kids that back then were "credits to their race" like myself. I would talk to them about some of the racial problems. I wrote an article for the *Daily* about the "miseducation" of Blacks in Seattle. I didn't know there was a book by the same name. The article was about how Blacks were being channeled towards manual labor, and white people were being channeled for college and running the show. And I felt that way all the way back to being one of the first twenty-five colored kids voluntarily bussed to test integration. I was "a credit to my race." All these first, only and youngest jobs I had, I was busy representing all my life. Mostly I wrote and learned the culture that wasn't mine. I did everything the white way because of Father Kappas, and the white way was where my mother had us.

I left the University of Washington January '72 and committed to the army because of finances, because they took away our Basic Education Opportunity Grants and forced us to take out loans to continue as students.[15] I was already kind of scared—what am I going to do out there by myself? How am I going to make the payments as a waitress? Foster care money was a hundred nineteen dollars, but because I was eighteen, I wasn't eligible for it anymore. I signed the papers for the loans, but the loan checks didn't come. Without the loan, I couldn't pay the rent. No security whatsoever, no rent coming in. I couldn't buy the books, couldn't concentrate on the classes. The army promised that besides the $280 a month I earned, they'd give me $20,000 when I left after four years. I thought it was a smart idea 'cause I would come out with all those benefits, and I'd have money and never be insecure again. By the time the loan check came, I was in the army. So, guess what, I just shot myself again...

Following a confrontation in with a commanding officer, Roxane received a general honorable discharge from the military. Roxane went on to work variously as a drug and alcohol counselor at Franklin High School in Seattle; at Youth Advocates, a nonprofit serving "high-risk" youth, and as a mechanic's helper with the Port of Seattle.

In 1998, Roxane was arrested, along with a friend, in a thirty-dollar crack sale, involving an undercover Seattle police officer. Both Roxane and her friend testified that Roxane had had no involvement in the sale, but had come by to collect an $18 debt that was the last of what she needed for a down payment on a new apartment. Though Roxane had no prior criminal record, she was sentenced to 24 months at the Washington Women's Correctional Facility.[16] The sentence was stayed pending the outcome of a Supreme Court decision with a bearing on the case. Roxane was arrested again in 1999 for possession, and in July 2000 on a charge of "criminal solicitation, delivery of [crack] cocaine," in what she recounts as a clear-cut case of entrapment by Seattle police. Rather than challenging the charges and risking a higher sentence in a jury trial, Roxane adopted an Alford, or "No contest" plea.

Roxane was incarcerated from "January 2001 through August 2002 on the 2000 conviction," and believed she was serving concurrent time for "both the 1998 and 2000 conviction."[17] However, following the 2004 resolution of the Supreme Court case that bore on her own, the Court of Appeals upheld Roxane's 1998 conviction; a warrant was issued and she was once again arrested and was returned to prison to serve out the two-year sentence. Roxane contracted the shingles while she was in prison. She reports that despite excruciating pain, she was repeatedly denied medical treatment at WCCW, and within weeks of the onset of the shingles, she lost vision in her left eye, which was surgically removed in September 2007. Roxane continues to struggle with PTSD, which she attributes to multiple sexual assaults beginning in childhood, compounded by the traumas she suffered during her incarceration.

CHAPTER 9

Delores Loann Winston

I met Loann outside Mary's Place in 2007, following a Women in Black vigil, and I was quickly drawn into conversation with her. It was only a few minutes into the conversation that Loann brought up her love of cooking and the enormous satisfaction she took from cooking for other women at Mary's Place. Food, family, love, and community were clearly closely connected for Loann. She had an energetic laugh and was eager to speak about her life and her organizing work with WHEEL and Women in Black.

Loann identified racism in its various forms as a central part of her life story, beginning with her childhood in a small town in Louisiana in the early 1960s. The love and security that Loann found with her grandparents, extended family, and in the African American community in Rayville, Louisiana, provided a sharp contrast to the threats of lynching and other forms of domestic terrorism and racial intimidation that she both experienced directly and heard stories about while growing up. Loann touches briefly on the 1955 lynching of Emmett Till, who was brutally murdered only four years before she was born.[1]

As a child, Loann also experienced violence in the form of physical and psychological abuse at the hands of a family member. After the death of her grandfather and her move to Seattle it would be several years before she would find refuge in a family that took her in following a random conversation with a classmate—now her cousin—on the steps outside of her school.

Looking back on the decades she's spent in Seattle, since moving to the city's historically Black Central District in 1968, Loann reflected proudly on her early participation in the Black Panthers' free breakfast program for school children, which began in San Francisco in 1968.[2] She spoke with regret of the transformation that the Central District has undergone in the wake of gentrification. Along with most major cities in the United States, as University of Seattle law professor and long-time Central District resident, James McGee has observed, Seattle has witnessed "a dramatic shift in the racial landscape of the Central District, Seattle's traditionally African American community. In 1990, there were nearly three times as many Black as white residents in the area, but by 2000, the number of white residents surpassed the number of Blacks for the first time in 30 years."[3] Red-lining and more contemporary forms of racial discrimination in home mortgage lending have played a central role in undermining the capacity of African Americans to retain their homes.[4] McGee cites a 2003 study by the Association of Community Organizations for Reform Now (ACORN), of "discrimination in home mortgage lending," that found that "Seattle African American loan applicants were 2.56 times more likely to be denied a conventional mortgage loan than white applicants in 2002."[5] He notes also that, according to a 2005 national study by the Center for Responsible Lending, "people of color were more likely to pay high rates for mortgage loans." McGee also observes that, in Seattle, as in other cities across the country, property taxes have spiked in areas undergoing gentrification, making neighborhoods prohibitively expensive for working class families.[6]

"Sometimes I still have the nightmares, the dreams..."

I had a mother who didn't want any kids. Being African American and born in the South in 1959, of course, you couldn't finish school. They took a lot of things out of her life. She didn't want me, but she had to keep me. Back then there wasn't a lot about abortions or giving up the children.

My grandfather did tell me the story one day. I was about seven years old. He said one day he came in from work, and my mother had packed up all my belongings, and this man and woman were on their way out the door with me, and he said, "What are you doing?" "We're going to adopt this baby." And my grandfather said, "No, you're not. That's my grandchild. " And he made my mother keep me.

At two years old, I was burned. I've never gotten the true story of that. I was beaten very bad as a child. I had surgery at two years old. I couldn't walk good. For some reason my legs would just give out. They sent me up from Louisiana to go to Children's Orthopedic Hospital. I had no skin on my knees. As I got older—I was eight maybe—I would be literally beaten on this leg with no meat on it and beat with an extension cord. Just beat me to pulps. Beat me until I would black out almost. Sometimes I still have the nightmares, the dreams...

I was shipped back and forth, back and forth, between Seattle and Louisiana, that's how my life was. I might go to school here a year and then go back to Louisiana. If my mother didn't want me no more, whoever in the family was on their way to Louisiana, she'd pay them to take me.

"My grandparents were very protective. They were my salvation. They loved me, good, bad, right, wrong. That's what I miss, is that love."

When my grandfather died, I knew then that all hope for me was gone. I had been alive that long because of my grandfather. They said that the last thing he said before he died was to my mother—to quit mistreating Loann and to take care of her. My grandfather's name was Robert Winston, but they called him Mr. Bob. Handsome man, he wore his derby hats, his starched khaki hats and his shirts, and he'd have a cigar in his mouth. We were buddies. My grandparents dressed me immaculately. I was dressed very well, fed three heavy course meals a day, because in the South it was about feeding, about eating. I was taught with manners and respect.

We lived in Rayville, Louisiana. Rayville, it was a little town. We lived in a part called Booker T. We had a little dirt road, and everybody had the big sun porches, and the screens. We had a smokehouse in the back, and we had the washing machine back there where you turned the handle, and we had chickens. I remember the bathroom was way back in the house, so at night we had a chamber pot. We had a garden, and my grandfather had a 1956 Chevy. He got to the point where he was kind of blind, but of course I was their baby.

Feeding in the South is a showmanship of love. My breakfast was grits, eggs, sausage, toast, orange juice, some milk. Then the school was all Black. When I went to school, the Black people in their lunch, we had greens, cornbread, peach cobbler, fried chicken, and when you went home, and you might have greens again. And everyday you got some steak and potatoes and cornbread. And whose house you went to, the first thing they said is, "Are you hungry?" To this day, even though it was me and my son, I've always cooked a whole chicken so that whoever came to my house could eat. There's enough for everybody. That's why I love cooking for people at Mary's Place. It really makes me feel good when I hear them go, "God, that was so good." I just feel like a star.

I never knew what my grandfather did. He was retired by the time I came along. I don't know if my grandmother ever worked or not. I know they were talking about how they had to pick cotton. I would hear sometimes my uncles talking, and they were saying, "When we lived on Mr. Filson's place," so I knew right then they were sharecroppers, and the land wasn't theirs. So, my grandparents, they lived on somebody's plantation, somebody's land.

The guy who owned the land, he had lots of cotton. I used to want to go out in the field, 'cause during the summer big trucks would come along with kids and the young people in them, and they'd be going to pick cotton and pick corn, so I used to want to go. But Granddaddy said, "I worked too hard so you wouldn't have to go do that. No, you ain't going to pick no cotton." So I never got to pick.

My grandmother was an Eastern Star. My grandfather, my father's grandfather, my father's father were all Masons. The women are called Eastern Stars. They came from Alabama, my mother's father. My father's father, I don't know where they came from. As far as I knew they were from Louisiana. Now, my great-grandmother was pure Indian, she had long white hair.

My father, he's never had anything to do with me, but you know, I've been thinking about taking a chance and maybe go see him. I'll find out why he never wanted me. I remember one time my father came to see me at my grandmother's house. My auntie Anna and everybody got me all dressed up. He went down the road. He told me he was going to be right back, and I remember standing in that window for hours and hours, waiting on him to come back. I remember my legs were hurting, but I never left that window. My grandfather came and picked me up and said, "He's not coming, baby. He's not coming." My grandparents were very protective. They were my salvation. They loved me, good, bad, right, wrong. That's what I miss is that love. Do you know that over the years, I still felt that love? I still feel like my grandparents are watching over me.

Me and my granddaddy would go places. We'd get on the railroad tracks and walk anywhere you want to go. And we would go to some of my grandmother's uncle's houses. I liked to listen to all the old people. Back then a child was seen and not heard, but my grandmother let me sit around, and I would listen to all the old stories that they would tell.

I was taught how to cook before I could reach a stove. The chair would be pushed up to the stove with my grandmother, and while she was stirring her pots, I was right there handing her some seasoning. I've always been an avid reader. They said that I was literally reading books at two. I would be right there giving her ingredients. With my biological mother having starved me, I do have a problem about not having food. I kind of go off the deep end if I don't have food, because food became a safe haven for me. My grandmother and grandfather taught me with food came joy.

"Of course we thought her father would kill me. Back then white people had no thought of killing Black children."

I remember I was a part of integration as well as segregation. You got to think about those little small towns were last to become integrated. In the sixth grade—what is that '66? I was eleven. That's when they integrated. I loved it when it was an all Black school. We had a parade—the homecoming queen—and the teachers would let even us little kids go out and be with the jamboree with all the big kids, and people doing the boogaloo, the skate, and the mash potato [*laughing*]. Oh, I used to dance myself away, and the big kids used to just look at me and go "Look at her!"

I have been thrown out of a classroom and my head slammed against the wall by white teachers because I didn't say "Yes, ma'am." The Black teachers had told us that we didn't have to say that anymore, but you know, be respectful, while the white people insisted that we say it. So, she slammed my head into a wall, and I remember the Black teachers really being upset and saying, "We've got to do something about this. We're not going to let them come here and mistreat our children." I remember when I went home, how upset my grandfather was. He was fighting mad. He said, "You know, I've worked all my life and did everything hoping that my grandchildren would not have to go through this." But my grandmother begged him not to go up to the school. There was no other schools in that town for me to go to.

One day we were shopping in the store. My grandmother was looking over in the frozen food department, and a little white girl about nine years old came and shoved my grandmother. I saw this, and my grandmother going, "Excuse me, ma'am. I'm sorry."

Girl, I chased that little girl around that store, and I caught her, and I pushed her into all the canned goods. All the food fell. My grandfather was just coming into the in door. She said, "Come on Mr. Bob, we got to go! She gone pushed that white child!" So my grandfather just turned around and we didn't shop that day [*laughing*].

Of course we thought her father would kill me. Back then white people had no thought of killing Black children. You heard about the Tillman boy in Chicago. He was only fifteen. They killed lots of children. I know a Black man in town that was hung because he tried to take a pair of pants back. They didn't fit. They shot up his house and hung him up a tree because he insisted on standing up for his rights. So, I've seen a lot of prejudice and discrimination that people don't think I've seen or been a part of, but I have. So, I try to use my experiences to tell other people it hasn't been that long we had Blacks got to stand on one side and whites on the other. I was a part of that having come from that small town in the South.

I knew about a lot of people that had homes burnt down. I don't remember their names. I just remember listening to my grandparents tell the stories. I know that we were mistreated. I know that we had to get in line for lunch, and if a white person want to come and charge in front of us and push us, they did. I grew up with a lot of hatred for white people at one time.

"God always sent good people in my life that were there for me."

We had a little church called St. Peter of the Rock Baptist Church. Now, down there, there wasn't a lot of pastors. We might not have had church but once a month, because a pastor might have preached two or three churches. I remember when my grandfather died, and they had his funeral. It was at this little church. There was so many people. When you came up the highway, by the time you got all the way to that church, say almost to the post office, that's how many callers were at that funeral. They couldn't even get into that church.

When my grandfather died, I remember my grandmother begging my mother to let me stay in Louisiana, and my mother said, "I wouldn't take her if I didn't need her, but she's the only way I can get on welfare." So that's how I came to be in Seattle steady.

She was a very greedy woman. I didn't even have a coat during the winter. The school all knew how my mother treated me. The counselors, there were many times they had to buy me shoes and stuff. God always sent good people in my life that were there for me.

I had a wonderful godmother named Ms. Lilly. Her and her husband have been dead for a few years. Very, very old-fashioned people. She never bought her clothes—she made everything. I can make a quilt, I can sew, I can knit, I can crochet. She taught me how to do all that. And I like making pickled vegetables like pickled okra, pickled onion. Jellies, I've done all that.

She went to First Day with me—the Black Methodist Church here in Seattle. I was always involved in the church. I was a missionary. The ushers—they called them "missionaries." She had gave me a duffle bag, and she said, "If you ever need to run, you keep this little bag packed if you ever got to get away." One day I had been beaten so bad, when I got to Ms. Lilly's house, Ms. Lilly took my sweater off, and my skin came off in my sweater. All this was raw, ripped meat on my back, and I remember Ms. Lilly just crying. She used to call my uncles and tell them to help me.

I came in on the last of the Black Panthers. I was thirteen years old—fourteen. I was involved with the Panthers for about a year. I still have my tam. It was right before I got away from my biological mother. I worked at the free breakfast program. Because I was young myself, I was serving breakfast to the children. I remember going into one of the panther houses and they had lots of weapons. I remember one of the panthers, he clicked something, and a wall turned around—full of ammunition, full of guns of every sort, every kind.[7]

You know how many ways I contemplated killing my mother? I probably would have never got out of prison if I would have killed her, so I'm thankful that I didn't. It had got to the point where I realized that my mother was crazy. I remember praying to God and asking God if he would just get me out of there, that I would serve him if he would just get me out of that house.

I was going to Franklin High School here in Seattle, Washington, and I met this girl. We kind of hung and stuff, but I really didn't know her. So one day we were sitting on the steps talking, and I told her what I was going through, and she said, "Well, I'm going to ask my Auntie if you could come and live with us." See, I had tried to go to the state to get away from her, and they would never take me away, and then I'd just get beat for telling. The next day, she came to school and told me that her Auntie said I could come and live with her, and that lady's my mother to this day. She adopted me and raised me, gave me lots of love.

"[M]y life took a turn further down especially after my best friend was murdered."

As I've gotten older, I've begun having some mental problems, dealing and facing the hatred from my biological mother, trying not to be like her. I am now diagnosed with bipolar too, but my psychiatrist says that my mother also was sick, and she was. I have come to terms with forgiving her, because I have to. I still have lots of nightmares, dreams, waking up in sweats, or thinking that she's there. But other than that, I'm trying to survive.

Now I have a child. I only had one because I want to make up to that child and do what never had been done for me. I didn't succeed all the way, but I definitely gave him a better life than I had. My son was dressed as sharp as a tack, had anything he wanted to eat. But over the years we've just kind of gotten not so close, and I think that happened when I started using drugs. It kind of destroyed our relationship.

I became a drug addict in 1986. My best friend, Ovetta, was killed by her husband.[8] My own illness began to really surface, and I started really getting into drugs, and my life took a turn further down especially after my best friend was murdered. My best friend came over that day, and I told her I knew her husband was going to kill her. When I tell you something, it's going to happen. Kind of scary sometimes. My grandmother says I was born with a veil over my eyes, which means I see things.[9] It's just a gift that I have.

I kind of lost it when Ovetta died. This is when all the things in my life also started crashing down on me. As long as I was high, I didn't have to think. I didn't have the emotions, the dreams, stay up for days. I wouldn't have to go through the sickening emotions. It kind of gave me the power.

My son did five years in prison for something he didn't do, but he didn't tell who did it. I raised him, "You don't talk—you don't say anything." There wasn't a lot that I was able to do for him while he was in prison because I was doing drugs. I did try to be there and be ready when he came out, bought him some clothes, and fixed him a big old dinner and everything. He got out by Thanksgiving. We used to be really close, but we drifted apart a lot. I just really have my grandson. My granddaughter, I guess she's only three, but I never really got to be around her that much.

"I tried to succeed in my life. I still have goals and dreams."

Crack became really epidemic for my neighborhood. They left their homes to the children and most of those kids lost their parents' homes. The Central Area is very accessible to downtown, very close to everything. That was my 'hood and that's where I grew up. That's where me and my friends rode our bikes, went down the street to our neighbor's house, you know? Now my neighborhood, my 'hood, where I grew up, is predominately white because they came back and took over all that property.

I tried to succeed in my life. I still have goals and dreams. I want to be a writer. If I ever succeed, being an African American, they dig up every bit of dirt they can about you. So, it will come out. Somebody's going to talk. So, I would kind of rather put it out there myself, and let the truth be known. There's not a person that's taken drugs that hasn't sold one. Nobody. I wasn't no big old dealer [*laughing*] riding around in a Mercedes. It wasn't nothing like that. But I did that in my past.

Like I said, I intend to succeed. I want to go on to get my master's degree. I have a year and a half to go to get my bachelor's degree, and then I'm going to go on to get my masters in journalism and history. I have spoken for many homeless women forums. I've always been a speaker at different things. I became very well known for my poetry. I sung with the Total Experience Choir for many years.[10] Drugs and all that destroyed my voice. I've been clean now over six years. I drink a beer every now and then. Other than that, I'm clean.

I moved to Texas—had a wonderful life there. I just wanted to get away. I've never cared for Seattle. In Texas, I worked at Texas A & M. I started off as a dishwasher, then I did prep cooking, server on the line, dishwashing. I've worked as an office worker—receptionist, secretary. And I've worked at a hospital as a file clerk, filing x-rays. I'd like to be an office person because I've always liked to dress and put on my heels.

I'm not always going to get disability. I suffer also with agoraphobia, but when I have my medication, I'm okay. I've stayed in my house for two years and never went out, but on my medication I do okay. But there's times when I don't want to go outside—I just don't want to see the outside world. It used to be really bad. I would get dizzy. I'd have to hold on to the side of a building, but I've gotten a lot better.

"I've taken in the homeless myself. I've clothed the naked, and I've fed the hungry, 'cause that's what I'm supposed to do."

I've worked with WHEEL for many years. I've been a part of the woman's forum, Women in Black. I've been in marches with them. We opened up a winter shelter here and at Lakeview. We helped the public become aware of what it's like to be homeless. I also did some public forums in churches to help churches open up their churches to shelters. We would go and speak and talk to these churches, making people aware and see that some of us were educated, we were women that worked, that tried to have a regular life. We were dressed decently and nice to make the public aware that there are homeless people out there that are very much trying to better themselves or get back on their feet. And really, there's a lot of homeless people that was homeless, and once they get back on their feet, they're never homeless again.

I've taken in the homeless myself. I've clothed the naked, and I've fed the hungry, 'cause that's what I'm supposed to do. Those are the things that give me joy. I wasn't homeless then, but I would be downtown because I didn't want to be by myself, and I had a house. Sometimes I would come downtown and just get people that needed a place to stay and take them to my house. I just like hospitality, you know.

Women in Black, it's in memory of people that have been killed while they've been homeless—remembrance for the people that have been here. One of them, Tessie was a wonderful friend of mine. Tessie was an Indian. She was living under the bridge, 'cause she got sick or something, but Tessie died.[11] Tessie was one of the closest homeless people to me. I had two friends, Caroll and Karen. Carol died a few years back, right before I left for Texas. It's hard on her sister because they were inseparable. We knew each other since kids.

Like last month, I had seen a lady named Pat. Not long after I got here, I seen Pat, and I hugged her and kissed her and we talked. Well she went to the shelter and went to bed. She had a heart attack in her sleep and died. I remember they're saying, "Pat died." And I'm like, "You guys are lying, I just saw Pat the other day." She was fifty-one.

Monique died about three months ago. She was murdered. Everywhere else she went, he knew where she was, but he didn't have no idea that she was staying with us. She was staying with me and my cousin. April 27th was a Friday, and she had called us, and told us that she was on her way back, and somehow he got her and chased her down the street and she was running, knocking on people's doors, and no one would let her in or help her. And the last door she went into, the lady hurried up and closed the door, and he shot her on that lady's porch four or five times. He killed her with a .357, so she looked nothing like herself in her casket.

I think I'm going to become really wealthy one day and when I do—you're going to put this in there too: that Loann has dreams of taking her wealth and having lots of children in my home—all races, abused children that have been mistreated—and loving them and having them be sisters and brothers. Another goal is I want to open up a domestic violence shelter, and I want to name it after Monique and Ovetta.

I had a heart attack about a year ago. I had the stroke a couple of months ago. A month ago I had bad pneumonia. About a month ago I had a stroke in the doctor's office. They're called TIAs. I have those quite often. I try to go to the hospital as less as possible. I take quite a bit of medication. I take two pills for my high blood pressure, and the other pill is a water pill for my hypertension. And then of course I have my mental medicine, you know.

"I love her because the Bible says you have to, and I've never disrespected her. I never said nothing wrong to her."

My mother lives in Ohio. She's still very sick mentally. You can just listen to the way she talks. She wants me to call her mom. I have, but I cringe inside when I do. I love her because the Bible says you have to, and I've never disrespected her. I never said nothing wrong to her. The Bible says you have to respect your mother and father so that your days will be longer on this earth. Sometimes you wonder why a lot of people die early. It's because of things that they did. Also because they didn't respect their parents. The Bible tells you that. So I never disrespected her. I tried to talk to her and be as close to her as I can, but she's not my mother.

When I was two years old, I had three dreams. Each of these three dreams were something to do with my mother leaving me. In the first dream, I had came up here, and I went to see Santa Claus at the store, which is now called Macy's. It used to be called the Bon Marche. That big window was where Santa Claus sat. My mother used to have this old song called, "Will the Circle be unbroken." It was by the Five Blind Boys, out of Alabama, if I'm not mistaken. Anyway, I was looking out the window and a chariot came and picked up my biological mother. There was six beautiful white horses—and she got into the chariot like a Cinderella chariot. She left me in this apartment that we lived in, and I stood there watching her get in this chariot, and then she left.

The next part of the dream, I was standing at Bon Marche looking with my hands behind my back like a little kid. I'm looking in this window, and there is this man with a white suit. He had a long white beard; he had a crown on top of his head, and he had a gold staff. I affiliated him with God and Santa Claus. My biological mother and all these people were just having a wonderful time. He was sitting in the chair like a king. Nobody ever paid me any attention. She never stopped and looked at me, and I just stood there and watched it.

Even then I knew she didn't want me. Even from very, very young I've always had a vivid understanding of God, you know. It's like I always knew that there was a God. Maybe that he would take her out of my life, which he did, because I credit my cousin with saving my life. And I told her, "You literally saved my life, because I'd probably be dead or in a prison, or probably would have been a whore on the streets or anything just to get away."

All my life, I've searched for love. I had it with grandparents. I had it with my godmother, Ms. Lilly. I had that love with the mom I have now, and Ovetta, and through my friends—my cousin. Like I said, I credit her with saving my life. I didn't even know her. We sat on the steps one day, and I told her the exact same thing I'm telling you. I told her, and she said, "I'm going to ask my auntie if you can come live with us." And she did. And you know, that was divine intervention. I know it was. That was God working in all of that.

CHAPTER 10

Mona Caudill Joyner

Figure 4 Photograph of Mona Caudill Joyner

I first met Mona at a meeting of the Women's Housing Equality and Enhancement League in June of 2006. That same evening, I ran into her and a female friend outside of Angeline's. Both Mona and her friend were staying at the emergency shelter there. We struck up a conversation on the street and then walked down to a nearby sandwich shop, where I conducted the first of my several formal taped interviews with Mona between 2006 and 2008.

Beginning with the first interview, Mona hearkened back repeatedly to the 1999 murder of her fiancé José Lucio. While Mona's involvement with WHEEL predated the murder of her fiancé, beginning in 2000 with the first of the Women in Black vigils in Seattle, she found an outlet for her grief at José's unsolved murder, and the circumstances surrounding his burial. Though Mona reports that she was listed as his emergency contact, it was days before she learned of his death at Harborview Hospital, and she was unable to gain the release of his body, which was cremated and stored for years at the King County Medical Examiner's Office, along with the remains of hundreds of other homeless and indigent people. In 2003 José's remains were laid to rest as part of a mass burial and service coordinated by WHEEL/Women in Black in conjunction with the King County Medical Examiner.[1]

Mona grew up in the midst of grinding poverty in the mining community of Harlan, Kentucky. In 1972, the year Mona turned sixteen and Harlan mineworkers declared a historic strike against Duke Power in their struggle for living wages and safe working conditions, the median wage of a Harlan County family was $4,600 a year.[2] In 2008, 33.9 percent of the residents of Harlan County lived below the poverty line, with a median family income of $23,648.[3]

Mona recounts growing up in the midst of horrific family violence, including child-hood sexual abuse at the hands of her father, and subsequently her brother-in-law. Three of Mona's brothers committed suicide, and a brief 1978 story in the Harlan Enterprise *reports the story of the death of her father, Ernest Caudill, 54, who was shot by her brother Jack, 34, during "a father-son confrontation," and subsequently died at Harlan Appalachian Regional Hospital.[4]*

Though Mona frequently broke into tears of grief, frustration, and outrage as she spoke about the dehumanization of homeless people and the deaths of homeless people on the street, she also seemed to draw strength from her own anger at injustice and her com-mitment to providing a voice for the voiceless. Listening to Mona's impassioned defense of the human rights of homeless and low-income people, I was reminded of the impassioned rhetoric, and the strength and defiance of the women of Harlan, Kentucky, whose voices are recorded in Barbara Kopple's award-winning documentary Harlan County USA. *I met with Mona on a couple of occasions to go over draft versions of the chapter, and during our last meeting in 2010, she told me that she wanted to write a more sustained account of her own life history, beginning with her childhood in Harlan. She was committed to speaking publicly about her experiences of sexual and physical abuse and had recently made contact with Harlan activists working against domestic violence. She was hoping to travel back to Harlan in the next few months to speak at a rally against domestic violence and access records relating to her family's history.*

"When I was a kid, I would go to the farthest corner and pray that my father didn't see me, but he always saw me. I couldn't escape his eyes—I couldn't escape him."

I come from Kentucky from a family of thirteen—seven girls, six boys. I had an alcoholic father, a bootlegger from Harlan County, Kentucky. My dad was the only child in the family, and he never saw his real father until he was fifty-one years old. My father was a coal miner. He worked hard. Worked during the Depression. He plowed the fields for ten cents, twenty-five cents, a day. So if it wasn't for my grandma, if it hadn't been for her, we would never have survived. My grandma was a very good lady. She was part Cherokee, part Blackfoot Indian. She worked very, very hard. There was always a garden in the back yard; there was always food on the table. It wasn't what we really wanted but we survived: beans and potatoes, corn bread, collard greens.

I don't know what made my father so angry. I don't know why he was an alcoholic. I don't know why he was so abusive, but he used to beat my mother all the time. It was a cycle: he would beat her, she would leave for a few days and then return. And when she would run away from him, the children that loved my mother more than they did him, we were the ones that got the beatings. Naturally, I was the one that got the most beatings. I loved my mom; she was a good lady, and it was a full time job taking care of thirteen children. And I never knew but there was one kind of men and that was abusive and very, very evil. I always thought my dad's name should have been Satan, because he was the devil himself.

When I was a kid, I would go to the darkest corner and pray that my father didn't see me, but he always saw me. I couldn't escape his eyes—I couldn't escape him. He always found me. Whenever he would get ready to start his tirade of abuse, he always found me, and I always got the other end of his fist or his broomstick or whatever he wanted to pick up. The only time he ever told me he loved me was on his deathbed.

I always had to be the baby sitter, the caretaker. Only had one toy in my life. Curious George, the Monkey. Worn hand me down. Only one toy, but I loved that little monkey. I still love Curious George Monkeys, so when I die, I don't want flowers; I want a Curious George Monkey in my hands. I've been curious all my life [*laughs*]. Everybody's got a problem, I'm right there trying to solve it for them: "What can I do to help you today? How can I make your life easier for you?" Give them the resources that I know of, all the time neglecting myself. But while I'm taking care of others, it lessens my pain. It takes my mind off myself.

My dad sexually abused us children; my brothers sexually abused us, and when I got older my brother-in-law raped me when I was four days short of my twelfth birthday. When one of my older sisters got married, she made me go home with her and start baby-sitting her three kids. So, every Saturday, she'd be out getting her hair done and sleeping around with all the policemen in town, and she left me at home with her husband. He used to rape me every time that she left. Every weekend.

I was innocent. I didn't know what sex was. It was my first time, and the bastard raped me with everything he could: sex objects, his hands. Everything. [Afterwards] he told me I had to go wash the bedclothes before my sister got home. I looked down at the bed—it was white sheets all covered with blood. I looked, and I could see the parts of my insides laying there. That was absolutely the most horrible thing I ever had happen, when I looked down and saw my insides lying on that white sheet.

So I got up and went through the laundry room, washed the clothes, and that dog went back to work. I felt like I was dying that day. I felt like my insides had been ripped out. I was scared to death. I was scared if I ever told Mommy or Daddy that they would kill him, or he would kill them, because he had threatened that he would kill me if I told. He threatened he would kill the family. So I just kept it locked up for a long time. Every weekend he was doing the same thing. The same threats. And finally one day, I told my older sister; she went and told my mom; my mom told my dad. They put me in a foster home to keep me out of the family, to keep my mouth shut. Eventually, they told my sister. They didn't believe me, and the ones that did believe me didn't stand up for me. So for thirty-five years that sister didn't believe me. She said it was my fault. She said I asked for it. She said I wanted it. Then I realized she was as sick and deranged as her husband.

I got pregnant while I was in foster care, and they wanted to take the baby. I fought the social workers on a daily basis so they couldn't take the baby, and then I wound up marrying a man I didn't even know—that was not the father of the baby— just to get out of the foster home. So, I've been running from something all my life. Running from one bad situation right into another—not knowing how to separate the two. Not knowing if there was anything but hating anywhere in the world.

My mother passed away with cancer; my oldest brother killed my father and got twenty years in prison for it. And I had three brothers that committed suicide. So life is not always nice. When my brother killed my father in 1979, I left Kentucky and never went back. My brother shot my father, and he was in the hospital for three weeks before he died. One day he called all of us in one by one. He called me to his bedside as he was dying, and he said, "Mona, I know you don't believe me, but I loved you just like I do all the rest of my kids." I looked at him for a minute, and I wanted to tell him, "Just because you're going to hell, don't try to ease your conscience with me before you go." But I wasn't as evil as my father, so I couldn't tell him that. So I told him, "Yes, Daddy, I love you too." But I didn't. I hated that son of a bitch.

I remember times that I had to sit on his lap while his hands was up our dresses. And he had this cute little saying for all us girls. Every time he called us over to sit on his lap, he'd always say, " The only thing in the world I need to make me happy is for you to sit on my lap and call me 'Pappy.' " While his hands was up under our clothes. I wanted to tell the bastard how I really felt before he died. I wish I could have. But I have a conscience. I can't. If it took him to say it on his deathbed and me to accept it, I had to do that, because [otherwise] one day I won't go to heaven. That was the only reason that I heard what he had to say, but it didn't mean shit to me. In all my life, the only time you're going to tell me you love me is when you were dying? Don't waste your breath. So, see he used me once again. He couldn't go to hell without trying to cover his conscience at my expense. I'm his daughter in name only; other than that, we're not connected.

"[T]hey don't have to have nothing on you to cremate you. You just have to be Mexican and no insurance…That's the cheapest way to go out— in a little box of ashes."

For the last ten years I've been a homeless advocate on the streets of Seattle. I'm always aware of what's going on. I keep up with what's happening in my community. I always speak out for the homeless. I always speak up for the poor. I don't need papers in front of me to know what I'm going to say or who I want to say it to. I've accepted homeless people as part of the family that I didn't have. I counsel them. I tell them where the housing is, where the food is, who to stay away from, what's going on, how to change their lives and not be doing drugs, not be drinking, stay away from that type of stuff 'cause it gets you killed.

In 1996, I met this Mexican guy. His name was José Lucio, and I fell in love with him, and guess what? He was an alcoholic too, but I always try to save the world, and I wound up getting lost in it myself. So, I took him into my home, and I cooked for him, cleaned for him, washed his clothes for him, done everything except marry him.

I had a restraining order on him because he had threatened to kill me. I'd finally had enough of psychology and therapy sessions that I had figured out that God made us in his own image, and he made us perfect, and he made us without blemish and without abuse. So, I put the marriage on hold, and I had a restraining order on him. I had put my boundaries out there: "If you're going to be with me then there's certain boundaries, and if you cross them, then good bye, because I don't need another man like my father." I was breaking that pattern, which was very, very, very hard to do. Lots of prayer. Lots of therapy.

My fiancé, he wasn't ready to leave his friends and leave the street, but he worked everyday. He worked out of the Millionaire's Club in Seattle.[5] He worked everyday. José and his friends were out drinking one night, and they got into a fight, and they pushed him off the I-5 and Mercer Street Exit and killed him. A lot of homeless people seen it happen, but no one would step forth and tell which one of the friends that done it, so it's still unsolved.

He was from Mexico, and of course if you're Mexican, they think you're all no good. He didn't have any family here. I was listed as next of kin on his papers in the hospital, but when he went to the hospital, they didn't notify me. They cremated him without even contacting his family in Mexico. They didn't even know his family, his mother and father's name, or the city that they lived in until I went and provided that information. They didn't have his social security or nothing. So see, they don't have to have nothing on you to cremate you. You just have to be Mexican and no insurance, that's all. Over a hundred and twenty seven dollars, they cremated him. That's the cheapest way to go out—in a little box of ashes.

I don't believe in cremation. I believe in heaven, and I believe in hell. I believe God made us all. He made us perfect. He made us in his own image, and for man to go and cremate a person, I just can't accept it. I grieved, and I grieved, and I grieved because he was sitting in that box of ashes in that Medical Examiner's office for four years while I fought to buy him his own plot and bury him separately, but they wouldn't do that. For four years he sat on the shelf in the Medical Examiner's Office before they finally buried him. And when they did, they buried 197 people at one time. And that just about killed me. We finally got him buried, and here it is a couple years later, but you know, when you love someone, the years can add up, but it can't take away the pain.

We're at the point now where we're working on getting the City of Seattle to let us put a homeless memorial plaque in one of the parks and make a memorial garden out of it. I came about that idea as a way to try to ease my pain with dealing with José. We want the memorial to be like a garden that you can just walk through, maybe an archway above it and have stones that's leading up to the plaque itself. Maybe have each person's name on it. Right now we have about nine places that we're looking at within the Seattle city limits, the downtown area. We want a place that is nice and quiet and respectful, [but] that is accessible to the tourists that come because our homeless needs to be visible. You can't put us on the run, because homelessness is here to stay, and when these people are come and gone, there's going to be more taking their place because housing is expensive, and you have a lack of housing.

You have the mentally ill and the physically disabled people out there homeless. You have the people that are mentally ill that do not have a hospital or an environment that can meet their needs. When Reagan opened the doors and threw them out of the hospital, he threw them out to the streets, and they've been here ever since. So, you cannot get rid of us. You may as well get ready, because we demand that you give us equal rights just like you do to other people. You're going to treat us with respect, and you're going to treat us humanely. If you don't, we're going to be in your face all the time until you do, because we're not going to let you just keep cremating us and doing away with us, thinking that's the end of the problem.

Last week we stood vigil for Douglas Dawson from Spokane, Washington. The man is handicapped. He was in his wheelchair at a bus stop, sleeping. These two young thugs had just robbed someone else a couple of blocks away. They set him on fire. His whole body and wheelchair caught on fire. When the fire department got the 911 call, they thought they were just going to put out a trash fire. They got over there and realized it was a human being in a wheelchair. They airlifted him from Spokane to Harborview, and he survived three or four days.

This man only had one leg and they set him on fire. This is what society has become. When you get burned to death in a wheelchair, that's just as low as it can go. If that man had had housing, more than likely he would be alive today. He wouldn't be sitting at the bus stop at two o'clock in the morning. It is a disgrace to see a homeless person out in a wheelchair. It's a disgrace to see an eighty- or ninety-year-old woman in a shelter. It's a disgrace to keep building new buildings and hiring more case managers when they're not even doing the job with the people that have been homeless for ten, fifteen, twenty years.

You stand out there, you do these vigils, they come along, and before they wouldn't even look at you. We have been in their faces for ten years now, so now when they see us out there, at least they start acknowledging you. They might look at you and give you a little smile. We stop the clerks [from City Hall] that come along. One of them came last week with a bouquet of flowers and laid them at our feet as we're standing there for Douglas Dawson. But the judges or lawyers are not going to come by and acknowledge you or accept the flyer. They're going to be on the other side of the street hoping you don't see them. We've been doing this for years so eventually—eventually—we're just praying that the mayor will meet with us after the vigils. The mayor needs to realize he needs to build more affordable housing for the homeless. Homeless people cannot afford a condo.

"These days when I have to do these vigils, I'm sick. I'm depressed. I feel like I'm going to a real funeral—it's just like it's a member of my own family."

We're going to stand again for the Women in Black. We're going to stand in vigil for Tonya Smith, the homeless person that was killed in the International District last week on Weller Street. This poor lady, sleeping in an encampment all by herself, stabbed over and over and over. Sometimes I think there might be a serial killer here working on the homeless people. She's not the first one that has died this way. She's not the first one that has died in the jungle or close to the jungle. There should be no such places as jungles people have to sleep, especially a woman.

The busses stop running at certain times of night, so you can't ride busses all night to be safe. There's not enough shelters to take everybody, so there's nothing but the streets, under the bridges, in the jungles, in the business doorways, wherever you can go, wherever you could lay your head and just pray that you'll be safe. You're speaking of a "jungle" encampment, you're speaking of places like you think animals would be dwelling. God created us and he created us in his own image, so why should we have to live in a jungle? There's no way you can justify [Tonya's] death. If she had a roof over her head perhaps she'd be with us today. So, I just sadly say, "Godspeed and God rest your soul."

Tonya's murder, it just makes me remember when my fiancé was killed. His murder is still unsolved. I wonder did the police ever work on that case anymore after he was cremated? Did they ever try to find his family in Mexico after I provided the information to them? I know you've never contacted me, because I certainly left you all my contact information. So it's just another homeless bum out there. It's okay. They're dead. They're murdered. What is it going to take to make this city wake up and realize that you need to pay as much attention to a homeless murder as you do to a person that might be in an elite neighborhood and have the best of the family and all the money that they need? Why is it that you don't pay that much attention when a homeless person is killed? You just can't devalue people just because they're homeless. I pray for the people that have been killed, and I don't understand the inhumanity. Why don't you feel the pain? We're crying out to be heard, and when we're not heard, then the Women in Black have to go and stand and cry out for you when you're no longer amongst us. What's it going to take for people to hear the cries of the homeless people? These days when I have to do these vigils, I'm sick. I'm depressed. I feel like I'm going to a real funeral—it's just like it's a member of my own family. That's how much I grieve for these people that don't have housing, these people that die violently in the streets. If it was not for the Women in Black, who would stand for them? Who would remember them?

"[N]ot only will your family rape you, the city and county will rape you too. Just in different forms."

Me, I had always had my home, and then about a year ago I became homeless myself. HUD, I lived in one of their buildings, but they're revamping the downtown area, so every chance they get to push a homeless person out of their housing they do. My rent was paid, and I still had three days to go before the first. I went to California because I wanted to move there. I went down to make sure everything was in order. I called [HUD] and told them I would be returning on Monday and planned on giving them a thirty-day notice when I got back here. But in lieu of that, I still had a seven-day grace period. They told me I abandoned my apartment, because I didn't give them notice before I left. I didn't need to, because I hadn't made no concrete plans at that point. That's how they took my housing.

So, I got me an attorney through Angeline's. They have attorneys that come in and represent homeless people. We took them to court. My attorney told them that they stole my housing, and they know they did. But I still couldn't win because this was up against a corporation, and there was only one of me. And even with my rent and everything paid, they still took my house. Here I am, I don't hurt nobody. I don't smoke, drink, or do drugs. One day I had housing, next minute I didn't. They took my housing from me with my rent paid. With a seven-day grace period. That's how dirty they are in Seattle.

The building still has Section 8. By law they have to have so many apartments that they rent to low-income people, but my apartment was on the thirteenth floor overlooking the Puget Sound downtown—exactly what an attorney or the professional people would want—and that's why they stole my apartment. All the homeless people were being phased-out of there. After the earthquake, they started renovating the building. That's when they really started getting rid of the homeless people, and that's when the professional people started coming in. Professionals get the big nice apartments for their offices. And all they're doing is building condos. Well, a homeless person can't afford a condo to start with. If you're a homeless person, it's a lot easier to get rid of you and rent to a professional person. They'll run you out and arrest you—like when we had the WTO—'cause they don't want anyone to see the homeless out in the street. Or they'll arrest you when it comes election time, because the homeless does not need to be seen. So not only will your family rape you, the city, and county will rape you too. Just in different forms.

"[W]hen you're running around in the streets all day from shelter to shelter and food line to food line, it makes you crazy. It makes you psychotic."

So, they stole my housing from me, and I have been angry and upset and devastated ever since. So, I walk the streets during the day, and I sleep in this shelter at night. Sometimes I just want to keep sleeping in the streets or along the streets because once you get inside the shelter, things are not all that they're cooked up to be either. See, everything goes to the organizations, and then it becomes like a dictatorship. The staff are desensitized—they're like drill sergeants. Open your mouth and you're going to get, "Sit down, be quiet, shut up." That's the way that we get talked to, and we rebel against that. You shouldn't talk to people like that in your family. You don't talk to people like that on a normal job. If you have to treat homeless like that, then that's not the job for you. Gently, that's the way you get it done. And medicine is not a cure for everything. Just a nice kind gesture will go a lot farther than medication. You don't get it done by force. Abuse is abuse no matter what form it comes in. So, is it safer in my father's house or in the shelter? It's hard to know the difference sometimes. All these years, I didn't smoke, drink, or do drugs, but I don't know what a peaceful place is like.

And kicking the women out because they're yelling, or because they talk too loud, or because they seem disoriented? Hey that's the truth, we are disoriented. Homeless women are so unpredictable because the streets beat us up so much mentally and physically, and it's so stressful out here that it keeps you depressed all the time so you don't know when you're going to be up or down. Some ladies have two, three suitcases and a bag and a purse, and the staff tells them, "Hey, when the van comes to take you to the shelter, you can only take what you can carry on your lap. Anything else, either throw it away, or you stay behind." So therefore they have to sleep in the street, and they do that in order to keep all their belongings. Then they might show up the next morning all bloody from being in fights—somebody tried to steal the stuff from them. Or they'll come in without it because somebody stole it from them while they were sleeping in the bus stop. A storage unit is another thing that people can't afford. They start to get behind on their storage; they can't get caught up, and they just auction it off for whatever the storage fees are. So, you wound up losing any way you go. You're always losing by being homeless.

If you're not sleeping and eating good and getting that proper rest, when you're running around in the streets all day from shelter to shelter and food line to food line, it makes you crazy. It makes you psychotic. One minute you're okay, next minute you feel like flipping out. And when that mood comes and goes and you're able to regroup, it's like a bulldozer run over you. You say, "Wow, what was that? Five minutes ago I was depressed, I was tired, I was crying or whatever." And then all of a sudden, you crack a joke, and you start laughing. You feel it in your belly, and then you think, "What was so bad five minutes ago?"

"The newspaper is a job. It gives you some respect. It gives you some dignity."

In our city, we have a newspaper called *Real Change* that was made by the homeless and for the homeless. We pay thirty cents for the newspaper, and we sell it for a dollar or whatever donation over a dollar people want to give us. The reason for the newspaper is so we know that we're valuable human beings—some have college degrees. The newspaper is a job. It gives you some respect. It gives you some dignity. You must go to orientation to get the newspaper, and you must be a licensed vendor. So, there's a proper protocol we must go through before we even get the paper. Instead of standing there panhandling, we have the newspaper. You may stand there eight hours to make eight dollars, but it's a job. And we still have our dignity.

But *Real Change* doesn't just cover homelessness, it covers how to get your voice heard in Olympia, how to give the elected officials there to hear and understand what is going on within the city within the homeless community. When the mayor won't listen to us in Seattle, then they bus us to Olympia, and we go up on the steps of the governor's office, and we stand up there, and we say, "Please do not cut human services. You say you want to work on ending homelessness in ten years? Well, you better just keep working on it for the rest of your life because it's in every city, and it's in every state; it's in every town, so it's not like it's something that you can look at it and blink your eyes, and it's gone. No, it's here to stay." If you want to end homelessness within ten years, you must talk to the homeless people. We can tell you what works for homeless people and what doesn't. If they're going home to their wife and family and riding home in a Lincoln every night, we will never solve this.

"Sometimes it just gets so overwhelming that I just can't even speak."

I have always believed in the Lord, and I always prayed to him as a child through all my abuse. I have never, ever, ever left him and I know he has never left me. I get embarrassed sometimes and I think, "Oh, God do you really want to hear? It's Mona again. Do you really want me to dump this on you today?" Sometimes it just gets so overwhelming that I just can't even speak. But my faith will continue to get me through all this. And that is the biggest critical issue that I see within the system right now, and why things are not working. Mary's Place is a church, and they have religion, they have God within the church. The same women [who] will be making a big ruckus and all out of control [at other social service agencies] will come to Mary's Place and just settle down because it's a peaceful, relaxing, safe place, and I believe truly in my heart because it's got God in it. God made us and he's never going to leave us, but as long as we leave him and keep him out of everything, we're not going to prosper. We're just not. It's that pure and simple. So, I'm glad that I know him. I'm glad that I've got him in my heart. I'm glad that he's held my hand all these years. I'm glad that he's still holding it, and that's how I survive.

CHAPTER 11

Jessie Pedro

Figure 5 Photograph of Jessie Pedro

When I met her in the summer of 2006, Jessie was volunteering in the office of Mary's Place. She told me that she saw her volunteer work as a way of trying to repay the staff and community for the support they had given her during her two-year struggle with homelessness. Jessie was active also with WHEEL and was a regular participant in Women in Black vigils, and was among the women who gathered to help honor Sonshine Smith and participate in a ceremonial cleansing of her murder site in July 2006. I interviewed her for the first time following the service for Sonshine at Mary's Place and again in 2007 and 2008 and met with her again in 2010 to go over the penultimate version of this chapter.

Among Jessie's contributions to the community at Mary's Place was her role in creating and helping to coordinate "Island Day," which she described as at an annual celebration of the women's diverse cultural heritages, and a much needed day-long vacation from the stresses of seeking permanent housing and other necessary social services. Jessie takes pride in her Samoan roots, and her family's history in the Tokelau Islands, a group of three atolls situated halfway between Hawaii and New Zealand.[1] Jessie's memories of her own childhood in Hawaii, however, are far less than idyllic and she traces her lifelong struggles with depression to a succession of traumas that she experienced in childhood.

A central theme that emerged in my interviews with Jessie, however, was her commitment to moving beyond the traumas in her past—and her critique of the dehumanization of homeless people and people struggling with mental health issues in the United States. Jessie's vocal critique of the stigmatization of people with mental health–related disabilities was clearly informed by her experience serving variously as a program assistant, director, and member of a mental health–focused advocacy center (PAIMI) housed within the Honolulu-based Protection and Advocacy Agency of Hawaii, known since 2000 as the Hawaii Disability Rights Center.[2] The Center's multipronged mission includes ensuring that "People with disabilities gain access to employment, public facilities, programs and services and transportation as established in the Americans with Disabilities Act," as well as providing for the "Independence, Productivity, Integration and Inclusion," and "Self-Determination" of people with disabilities."[3] Jessie clearly finds affinities between the Hawaii Disability Rights Center and the emphasis on community and empowerment in both Mary's Place and WHEEL. For the last few years, Jessie has served as emcee for WHEEL's annual Women's Empowerment Luncheon. She is currently in the process of pursuing an Associate of Arts Degree at North Seattle Community College and hopes to go on for a doctorate and teach psychology and English literature at the college level.

"I don't remember anything 'til I was in the third grade. I'm seven—eight—years-old, and a man's head—his brains—were flying underneath the stairwell."

When people tell me, "So what was the happiest moment in your childhood?" I look at them and go, "Gosh, you can ask a weird question. I'd rather not answer the question." I don't live in the past. I live in the moment—in the present. Before, my past would take over me, and it's not like that now. I live now. My problems are in the right order. I've dealt with my past; it's the present that I'm dealing with now.

My great grandmother, she's Tokelauan, and my great grandfather's from Spain. My great grandfather José Pedro used to be a trader on a ship, so he was like a Casanova. First he got this other lady pregnant somewhere, and after that I guess he jumped the ship, and then he swam to the island, and next thing he knows, he married my great grandma. She was the princess of the Tokelau Islands. And her parents were the king and queen of the island.[4] My grandfather, the one that I call my dad, that's his parents. They have a book on the family history.

My trauma started when I was a baby, when I was abandoned from one home to another, to another, from one place to another to another. My mother gave me up, but I don't know why. I'm not going to ask why anyways. I'm done with that. I wasn't even adopted; I was just put from one home to another. The second family I was with, I was the outcast of the family. I was the outsider. The third family I stayed with, that's actually my grandfather and my step grandmother. They're my parents, because they took care of me, and I'm grateful for that. But I never belonged anywhere, even in my blood side's family. I was just a nobody.

I don't remember anything 'til I was in the third grade. I'm seven—eight—years old, and a man's head—his brains—were flying underneath the stairwell. He beat up his wife, and he came out the door. We lived in this apartment, seventeen floors [down]. Me and my friend went to go play. He jumped from the sixteenth floor all the way to where we were standing at. He committed suicide right in the front of us. And all I saw was this man with his brains underneath the stairwell. And the old lady laughed because you can see his ding-ding. That's what I learned when I was small: that when you die, it's funny.

And then three days later, this guy jumped over from the ninth floor, and I saw it again. He jumped from the ninth floor down and died and his blood was…If you ask me if I had a happy childhood, I don't think so, 'cause those are the things that I learned. I don't know even why I don't even remember from third grade on down. I don't remember anything. That's my first memory of my life. I was raped by a kid who was a year older, then I got molested when I was twenty-eight in an emergency room by a doctor.

"I emceed three statewide consumer conferences for the Hawaii Department of Health."

When I was younger, I wanted to be a lawyer. I wanted to be a doctor. I wanted to be a singer. I finished my high school, I took some college and that was it. I was working at McDonalds in Hawaii, and then again in California. And then I became a director of a psychosocial rehabilitation program in California for people with mental illness.[5] At first I was hired as a program assistant, and then next thing I knew, I became the director. We used to teach classes, had groups about four days a week. There was just two employees, me and this other lady, and we had volunteers, which was people with mental illness. We got to say, "This is what we need. This is what we want." That was the cool part, that you did have a voice.

PAIMI, it was an advocacy place. They had lawyers that advocated for you. It was trip when I became president of the PAIMI board.[6] "Dang, tiny old me, Jessie Nobody! Who am I? I don't got nothing." I mean, that's a chance of a lifetime. For me that was humbling. I mean, me, a person with a mental illness that only have a high school diploma, to be asked to be on the board of directors. My friend in

Hawaii—we started out the same program, we did the same thing—now she works for the State of Hawaii in the Office of Consumer Affairs, for people with mental illness.

I emceed three statewide consumer conferences for the Hawaii Department of Health. I also organized two of them, because in Hawaii, the people with disabilities organize it, not a provider, not the state. All the state do is give us the money. We come up with workshops, come up with keynote speakers, the whole shebang. So I did that. I emceed for three years. We had about 300 people. We had people from the other islands flown in from the outer islands to Hawaii just for that day. The first year, the emcee got sick, so they asked me to emcee the thing. At first you get kind of shaky, but then it's like you don't see anyone; you don't see the audience. The strongest part of me speaking is I speak from my feelings, and I love to do it. Even with Mary's Place, I go out and speak, and I enjoy it. And the more I do it, the more I love it.

In Hawaii, for all of the mayors that they've had, it's like the homeless people are garbage, so we have to sweep them up, because it's a tourist place. You sleep daytime at the beach or the park, and at night you just have to go walk the streets. You have to keep moving because you'll go to jail. If you sleep at a park, they'll put you into jail for thirty days, or they'll give you a thousand dollars fine. You get out thirty days later; next thing you know, you're back in jail again, and it's a stupid cycle that's a waste of the state's money. We don't want to show the tourists this is the real world. This is real. This is how life is. And at the homeless shelters in Hawaii, if you don't have a job, you sleep on a thin mat. That's no way for a person to be.

"I wish there was a school for homelessness. Homelessness 101 you learn when you're homeless."

I ended up in Seattle, thinking, "Oh, yeah, okay, I'll come to my mom's family." Instead I was abused emotionally and mentally, and I ended up in the hospital every month. When I was in the hospital, I thought the doctor would redirect me to a group home. That's the day they redirected me right in front of DESC.[7] They put me in a taxi and dropped me off at Third and James in the front of DESC at five o'clock p.m. When you say you want out of the hospital, you're going to end up on the streets. I didn't know that. It's in the news how—not this state but other states—how hospitals just go dump the person. I mean, even if they came with a wheelchair, all of a sudden, they're on the on the sidewalk of the street.

I didn't know what DESC meant until I got there and thought, "Oh, shit, what the hell!" It was scary because I didn't know what the hell I was supposed to do when I walked in the door. I felt like I was in the psych ward again. I mean it was like I would wake up at three o'clock, go shower, leave DESC at four o'clock in the morning. It's dark, and I would just walk around because I didn't know where I would go. I stayed there for a week and a half until I went to go see the nurse, and she goes, "Excuse me, do you know that there's male predators here? What you do is get out, leave this place. Right when you talk to me, you leave this place. Go to Angeline's."

Even when I went to Angeline's, I was like, "Oh, hell!" I mean, you walk in Angeline's, I mean its scary. Over there, they don't have groups. It's like you walk in, all you do is just sit over there and fall asleep on the chairs. I would go to the women's referral center in the evenings. At six o'clock we'd meet over there, and it was like, "Okay, where am I going to go tonight? I don't know." The first night they gave me the bus ticket—I don't know where I'm supposed to go. It was scary, and then all of a sudden people just kind of take you under their wings and say, "Okay, here, I'll show you where there's good food—better food than over here."

I used to catch the bus all night long with the hour pass. I would go bar to bar, and I'd pretend that I was going to use the bathroom or whatever. I'd sit down, I'd order a soda or a water, and I'd stay there until the bar closed, even though I don't drink. The next thing I know, I'll go on the bus, get an hour pass, just ride the bus. I never slept on the bus. I just stayed awake and I'd catch the bus like, "Okay, I'm surviving the night. At least I'm not outside." At the time Angeline's opened [in the morning], I'd go to Angeline's. About seven o'clock, seven thirty.

When I first went to Mary's Place, I never talked to anybody, I didn't even talk to the staff, I always covered my head with my hood, or I would curl up in a ball or fetus position because I was always scared. I wouldn't talk for anything, and I wouldn't even talk to the staff. I would be talking inside because I would be having panic attacks like crazy.

There is trauma in homelessness. Because you have no one. Your family is not with you. Your mom is not with you. Your sister is not with you. Nobody's with you. It's just yourself. I wish there was a school for homelessness. Homelessness 101 you learn when you're homeless.

I was homeless for about two years. We call it the "Shelter Shuffle." Shelter to shelter to shelter. At first I didn't know nothing. I was scared. All I had was the clothes on my back. I'd go stick my clothes in the laundry and go wash up and put them back on. All I had was shorts, a t-shirt. I don't think I had a bra. I had a jacket. When I left the hospital, that's all I had. I only had my walkman. I had my wallet with me, but for my clothes, that's all I had. I think I went about a month, a month and a half without anything. I was kind of scared of getting clothes at Mary's Place. Next thing I know, I was kind of "Okay, I'll go and get a shirt or pants." I'm grateful for Mary's Place. I don't know how many times they've saved my life.

"For me, I never knew what love was. I never learned that from my family. It's here where I learned it, and I'm still learning."

I mean, look how bad the system here in Washington is with mental illness. You know, when NAMI [the National Alliance for the Mentally Ill] graded them, they were like forty-nine, forty-eight. I mean, the low, low, lowest.[8] The caseloads are like—when do you ever get time—really give time to a client? When I was homeless, and I was seeing my therapist in the mental health system, it was okay, but she had to leave. I took it very hard. It was really hard on me. You know when the mental health provider person is genuine or they're just there because they're getting their paycheck or they're just book smart. After that I ended up in another place. I didn't have no control over my life. I know how to take my medication, but no, I had to go to them, take my medication, open my stinking mouth and show them. "Hello, I don't have any medication in my mouth!" That's degrading, to me that's degrading.

At times I would be suicidal. One day I went in to Mary's Place, and Pastor Pat was teaching one of the classes and tells me "Promise me you're going to hold on for one more day—just one day. Just tonight, hold on and come back tomorrow." So I said, "Okay, I can hold on then." Next day I come: "I want you to hold on for one more day." I mean, that's what you call caring. I never had that before. I didn't know what that was. I didn't learn that. Love was the end of the high heels, or the curtain iron rod, or the belt. That's what love was.

When I had my mental illness, when I got sick, I would be depressed, and it was harder when I was actually at Hammond House. That was the hardest because I was staying with forty-one other ladies. And when I first went there, I was scared, big time scared. They made me sleep on Bed Ten, and I wouldn't sleep on that bed. I would go to sleep on the sofa by the bathroom. I was scared. I didn't trust. And it was funny because the staff would go to Kim Sather, the director, and say, "Why's Jessie not sleeping on the bed?" And Kim would turn around and tell them, "Just leave her be. Just let her sleep on the couch." Because I didn't trust them, I couldn't sleep. I was like, "Man, there's forty-one women. I don't know what the heck I'm doing." And I think it was Barbara, Pam and Kim, after the three months they said, "No, Jessie needs to get out. Jessie needs to go to a transition home, that's where she belongs. She don't belong on the streets. She don't belong here." I was grateful. They're the ones that actually got me into Compass Cascades, which is a transitional house. Even now at the transition houses, they have the alumni come back every month. I go once in awhile, and I would crack up laughing with the other ones I that I used to be with, and we talked about stories about when we were there. I can laugh now because I'm not in that situation any more.

I think I applied for ten or fifteen apartments, never got nothing. Just housing authority 'cause I don't have Section 8. They closed Section 8, so how am I going to apply? And plus I looked at the waiting period for the lottery. Excuse me, do you think they're going to pick my name? Who knows, maybe I'll be the ten thousandth person. You think I'm going to get a home now? It's not realistic. Actually I got subsidized housing by chance, because I had a person who was homeless tell me that her apartment was open. That's how I got the place.

To tell you the truth, the homeless people know more of resources than even the providers. You go ask, "Excuse me, do you know how I can get a voucher for Jubilee?" Jubilee is this clothes place, where you can get clothes. They didn't even know. It's like, "Excuse me, I'll tell you: you as the staff need to sign a voucher so the person can go get clothes. That's all you got to do." I mean, that's like the simplest thing. The providers don't know or the people that have programs don't know.

A lot of the women [at Mary's Place] have been in domestic violence—abuse. For me, I never knew what love was. I never learned that from my family. It's here where I learned it, and I'm still learning. You go through life, or you go through homelessness, and it's like we don't trust nobody. Out there you don't trust nobody, but when you come in here, you trust the person sitting next to you, and it's like they understand more of what you're going through than people in the real world. You always have a safe place to come to.

"They think that homeless people have no morals, that people that are homeless have no brains, that homeless people have no heart."

I have a support network. If I don't have that support network, I know I'm going to end up on the streets again. I know that for a fact. You just cannot throw a person in the apartment and think that they're going to keep the apartment or they're going to live in that apartment. I mean, be real. I mean, it doesn't matter to me if I eat, drink, whatever or get a house, because I know that for my life I need the love, the care, the compassion, acceptance. You're gonna need these things just to survive, because the real world is scary. I've never been terrified in my life like I've been since I've got my own place. So I have to work extra hard now and keep my support network and get through whatever, so I don't end up homeless again. I'm glad that I can come back here because what Mary's Place has done for me. This is the only place where I feel safe, where I know that I can come to work out whatever mood or whatever question I have. Nobody criticizes me. They accept you for who you are. They love you for who you are. What I'm learning is confidence. But I learned a lot from my whole experience.

The problem with homelessness in general is that society looks at the homeless as garbage. That's how I felt when I was homeless at times. I was nothing, you know? Because we're invisible to their eyes. Who I am is not homeless. I'm a human being named Jessie. That's who I am. You know, some people are scared. They think homeless people are dangerous. They think that homeless people have no morals, that people that are homeless have no brains, that homeless people have no heart. I can see why they say that. It's because their own self is empty. They have no heart. It's society's problem. On T.V. you see those commercials about, "Look at this person who is so famished." They are skinny with bones, but yet why don't we address our own issues over here? Everybody thinks it's about alcoholics and drug addicts. That's not the case.

"The best place to learn the Golden Rule is when you're homeless. You want to learn the real truth about it, be homeless for a week and then you'll find out."

In Seattle, we hear, "Let's take the low income houses and demolish it, and let's put up a condo so you can pay your rent for a thousand something dollars—almost two thousand dollars. Or okay, let me buy a condo for two hundred fifty-six thousand dollars. Just for a small one-bedroom apartment? When you can use that to have a family of four go into that place that really needs it? That doesn't have enough money to live on? I think when the people higher up, maybe when they hit rock bottom, maybe they'll find out how it is. But you know what? When they do, the homeless people will open their arms and take them in.

What struck me about Mary's Place, one thing that hit me in the heart, was when the women would say in our community meeting and prayer, they would say, "Help those who are less fortunate than me. Help the women who are out there that don't have any shelter, and the men that don't have any shelter that they are safe tonight." When Katrina happened, they had a community meeting, and the ladies decided that Katrina was worse than what they went through. They told the staff, "You see those underwear in there, those two boxes of underwear? We don't need it. Send it to the relief in Katrina, they need it more than we do." They actually sent two boxes of lingerie. Come on, man! It's a bunch of homeless women—that care more about people than normal people that are out there, because they know how it is. They know how it feels. They know they're still just basic people. They understand it way more than everybody else, because they're living it.

Sometimes people think that homeless just take, take, take, but they don't know that they do give. I mean, it might be the smallest thing: to help an old lady across the street. They go to a program, and they clean outside or clean the toilet. Excuse me, but they're doing something 'cause it makes them feel proud and to let them have ownership of something by giving back.

When I was a volunteer at Mary's Place I came in twice a week from maybe nine o'clock to one or two o'clock. I did office work, I did computer work and took the phones, did signs, sent out the fundraising letters. When I was volunteering, I owed them so I was repaying my payment for what they'd done for me. And then when I started working there, it felt odd. It was like, "Wait, you guys do this for me, and now you guys pay me to do this for you guys?" That's weird. For me, if you help me, I owe you. When I say I'm finished with paying my debt, then I'll say "Okay, I'm done paying." That's how I always was: if you help me, I have to pay back. I have to pay back what was given to me. I feel like I don't deserve that paycheck because of what they've done for me in my life.

It's not going to be ten years to end homelessness. It's going to be longer than that. I think that the numbers are going to quadruple. But that's just how the govern- ment is. It's that pretend. It hurts me inside. It just makes me sad to see these people, and at the same time say, "Aren't you grateful that you have a home? Are you grateful that you have a bed to sleep tonight? Are you grateful that you're not going to be murdered tonight? Are you grateful that you're not going to commit suicide tonight." The governor and the mayor should walk in our shoes for a week. I'm one hundred percent sure—that your perspective will change. You'll see really how it is, not the stigma that society puts on the homeless community.

The best place to learn that Golden Rule is when you're homeless. You want to learn the real truth about it, be homeless for a week and then you'll find out. I open my door to those who are homeless. I open my door, and I used to be homeless. Sometimes I let them sleep in my apartment. I don't want them to get murdered. How many murders have been happening? How many times have we stood for men and women that are homeless? I don't know what it's going to take anymore for all this to end. Friends of mine died. What can you do? There wasn't any place for us to deal with it. When it happens, where do you deal with it? How do you deal with death? Where do you deal with death? The Homeless Place of Remembrance Garden, we want to go somewhere where we can grieve for these people.

CHAPTER 12

"Marie"

I met "Marie" at a meeting of WHEEL and interviewed her on three separate occasions between 2006 and 2008. Though Marie had struggled most of her life with fibromyalgia, she could easily have been mistaken for someone in good health. There was something distinctly maternal about Marie. Concerned with my continual rummaging around for random notes—not to mention my ongoing struggles to operate the voice recorder—during our first meeting, she came to our second meeting a week later bearing a file folder to help me better organize myself. She also brought along a manila folder filled with notes and citations that reflected her ongoing independent inquiry into the links between stress, trauma, and cognition. By our third meeting, Marie had moved into an apartment and brought along a portfolio of her work that included a mix of charcoal sketches and intricately rendered naturescapes in vibrant watercolors that provided evidence of her evolving voice as an artist.

Painting, it quickly became clear, had become for Marie a critical medium for coming to terms with the traumas she'd encountered beginning in childhood, which had been exacerbated during the four years she'd spent homeless, following a succession of events that snowballed when her I.D. was stolen, along with her jacket, during a Greyhound bus trip. Marie's concerns were not limited, however, to her personal traumas; she clearly spent a great deal of time meditating on collective social—and environmental—traumas and strategies for addressing them.

Marie's vision of alternative housing—and community—for homeless people resonates in a number of ways with Portland's Dignity Village, a democratic, self-governing community of otherwise homeless people that was officially sanctioned by the city in 2001 on a semi-permanent site seven miles from the downtown core. Like SHARE/WHEEL's tent cities, the Village forged broad community collaborations, with churches, schools, artists and nonprofits, including Sisters of the Road Café and Portland's street newspaper Street Roots. In a collaboration between Villagers and the nonprofit City Repair Project, tents and shanties were eventually replaced by green-built houses constructed out of light straw clay. The Villagers tend flower and vegetable gardens and much of the energy for the community is generated by wind and solar power.[1]

"I'm going to watch for the red flags of a dangerous person…and I'm going to trust my instincts. I'm going to protect my own boundaries."

It took me a lot of years and counseling to be able to understand everything that happened to me, that eventually led to homelessness for four years. It took me a lot of years of counseling to recover from sexual abuse, mental abuse, including mental sadism. So it's very difficult to just say, "Okay, I'm going to talk about my life story." I was protected more than some people are. I was able to kind of hold on to myself inside. I never became mentally sadistic and abusive, and I never became sexually abusive. I just turned fifty-seven in May, and really it wasn't until I was homeless that I realized that I still had something I might contribute to the community [*laughing*].

I went to college off and on before I was homeless, but because I had fibromyalgia—which ended up being connected with all the trauma too—I had a lot of physical problems. I never ended up getting a degree, but I got a few years altogether, and I did my own research to deal with the muscle condition that they ended up calling "fibromyalgia," finding out what triggers it. It's severe physical and/or mental trauma.[2] Nobody knew for a lot of years what happened to people's muscles from trauma—that it triggered fibromyalgia.

My first job after high school, I was a periodicals clerk at Seattle University at their library. Then I started getting ill. I was young, and I didn't have anybody supporting me and saying, "Let's find out what is wrong with you." I thought there was something wrong with me as a worker. I was sleeping through my alarm clock—I couldn't hear it. I was on medication, and it ended up affecting my kidneys, and I was starting to get really ill and finally quit my job. I thought maybe I'm not responsible or mature enough to have this job, and here I'd already had it over a year.

For a while they thought it was just clinical depression, so they put me on depression medicine that I'd get a bad reaction from. I went to look for work again here in Seattle. I worked for a retail clothing store in credit, and then I worked for awhile at the Port of Seattle. Next thing I know I wasn't holding down a job longer than six months, and it was like, "What's going on here?" I am conscientious and responsible…

The doctor found out I had really bad low blood sugar. When your blood sugar is really low, you can feel depressed. I spent a few years trying to help myself with diet and doing whatever I could to take care of myself and those around me. I spent years in therapy to deal with childhood rape and adult rape. Since therapy didn't help, and my fibromyalgia got worse, I had to come at it from this direction: "Okay, so why was I in shock?" Because the shock itself makes you enter into dangerous situations easily or you'll act impulsively. The brain is set up to put you into shock so that you can live, survive, until you're strong enough inside to begin to understand what happened and change your life so it doesn't happen anymore.

I was ready or willing to remember and to actually experience a little at a time the horror, the terror, and the feelings that young people cannot bear. If they had to bear it all at once, they'd be totally insane. I had to go through therapy to give myself permission to face reality, and to get strong enough inside me to say, "No more. I'm going to watch for the red flags of a dangerous person. I'm going to listen more carefully and I'm going to trust my instincts. I'm going to protect my own boundaries. I'm not going to be sweet and nice and polite and friendly when somebody is violating even the smallest boundary."

I went back to college in my late forties. The last couple of years, I was very sick with the fibromyalgia. Sometimes I'd feel so much inflammation around my upper spine and head, it was so hard to focus. It was hard to sit up and hold a book, but I got through a few courses, and I felt like, "Okay, I accomplished something under my circumstances." I had to focus on taking care of myself physically, so I couldn't finish my last quarter. I have a student loan outstanding, didn't even take the class. They wouldn't let me drop the class, and I was trying to tell them how sick I was.

I had to stop and start my own research on muscles, shock, trauma, nutrients the muscles need, nutrients the brain needs, the immune system, everything. I spent five years doing this—an independent type study and worked with doctors. I had been working to try to take care of myself, to take care of other sick people in my home and other family members. I was taking care of my husband, who was not well. But I realized I couldn't handle these very toxic relationships. In some ways I ought to have stayed where I was because at least I wasn't homeless. In a way it was impulsive, but I just felt that mentally and possibly physically I was in danger. Without dishonoring somebody, I'm just telling you it was unbearable. This one day I got up and just did a couple of things in the house, and then I walked out the door. Hitchhiking is very dangerous. I don't recommend it to anyone, but I hitchhiked out of there.

I ended up trying to find work in another state. My muscles started feeling weaker, and it just didn't seem like the work that was available I could physically do. Then somebody stole my jacket that had all my I.D. in it. All of a sudden I'm stranded with no I.D., and at that time they weren't even letting people get on a Greyhound bus without picture I.D. It was right after 9/11.

The first couple of months after I was homeless—in Arizona—I was exposed to the streets, the terror of being homeless. I never could handle that idea. It was terrifying. It's just absolutely overwhelming to all of a sudden not have a place you're going to go that night, and you start looking, "Where am I going to sit all night?" And then you have people approaching you. I'm fifty-seven now. I was just over fifty. A couple of months ago, someone assumed I was a hooker, and here I'm out there struggling to survive. I'm sick. I can't sit up that long. I'm desperate. I don't have any nutritious food.

I did have help from a volunteer during my first exposure to the streets and the hard life out there. This one woman paid for ordering a birth certificate, paid for I.D. Usually it only took them about a month, but it turns out she accidentally wrote something wrong on the order for my birth certificate. I ended up there for four months.

The whole thing was a mess—being down in a hard area of the streets with another subculture that I wasn't used to. Plus it was another culture to be in shelters. There's indignities. People are doing the best they can, but you're hungry and you're malnourished all of the time, so you're eating. I went a few days when I was first homeless without eating anything, so the first time any food was offered, I ate it. The first year I put on like fifty pounds because I'm eating other people's food—whatever comes in—and it was not nutrient dense. Here I had worked so hard on my diet, to help my muscles and release some of the symptoms, and I'd even started to lose weight before this happened.

Homelessness causes a lot of problems just because you don't have the same control over your life. And it doesn't indicate you have some kind of gluttony-eating-disorder-personality-character-deficit. Your brain is driving you to get nutrition because you need it. It happened to every woman that I know. Unless they're on hard drugs, they seem to get skinnier. But the point is everyone else gained weight. And they weren't any healthier for it. Living in community situations that were very unhealthy, you're exposed to more things. Even the Health Department will tell you, we've started to have more TB in the last few years. It's because we've had an increase in homeless people. They were in communal living situations, or day centers, or out in the streets where people have TB. And so, all of a sudden you're exposed to that.

"[I]t was a voice I could [use to] deal with grief about the environment and family and things that I can't say. Art became that: like a voice and it still is."

While I was stranded down there and going through shock—I was terrified—there was this nonprofit group that created a little painting workshop in a building near the shelter where they served meals to the homeless. I'd never painted in my life. I had told everybody for all those years—fifty years—that I had no art talent. One evening I went down there, and they said, "Well, why don't you just put some color on the paper? Just have some fun. Don't worry what it looks like, and don't ever expect anything that you put on the paper to look like anybody else's stuff." This lady, she said, "Just keep going and don't stop. Go from one to another." And I did that. They weren't that great, but you could see already by like the third time I tried something, I was starting to form little naturescape things, kind of crude, but I was trying to say stuff with it, things that were important to me.

When I did get back up here, volunteers in programs gave me paints. By the end of that first year, I started working on detail. So, I wanted to show you what I did about three or four years ago. You can tell it's simple, naïve, primitive. But just having the encouragement of people saying, "Okay," even if it's simple, a naïve, primitive art style. I was told to keep going and I did. It's sad that I had to end up homeless to have the time to put into overcoming that stunted part of my growth as I was growing up. I found it was a voice. I could deal with grief about the environment and family and things that I can't say. Art became that: like a voice and it still is.

About three years ago I started going to a mentoring program through Antioch University for homeless and formerly homeless women. They had a city council member come in and speak to us. I had some of my artwork out and another artist—a homeless woman who was an artist—had her piece of art there, and for a month we ended up having our exhibit here in the new city hall building.

This one lady saw this one painting I did called "Winter Peace"—even I have to admit it was very striking—and she said, "Oh, I have to have this painting." She paid $180 for it. And just the way the colors were, even I was surprised how it turned out. I called it "Winter Peace," and she loved it.

I think a lot of problems people have are caused by those original traumas—maybe neglect, maybe malnutrition, different kinds of abuse, terror and things like that—and I really think that it affects their learning process. Because if we can just understand, if we can encourage people who are disabled physically or in their learning, even after they're adults to do just what I did without even realizing I was doing it...

I love working with watercolors. I've already put forty, fifty hours into this one painting. I have to take all the time it needs but look at how that taught me patience. Because I told you sometimes I act impulsive when I was terrified or if it didn't feel safe. Like just taking off. I still have to get up and leave situations if it doesn't feel safe in some way, but I don't act impulsive anymore that much. I think painting helped me with that. It taught me patience. At least one show, I must have spent six to eight hours a day there. I hadn't been able to hold down a job where I could work that long doing other kinds of physical movements, but with this kind of watercolor, I could sit back and rest, you know, let my muscles relax if they start to stiffen up and hurt, and then I could go right back into the painting. I could hang in there. And that made me feel good too. "See, I can work! [*laughing*] I'm an artist!" [*laughing*] I wasn't expecting it. So, out of this horrible experience came an understanding about my own ability to learn.

You can see my colors are changing, making statements about different things that's happened to the earth. So this one, when it's done, is called "Early Morning Weepers." When I was a little girl, when things would get rough, at this one place we lived in, I remember going out into the yard, and there was this huge weeping willow tree, and I'd crawl under it and stay there for awhile. The few memories I have make me think I was probably dealing with some pretty overwhelming things even during that time. I was about five years old then. There's a message of hope in every painting.

I just recently in the last two months moved into my own place, I'm real happy for that; it's given me an opportunity to get back to these stories, get back to these paintings. I don't have to pack things around in a bag. I couldn't have got this far in this painting if I wasn't in my own place right now. You can see that the skill level is changing. That's why I wanted to show you these paintings so you can see, okay, this happened while I was homeless but it's just the message: "Don't give up on people who are homeless. Don't give up on them because they're chronically homeless for awhile, or they're disabled or they're depressed or something." Maybe it's better to let them begin to dream and to give themselves permission to dream, to not give up on an original goal.

"You can't herd people into this kind of unnatural communal environment and then take away the very last things they have..."

I've been around women who've been homeless, and you would not believe how highly talented they are. This one woman, I think she has some pretty severe mental problems that are different than just our usual. She's been in the homeless system for several years that I know of. She's a college graduate; I think she played classical piano for several years. You can tell she's intelligent, and I always tried to respect her boundaries. She'd say things people didn't understand—it seemed like she was coming off the wall. Some people would get angry with her and even harsh, and I felt their harshness was unnecessary. The things she was saying—even though it sounded kind of crazy—that is the only way she can protect her boundaries, her mental, spiritual, and physical boundaries.

These are not paranoid things that homeless people are worried about, both those in shelters and those who prefer to sleep outside instead of being in the shelters where they can pick up communicable diseases more readily. They also have to take mental abuse—and no one ought to have to live in a mentally abusive situation. They're kind of thrown into shelters with people who are violent either mentally, sexually, or physically, and bullies. You're thrown into that and told you just have to handle it the same way everyone else does. You have to act all peaceful and nice so that the staff around you don't have to deal with anything. You have to take whatever is done or said to you no matter how it affects you and, you have to do it quietly and sweetly. Or else you're the troublemaker.

Perfectly healthy people would stress out trying to be in the system. So here we have people who really are just grief-stricken, overwrought by the physical stress of it, the mental stress of it. They are dealing with stuff that's too much for them to deal with because they're already bludgeoned; they're already damaged. You have people with severe clinical mental problems who are also thrown into that same system that's unbearable physically, mentally, for a perfectly healthy person. This person with this great challenge is thrown into this community situation and basically told, "You have to take whatever said and done to you. We have these rules that say it has to be a safe place. But if we hear you complain that it isn't safe, or you verbally stand up for yourself to protect your boundary, or to get somebody to back off, we are considering you to be the trouble maker and we're even going to have to ask you to leave."

The staff jumps in. These are intelligent adult women, and to jump in like they're one- or two-year-olds, just because their voice is raised a little bit because they're upset or because they're angry, this is not appropriate, and it's not respectful. I'm a vegan so I don't even believe that animals ought to be handled except briefly, and I don't believe in cattle and all this herding animals or people. It's easy for the staff. It's so they don't have to hear things, and they don't have to listen. Allow people time to resolve it. To stop people from doing any kind of resolution themselves reaffirms the message they maybe got while growing up or in a marriage situation or any kind of personal relationship situation, where they were forbidden to speak unless spoken to, where if they started to get upset, they were punished.

You can't herd people into this kind of unnatural communal environment and then take away the very last things they have: the natural instinct to protect their boundaries, their humanity, and their dignity and their civil rights. And you tell them they can't work things out with one another because you don't want to hear it, or you're worried somebody else might get a little upset. That's what abusive relationships do. I will stand up for myself now. A lot of years I didn't, but I learned to do it, and I'm not giving that up now. I had to get to the point where I could do that: defend my boundaries.

"They just would like to be part of the garden."

But what will help in the community is if other people can begin to understand that themselves and not judge all the homeless people as lazy, useless, or it's too late for them—all they are is the dregs of society, and they're just a burden. I don't think everyone intends to give that message, but you do get the message sometimes, and sometimes people say it overtly, and its very painful 'cause you're trying not to give up in your situation, you're trying to stay encouraged. "Get a job," I had somebody yell at me on the street here in Seattle. This was about three years ago. I'm going down the street. I had a bag. So there's a couple of things I'd say to people: We're trying not to give up on ourselves, so please don't give up on us.

The city should put out the word that they're willing to take proposals for building programs. I think that there ought to be land allocated, and then put out the word to people who would create these proposals for natural self-sustaining units, even if they're in the old motel style village-type units with a courtyard garden in the middle. I have a vision for these housing units—there are inexpensive, natural ways to do it that are self-sufficient with solar power, incinerating toilets.

There's straw bale and cob or straw bale and adobe. These are being done other places. If you had a separate solar power system with a solar charger and an incinerating toilet setup at least as a back up, and then all waste ends up clean ash and easy to clean up, and nothing's toxic, and nothing goes down into the earth that's toxic. And it's healthier. It's hygienic. They could actually have a small space garden in a small yard, backyard or courtyard that they actually meet all their needs, and not just survive, like they're doing out while they're homeless. I have been studying too what plants are zone appropriate for here, in a small space garden that will provide protein, vitamins, minerals, enzymes, carbohydrates that people need. They can thrive. They'd be healthy. Then, if ever they earn the money, and they want to get some special foods or some extra things, they can go out and buy it.

But you have to have been homeless for four years and saw your whole life flash before your eyes to understand the seriousness of what I am saying. You can't depend on Social Security. There are people out there on social security that have been homeless for a few years because it isn't enough. The lowest rent is a little more than what GAU gives, so even for people who aren't spending it on drugs, it's not enough to pay rent.

You don't know how much that art helped me through the last three years. There were times where I couldn't handle anything, but I'd get into a painting, and for a few hours I just, like, could tune it out. Once in a while I'll go to an AA meeting and share what they call a testimony about overcoming a lot of odds. And the last thing I said a few weeks ago at this one when I went was, "Just being sober isn't enough. You must also make a commitment to understanding that you are valuable just as a person, no matter what you do, are able to do. But once you know how valuable you are, you know you are valuable, and you have potential not only to take care of yourself, but to contribute to others and to care about the earth and others around you."

I told all the women that you grow personally, you reach your full potential, and you find you don't have time to get involved in those relationships that harm you. You start saying, "I don't deserve to have my boundaries crossed, and I have the right to say no and defend my boundaries."

About two and a half months ago, when I got my own place, I told [the faculty/staff at Antioch University Women's Education Program], " I'm a fairly new artist, and I'm a little nervous about my ability to facilitate a workshop, but I have some ideas..." So the next week I brought some of my paints, papers, and I said, "Now, just make any design you wish on that little paper, and then I want you to think up something you'd like to say that's wise. Some kind of wisdom and encouragement.

I talked to people about a little bit of folk art, and how it was just the average folk, that they expressed themselves. They used what they had; they freshened things or made things pretty that were old. It became usable, useful art. Folk art, it isn't just random. Folk art is about the folks. It's what the folks do to express themselves, whether its pottery in different cultures, whether its painting your cob or adobe house or fence, you design and sculpt an outdoor fireplace, or you do a cob floor, or whether you take an old frying pan you can't use anymore and you paint it, and you make it a pretty design, you say something on it, to encourage your family. That's folk art.

It's proven if you can develop some kind of creative outlet, it helps your brain neurons to begin to function better. Painting was helping me not only resolve grief and have a voice, it actually was helping me learn faster other concepts, other things. I just was reading about how that happens for children, that if they have a consistent ongoing continuing creative outlet, that it helps their growth, development, and learning process. And when I read that recently I went, "Oh, my gosh. I bet part of my brain did take over when I started doing this art." So, I don't think the people in that workshop down in Arizona realized how much they really were going to help me.

The other thing we need going into these housing programs, they need mentoring, how to get all your nutrition in this garden, how to do composting, how to do soil management, wildlife habitat, just learn some basic things like that for responsibility. They have to be taking some kind of education training. In order to be in the housing they have to be bettering themselves; they have to be learning, and learning how to work, toward a creative endeavor and/or another skill where they could maybe make money later. And they need mentoring. They need these mentors that come in right there with them; make sure they're learning gardening; make sure they know what to do; encourage them to provide their own nutrition. And help them with learning, training, develop skills, creative and otherwise. Every business, every career, you have to be creative, 'cause you have to be creative problem solvers.

In several of the paintings I've done since I've been homeless, I put sunflowers, because I've been doing a self-study on nutrition, and one plant I found was very nutritious was the sunflower. It provides not only seeds, but it provides high-protein nutritious leaves that you can dry and add to breads. Another thing in the last few years that I learned, I read somewhere that the sunflower absorbs toxins from the soil, from the earth. I began to use metaphors in my paintings, and the sunflower is one of the metaphors. I decided that maybe there are some among us that absorb toxins from the earth, like the sunflower, and that if we take the time to find out about them, we're going to find out how much they have to give and how qualified they are, what gifts that they have.

I have been around a lot of the people—people who are heavy into drugs or alcohol or even drug dealers or prostitutes. The point is that they still need their needs met. But I've been around a lot of other people, some of them included, who if you just listen and are around them awhile, you'll begin to hear and see beneath that surface. Maybe their brokenness is manifested through those problems. But other people who don't have those problems, their brokenness is manifested in other ways: chronic physical problems, illnesses, things that. Even when you have a home, they're difficult to deal with. And they're trying to deal with packing things around, going from place to place. Doctors are telling them to go rest. They can't. They have to carry heavy things. They have to go here and there, right, but to late at night. Packing things on and off buses and up hills.

So, I guess what I'm saying in the paintings, I'm using a lot of sunflowers because that's one way I can speak for many of the problems of not only women, but men, who I think are little sunflowers, you know? And beautiful—they're beautiful in their own way. And yes, like the sunflower, they might stand out. And they might seem kind of like they're overpowering, but they're not trying to be overpowering or to be in the way of the other plants. They just would like to be part of the garden.

CHAPTER 13

Janice Connelly

*I met Janice in the summer of 2006 at the WHEEL-run Women's Empowerment Center
and interviewed her on two different occasions that summer, meeting at the public library
and at a café overlooking the Puget Sound. Between going to school, interning as a legislative assistant with Tom Rasmussen, who chairs the Seattle City Government's Housing,
Human Services and Health Committee, volunteering time with WHEEL, and sporadic
volunteer speaking engagements on homelessness, Janice had to work to squeeze me into
her schedule. Janice's juggling act was all the more remarkable given that she had been
living at the Lutheran Compass Center–run Hammond House women's shelter for the past
year while waiting to get into permanent housing. At Hammond House, Janice slept in an
open dormitory space that she shared with thirty-nine other women.*

*Janice struck me as someone with a kind of unshakeable will to succeed and to rebuild
the life that had been "derailed" following a police call on a domestic violence incident
that had led to a felony conviction for drug possession. Unlike many of the women I interviewed, Janice described her family growing up as loving and supportive, but most of her
immediate family had been dead for more than two decades, including her brother, whose
gun-related death remains something of a mystery.*

*Beyond the heart murmur she was diagnosed with in grade school, Janice is athletic
and able-bodied, having recently trained as a forest firefighter, but her story foregrounds
the physical stresses involved in homelessness, which pits the unhoused against each other
in a daily race for lockers, jobs, shelter beds, and resources. In the absence of any major
physical or mental health issues, and with a kind of steely will and determination to
succeed and rebuild her life, Janice has been able to make the most of educational and
vocational training opportunities directed at homeless and low income people. It was clear,
moreover, that Janice derived meaning, direction, and a sense of community from her role
as an advocate for homeless women and found creative and intellectual challenges and
satisfaction in her political organizing with WHEEL and in her internship at Seattle
City Hall.*

"When I had all my money, and I had my place, the lifestyle just enabled me to isolate."

What I've learned from homelessness is that, regardless of my circumstances, I'm not defined by them. Homelessness is not the end of the world. Although it's a contradiction, on the one hand I say that, contrary to popular belief, hard living does not fortify your character. It diminishes your spirit. But on the other hand, for me, [*laughing*], homelessness has really been a blessing. We get here from many different avenues, many and varied and heartbreaking. Nevertheless, we are all here, and you don't have to feel powerless just because you're without a roof, when you're without a job, you're without finances. Where I find myself does not define who I am. I found that it's made me more human.

I was very selfish. I had a very easy life, and you get so caught up in your busy little life, and you don't have time to even listen to another human being. When I had all my money, and I had my place, the lifestyle just enabled me to isolate. It wasn't until I became a WHEEL member when the responsibility, the focus, was no longer on me. It became "we," and that was where I started growing emotionally and spiritually. My life took on new meaning then. I gained empathy and understanding. Once the responsibility of it was really made clear to me: that we're homeless, we need to look out for each other, we need to further this cause of housing and equality, my life had meaning from that point forward.

The church that I spoke to today, I told them that as a child I had great role models, that like any child, they taught me; they wanted me; they raised me to have a good life and to achieve happiness. Does not everyone want that for their children? What happened is that I had a life-altering event happen in my life when I was twelve years old. I was very athletic, and I represented my school until this health issue was discovered. I had a heart murmur, and I couldn't run. I played basketball, volleyball, track, and stuff. I had to sit on the bench. I could go to games, but I could not participate. I couldn't exert myself. I felt like damaged goods, and my whole life changed. I was no longer interested in school. I said, "Why bother? Why bother?" And I started drinking, and I started hanging out with the bad kids, and I started skipping school. I just ran amok, and I became a very angry young woman because I didn't know where I was headed.

Everything's just drama when you're a teenager. I broke up with my boyfriend. I didn't want to go back to that school for my sophomore year, so I talked my aunt into allowing me to go to Indian boarding school in Oklahoma. I was far removed from my family, and I'm young and I'm angry. So there I was far away, and I was party, party, party.

I don't know how I made it through school, but I did, and then I'm out, and I go home, and within a couple of months, I was kicked out of the house. I got on the bus, and I came north. I had been to Seattle with a friend that I went to school with; that's how I ended up getting to Seattle. I was seventeen. I left home and I was gone for good. Never returned until recently.

I didn't get in touch with anyone for five years when I left. In the interim, I cut it as a railroader. I'm a third-generation railroader in my family, so that was a dream come true. When I got in touch with my family, my mother had died, my brother that I was raised at home with—he was my cousin but he was like a brother—he'd been shot and killed. They don't know if it was an accident or if it was suicide. He was gone and all of my grandmothers. All of a sudden here I am, an alien once again. I have no family. I have no connection, and I'm way up here and making tons of money. I don't know what to do with it but be destructive. So my train derails [*laughing*]. It crashes and burns, and some years later, I find myself in the homeless system.

I was a customs specialist, a bridge operator over the Snohomish River for the railroad. I was there for twenty-four years, and it was pretty responsible—decision making, communications, multitasking everyday. What happened was I was doing drugs, and the police were called in on a domestic situation, and it so happened that they searched me, and they found these drugs. I was hauled off to jail, and I resigned on the spot. Everything that I ever did in my whole life was being responsible in positions with men and equipment and the public. Operating the bridge where human lives are at stake, I don't feel good about that. I've forgiven myself when I had to. So I resigned on the spot. [The sentence] was thirty days jail time, one year supervision by the Department of Corrections (DOC) and a $600 fine. I did thirteen days in jail—for good time—was released from DOC supervision after six months, paid restitution in full, and I was able to leave the state.

"My first real memories after having gotten clean and took stock of where I stood, it was like having no skin: 'I'm homeless, I live in a shelter.'"

When I went to jail, all of a sudden I was with other women. I saw women for the first time. They just weren't in my life. I worked in a male-dominated field. So it was like landing on a different planet, getting to know the population. I thought, "Oh, wow, this is like camp or something." And later when I went to the Everett-Snohomish County Jail, I heard a lot of them didn't have any place else to go because they got there via domestic violence like I had.

I ended up doing thirteen days in jail, and then I became homeless after that. I gambled, so I had no money saved. It was probably the hardest part losing my dog, my little Llapso Apso, Baxter. While I was doing my time, my neighbor was supposed to be watching my dog, but he ended up mistreated. He was tied up to a motorcycle outside in the rain, and one of my neighbors had seen him and brought him in. So, thank God he was fed and sheltered. Once I got out I had to find a place for Baxter to continue to live while I found my own way.

The Union Gospel Shelter in Everett for women, I started my first homeless experience there. This was my first time, really—just out of jail, no job, no home, no dog. My first real memories after having gotten clean and took stock of where I stood, it was like having no skin: "I'm homeless, I live in a shelter." You're stripped bare of everything, and you begin to take notice of life going on around you. I found that most women in homeless shelters are not looking for a handout. They come from such diverse backgrounds. Homelessness is a real equalizer. I don't know how most people deal with it. There is just so many people with mental illnesses and drug addictions. They have programs for those people, though, so I don't know what they're doing on the streets still homeless.

It was around the holidays, and I'll never forget that holiday. I'd go to A.A. meetings downtown, and I would stay out of the lower part of town, where the bars were and where the drugs were. I'd go to meetings downtown, and I'd notice for the first time people—normal people. People would say, "Come on in, have a meal." So there was lots of good memories. The kindness of strangers never ceases to amaze me. I think that the most wonderful thing about my experience with being homeless is having these for real experiences with for real people. I was too busy in my former life—I didn't have time for "you," much less myself.

While I was in Grays Harbor, I went to the Union Gospel Mission shelter on the harbor, and I said, "Do you have a branch in Seattle that I can call?" I explained my situation—that I was coming up here, but I had no resources—so they gave me a number of their women's branch down in the International District. I must have called everyday for a week, and every day they'd say, "No, we have no vacancies." So finally, in desperation, I said, "Well, can you refer me to any place else?" And they gave me the number to Angeline's so, I called them. I asked them, "If I come up will you guarantee me—will I have a place? 'Cause I don't want to sleep on the streets? Are you sure that I will be indoors?" And they assured me I would be. My friend loaned me twenty dollars, and I got on the bus and came to Seattle on the Greyhound. I got registered and I was able to stay at Angeline's.

"It's like being on the front lines every day, and you get burnt out after a very short time."

I don't qualify for any government benefits. I don't even know how to talk about them, because I don't know what they are, nor did I want it, because I'm able to work. Having a felony, though, makes it more difficult. I decided the only thing I could do is put one foot in front of the other, breathe in between and try to sleep indoors, try to have a little walking around money.

A lot of Native Americans work seasonally as forest fire fighters. I did some research, and I applied while I was on the harbor, so when I got here, I had all these applications all over the state of Washington. What I had in mind for myself is that I would hire myself out as a forest fighter, part of a bunk line crew where they housed you and fed you and paid you a lump sum at the end of the season. That was my grand plan. But because I didn't have a license, or an address, or a phone number, I would not be considered. That was my first experience with the reality of no address.

I stayed at Angeline's for four months. I came in April—April first, like a fool [*laughing*]. A month later, in May, their winter shelter was over, so [only] twenty-five could stay there. I'd see people hauled out every night to go who knows where. I know they went to other shelters, but it's so inconvenient. Everything about homelessness is inconvenient. You're tired from either having worked all day, packing your pack, steel-toed boots, not enough clothes. You need a shower. You need food. You need a bed, and there's rules, and when you're new, you don't have any clue. It must have been two months that went by before I had any inkling of how to get a locker, where the coffee shops were, where the library was, where to get a shower.

That's the big thing about homelessness. It's not set up to accommodate people who want to work. First of all, you have to take your stuff everywhere. You have to wait around to get a locker, and you're not guaranteed one. Fortunately I was pretty fast, 'cause they trained me. Forest fighter, you take a pack test. I was in shape! Three miles in forty-five minutes. Set my stuff in a locker and, if you stay there, you can keep it there all night. They take it out in the morning, and then they do the shuffle, the mad dash in the evening to have lockers again. That's why you can't work, because you can't pack all this around. But most of the time I would get up in the morning, put my pack on, go to Labor Ready and try to get out on a job. Sometimes I did, sometimes I didn't. It's pretty depressing.

It was like musical chairs in Angeline's lobby all the time. At six o'clock, people would just up and vanish in thin air so that seats would become available, so it was a real circus. There was always so much tension and so much craziness, and a lot of racist shit going on. I'm normally a person that really likes to stand up for the underdog, but when you're in that position too, sometimes I found it's really best to pick your own battles [*laughing*]. You don't know what the situation is. Because you have your own stuff to protect and your own little area to protect, you really can't get involved. It was a stressful time, you know, because there are no boundaries. It's like being on the front lines every day, and you get burnt out after a very short time. It was like a pool where the fish—the more aggressive fish—would eat the little fish. There wasn't any actual physical violence but in every other sense of the word. Where I came from, I was never—I was never—involved in an altercation of any kind. It wasn't worth it. Nobody's worth my freedom, you know.

While I was at Angeline's, I participated in a focus group through the Chief Seattle Club, which is a club for Native Americans, Alaskans, Pacific Islanders. They provide a place to nurture your soul. The group was over, and I didn't have any money or bus pass, so I had to walk or find out how to get from Second and Cherry across to Belltown in a timely manner. I had a note saying that I would be in late to Angeline's that night. But when I got back that evening, they told me I had to go to Hammond House. Being the creature of habit that I am, I didn't want to go to Hammond House. I don't like change. There was a few women at Angeline's that I spoke with, I identified with, that I felt comfortable with. We'd put our mats in the corner, talk and read and do crossword puzzles. They were my little support system. But the Women's Referral Center didn't give me a choice. It was like holding a gun to your head. So, I participated in a homeless group, and I came back and I was homeless from my shelter where I'd been. So, I emptied my locker, I packed my bag, and I went trudging down a block a half away with a heavy, heavy pack. You just somehow accumulate stuff when you're here. I guess because of the insecurity, you just get more stuff.

At Hammond House it was like being new all over again—this whole uncertainty. I got there; I check in, they give me a bed, give me the tour, and I spent the night. In the dining room at Angeline's, you're kind of herded in, you sit down, hurry up, and get done and get out. It's like cattle-feeding time. And [at Hammond House], I could stay up all night. I can shower anytime I want to. I can watch TV. I can think. I can smoke. I can play on the computer. It was like, "Ah, this is paradise. I can drink coffee all night if I want to. I can sit at a table like a human being and have my own cup and my own space to write, and not be bothered."

But it was kind of scary when I first went to Hammond. I didn't know anyone's name, and only one person spoke to me. Some women were really mean, and I don't know if it's because I was different—a person of color. And so I said, "I don't care, I've been in rougher places. It's not bad." It didn't matter. I had a busy life outside of that. I just came to sleep and rest and all that. So that was my new residence, and again, I began the whole process of not knowing anything about anything all over again. Not ever being sure, not understanding the process.

Somebody down the road told me about Mary's [Place]. I was leery about it because I'm not a religious person, but it was something other than Angeline's, and it was my beginning of exploration in the Seattle area with the services. So I found my way over there, and I walked in there, and it was huge, and there was these ratty couches, and people parked on them, and they were sleeping. They offered lunch, so that was good.

"My world was so miniscule, and all of a sudden it grew. Over night, it mushroomed into, 'Let's take on the city. Let's take over a plot. Let's build a garden of remembrance.'"

WHEEL's Empowerment Center gave me another place to be. Because when you're homeless you can't be in the parks all the time, 'cause the same homeless people that you're trying to get away from are there or the library. It was summertime, it was hot, and I wanted to go indoors where it was cool. But they're open three days a week, Saturday, Sunday, and Monday, and I got interested. They were active. They were intelligent, and they were making a difference from what I could hear, but I've got to investigate that for myself. I like to do my own research. As time went by, they got talking about this forum, and they needed poetry and writing, and they had workshops. I won a journalism award in high school and anything that has to do with reading or writing, my skills are over the top. They talked me into becoming a member of the editorial committee for the Homeless Women's Forum. It was the art stuff that really got me. For "The Revolution of the Heart" [program], I drew a phoenix rising. That was my idea. I wrote a poem called "Ground Zero," and I was a speaker. And the whole process of finding a venue, meeting, starting up, parking, catering—the whole package—it was really exciting to be a part of it, and to see a project and the results in person, to have a deadline. It was like soul food—my creativity needs to be addressed. I got into action. I got involved in fundraising, speaking and lobbying, and volunteering. My world was so miniscule, and all of a sudden it grew. Over night, it mushroomed into, "Let's take on the city. Let's take over a plot. Let's build a garden of remembrance."

Every time somebody dies homeless—outside or by violence—Women in Black stands vigil to bring about the message that "People are dying on the streets," and that "We need shelter and we need it today," you know. The Ten-Year Plan to End Homelessness has really left a big gap. They've cut the programs that house people, sent them out. Those women are getting killed and raped and robbed and hit over the head and blankets stolen.

We ended up winning the Safe Harbor Campaign. Our issue was protecting our identities. At first I thought I was okay with giving my name and that kind of information, but the more I get into the workforce, and the more I look around, I'm changing my mind about that. What if I don't want them to know that I was homeless at some point or that I used services? Now that I'm getting out in the workforce again, I really don't want that sensitive information [out there.] We have a right to our privacy. So, we fought it, and we won and there was a concession.

The self-managed thing that SHARE and WHEEL do is so very important. If you're in the SHARE shelter, being a part of that process, you really have to show up; you have to be a voice. It's all about action—that is what's empowering. Because it's self-managed, you have to be involved. You have to build that network of trust and watching each other's back. It's a little village, and anytime that people are entrusted or supported with doing the good of the whole, you can't help but be empowered. Your life takes on new meaning, being part of something.

When I was at Hammond, I decided the Labor Ready thing wasn't working out, and I knew that there was an Indian center there from previous dealings in Seattle and the Indian Health Board. They were offering a training program in computers, which is what I needed to learn. It was in the plan all along: to be able to change careers, I would have to know something about computers. So, they signed me up for the program. It was from nine to one o'clock. I did that for eleven months, and finally got my certificate. It was very challenging because it was my first time back into school really. I had a stipend. It was five dollars an hour, which is what, twenty dollars a day? So I didn't have to go to Labor Ready anymore—really early in the morning and not being guaranteed of even getting out.

After my eleven months [in the computer training program] I went to the Learning Center above Angeline's at the YWCA Opportunity Place, and I discovered the Homeless Intervention Program (HIP) there. So I went to an orientation. A year later, I'm a legislative assistant interning with Councilman Rasmussen at City Hall in the Housing, Human Service and Health Committee. I'm interested in nonprofits, and

I'm meeting a lot of professional networking people like I do in WHEEL. So that's where I'm at today. It's really been a fun journey for me, really odd, but I've learned a lot from just observing. I'm curious. I'm a good student. I found I actually enjoy learning this time around. I know what I want for myself, and I'm using these skills and knowledge to give back to the community.

"[S]uddenly you have a responsibility and you do whatever it takes for as long and as hard, in any kind of weather, to see that people stop dying on the streets of Seattle."

After those earlier experiences of living destructively, doing myself bodily harm, suddenly I get a wake up call. Homelessness is my wakeup call, and now that I'm here, I set some responsibility to myself and others around me, and particularly women—this foreign species that I encountered. All of a sudden, I identify with another human being. All of a sudden I want to protect them. They lift me up, whether they know it or not, just by being my sisters in homelessness. They make it possible for me to have the courage to decide that I could sacrifice myself for them, in the sense that you can know everything about me if it will help you understand us. If it can lead to change, I am willing to go there with you. WHEEL gave me that.

I talked to some of the WHEEL members that were at the vigil for Doug Dawson. They are not able to get out of their mind how brutal the murder was. They feel like I do: that they did it to us, and "us" is homeless people. We bleed too. Can't they see that? It hurts your spirit and your heart to know this thing that people do. Stop hurting us. Stop. You know we have feelings. We are taking action to make a change in housing, in the resources. But we do it all the time, and they don't hear us. It's frustrating. It's disappointing, and it's too important to stop, so we will never stop. We're few, but we have our voice, and we do make a difference. They ask us why do we do it, and I said, "Because we are not sitting around waiting for somebody else to do it."

The memorial garden that the Women in Black are proposing is right there at Victor Steinbreuck Park. People can take their children and say, "These people died on our streets." And educate their children that lives were lost right here on these streets, that if everybody cares more, they too can change the direction. Human dignity needs to be restored.

What I spoke about at my commencement is that my job today is a very responsible one, and it's to *bring attention* to the social injustices that people without means endure at every level. You're going to hear about the experience of how we're stereotyped, that we all have issues, or we're all dirty or lack ambition. I believe the system is set up for keeping you there, because we're a multimillion dollar industry, homeless people. If we all got up, if God came down and laid hands on us, and we all got up and walked away, there would be lots of money lost to lots of service provider type people. They need us. It's a business. I think it's a conspiracy. If it weren't for homeless people, they wouldn't have all these resources. I've always said I hate the word, "case management" because it implies that you can't manage your own affairs. But for lack of a better word, in order to navigate the whole labyrinth of services, to cut through the crappola, to get through the real heavy bureaucracy, you need at least ten to coach you. It's almost impossible to maneuver it on your own.

I think [tolerating homelessness] makes people callous and unfeeling, whether they realize it or not. If you stop seeing suffering, how can you call yourself a good person? You know, it just confounds me how callous people have become. I can see myself as a callous unfeeling thing before I got here. I guess the hardest thing about being homeless for me is being invisible, the shadow survivors that we are. That's what motivates me to get into action, is that you will hear from me; you will address my needs. I will tell you, and I will keep telling you until you hear my voice.

In the hero's journey, you start out. Something happens; you get lost; you find your way, and then you come back around. That's where I'm at. I'm on the down swing, I'm in the up swing, I'm arcing, I'm right there, and since I've been homeless, I found myself, which was the goal all along. All I can say is that there's so much goodness in the world, in people, in my life today that I have faith that I will survive, so that fear is gone. God's alive and well. I mean, what's there to stop me now, you know? I'm using my training and volunteer work to finally meet the goal that my wonderful role models raised me to achieve: happiness. But to give back is what I feel most grateful for—that I can contribute in some way. There's always alternative solutions to problems that seem momentous or insurmountable, but there's a lining—a silver lining—a good lining, to being human and having hard times.

At this meeting on Tuesday for Health Services, they want to know what they can do to better serve people like me, and boy, am I going to tell them [laughing]. When I speak, it will be about education and training and opportunities for people like me who have fallen through the cracks. I think it's a shame that one of the richest counties in the country, King County, has people to the tune of fifty-six plus a year dying on the streets by violence or from the outside elements. And that needs to change. That needs to change. At whatever level, whoever decides needs to have the experience I've had, the revolution of the heart, where suddenly you have a responsibility, and you do whatever it takes for as long and as hard, in any kind of weather, to see that people stop dying on the streets of Seattle. That's what I'll tell them.

CHAPTER 14

"Flower"

Flower is obviously a particularly well-loved member of Mary's Place, and it's easy to see why. I number her among the most gentle, soft-spoken women I have met in my life—housed or unhoused. She is quick to listen and support other women. Though her grief is palpable, she seems utterly without cynicism or anger.

When I first noticed "Flower," she was deep in conversation with Sonshine and two or three other women in the smoking area outside Mary's Place. She spoke of her struggles in her marriage to a longshoreman several years her senior with a controlling streak. She talked openly of the grief that she felt over the murders of the two stepdaughters—one by the woman's husband, the other raped and murdered by a stranger—she'd helped raise and of her struggle to recover from her first stroke.

I talked with Flower intermittently during my visits to Mary's Place during the summer of 2006, but having already gained some insight into the depths of the traumas that Flower had suffered in her life, I hesitated to approach her for an interview. But after I had interviewed a number of women at Mary's Place, she volunteered to tell her story. I interviewed her on tape on three separate occasions in 2006, 2007, and 2008. It was only during the first formal interview that I gleaned some semblance of the depth of the traumas that Flower had survived, beginning with a succession of abusive foster homes. In the last, she was systematically molested and prostituted, beginning at about the age of eight.

Though she was a regular at Mary's Place, I had no knowledge of Flower's involvement in Women in Black until after my first interview with her, when I encountered her at the cleansing ritual and memorial service for Tonya. Flower was struggling not only with the death of her friend, but with the recognition—hardly new to her—of how easily she could have shared Tonya's fate. Flower was forty-six at the time of my first interview with her. Given the succession of traumas she had sustained, the multiple strokes she'd already suffered, and the diabetes with which she had recently been diagnosed, she looked much younger.

"In the Bible, it says about how people suffer, and I believe that it's sometimes people's destiny to suffer and that's just the way their life was written out..."

My dad came from Louisiana. I don't know what part, though. He moved back to Louisiana or somewhere and went and started another family. I never met him or nothing. He died at seventy-four, before I turned eighteen—a lot of years ago. He lived to be in his mid-seventies. I seen a picture of him when I got older. I met one of his brothers and my dad's nephews—which is my first cousin—as I got older, and we became kind of familiar with each other. Not real close, but we got to know each other.

My family background was like a real big secret. I kind of remember a real bad tragedy happening, due to my mother's mental illness. I think my dad did something—killed one of the babies or something—and my mom went crazy. You know how you kind of get bits and pieces of stuff? So I think it was a tragedy like that. Whenever I asked any of my cousins about it, it was real hush-hush. Stuff that they don't like to talk about.

We were abandoned by our parents. Before my mom took sick, we were abandoned in that house. My sister was about seven or eight, 'cause I was like five or six. My sister used to go to the store and steal bread, and that's what kept us alive for a couple of months. Finally the man that owned the store, he followed her home, and that's how we got discovered in the house.

My mom had left a note for us to go to that one foster home. I guess she probably didn't know that the woman was like that. I had braces—I couldn't walk—and the lady she was really, really abusive. She used to beat us, but the main thing: she would take pliers and pinch our skin off. I wasn't really badly pinched like my sister. My sister's whole back and her legs and everything is scarred up from that, but I only have a few because I had braces from here on up. *Flower points to an area that extends from her ankles to her thighs.* So I only have little spots from the pliers pinching.

We stayed there a couple of years. How they found out that it was abuse in that home was because my sister fell out of a tree on Friday, and she broke her arm, and that lady didn't take her to the hospital. She went to school, and she was crying about her arm. Back then they had nurses at the school, and they took her into the nurse's office, and they seen all the scars, and then they came and took us out of the home and put us in another foster home.

We had three foster homes. I'm the kind of person right now that believes that you have a destiny for different things. In the Bible, it says about how people suffer and stuff, and I believe that it's sometimes people's destiny to suffer, and that's just the way their life is written out, that they always kind of have grief and tragedy in their lives. And I just believe that I'm one of them people.

"It was like breathing. I thought that's what you do."

After that one, we went to this other foster home. That's the one I stayed in until I was eighteen. The foster mother, she started selling me to men at eight years old, and that went on all the way until I was old enough to move out of there. When I was eight and being led to do it by my foster mom, it was a way of life for me. It was like breathing, was just something that I thought you were supposed to do. At some point in time—I don't remember when—I knew it was wrong. I was doing my foster-father by then. It was confusing is what it was. Being a good daughter in the daytime, and then at night having to have sex—whether it was for money or not—it still was very confusing not really knowing what role to play...

My sister got pregnant by thirteen, and she got sent to an unwed mother's home. And then the foster home we were in, the state came in and took all the kids out of the home except me. Isn't that weird? They said that this isn't fit for a child to live in, but they left me. They took all the [other] children out of that home—my sister, my brother, and other kids that they had. And they left me. Isn't that weird?

My sister went to different foster homes, but when she got pregnant, she ended up staying with the father of her child's parents. They were good people. She got support, and she did good. She's successful. She's an administrator of a hospital. She owns her own home. She's doing real good. I'm real proud of her. I love her. She's like a mother but a sister cause she's always been... We still see each other—not a lot—but I see her at least a couple times a month.

All the way from elementary, all the way up until my junior year in high school, I was one of them girls that everybody picked on. I was basically a loner. And the neighborhood I grew up in, they had little cliques that girls would hang in, and they would jump on me. Ten and fifteen people at a time jumping on one person. I wouldn't want to live through it again, but it wasn't so bad. At times it was pretty intense, but I got through that.

The neighborhood I grew up in, there was a lot of drugs and prostitution. You try to escape from one thing, and one thing seems better than the other. I started on drugs when I was really, really young. About twelve, I started shooting heroin. My friend was doing it. I really looked up to her, and she was like, "You don't want to do this." And I was like, "Yes, I do," and so she put it in me. And from then on, I started using that sort of thing. I was smoking pot way before then, and I got involved in drugs and prostitution, and I had pimps and all that. But I did finish high school. I graduated in '78 from Garfield High School.

"I had changed my whole life. I started working a regular job."

I had a stroke in March—March 12th of '05—and my memory was pretty well wiped out. It's really shot. This one girl walked up to me, and she said I used to come over to her house and she would come over to my house, and I don't remember her. It's from the stroke.

I got married at eighteen. He worked and he took care of me, so it was nice. I had changed my whole life. I started working a regular job. I was working for the state with stroke victims. Just think, I had a stroke later on in life... I was working with stroke victims, home health care, starting their day, getting them dressed, taking them for walks, making breakfast, lunch for them, dinner. That's what I was doing. And then I got pregnant.

He was real jealous, but when I got pregnant, he swore up and down that it wasn't his baby, because once you've been a prostitute, when you have a relationship with a man, they don't never let you live that down. They never let you live that down. So he'd always throw that up in my face. And when I told him I was pregnant he's like, "That's not my baby," and put me in a lot of stress. I was like five and a half months, and I lost the baby. It was very painful. It was just like having a baby. It was five and a half months.

He's dead now. He had stomach cancer. It was after we had broke up. My second marriage was short—it was like two years. He was already married. He was a biga- mist. I come to find out he was married. I was trying to get pregnant and come to find out he had a vasectomy. Our whole marriage was just a big lie. So that was only short term.

Shortly after that, that's when me and my third husband got together. We stayed together about fourteen years. But our relationship was very unhealthy, 'cause he stayed drunk all the time, and I stayed high all the time, and we fought a lot. It was very unhealthy. We were together a long time but it was mostly the same thing: he got paid every week; we'd get loaded, and that's why we'd fight. I never had any kids by him. But I helped raise two of his kids, and they called me "Mom."

One of them, one of his daughters was killed and found behind a dumpster, so that was pretty painful. She was beaten and raped and sodomized. When she died, he went in and identified the body. But when they had the funeral, it was closed [casket], and I wanted to see her. And he didn't let me, so we broke up, and we stayed broke up. He said that I wouldn't have recognized her, but I think I would have. That's what ended that. The other daughter was shot by her husband, but I didn't really help raise her. Not like I did the one that was found raped in town.

I had the stroke after I had gotten evicted from my apartment. This is '06 now— it's been over a year now. I had it March 12th '05. I have really bad hypertension. And I'm diagnosed with diabetes, and so I'm just trying to keep myself as healthy as possible.

I was going to school for a while, but then my new boyfriend didn't want me going to school. He's too controlling, so I'm writing him a letter now telling him he can't live with me no more. I'm going to drop the thing off at the post office and let him know he cannot stay with me anymore, 'cause he wasn't paying rent or nothing. I won't say he's using me, but I can't support him like that. He likes beating on me. He likes to fight too much. I'm getting too old for that. Plus I'm not all that well to take all them punches and stuff.

I think this year has been a good year for some of the people that's been home- less. A lot of women has been able to find homes and stuff. They've been placing a lot of women in homes. They've got a whole bunch of programs together, and they are finding places for women to live. So I think it's been up to a lot of women to really do the footwork and do the paperwork to get homes. Me, myself since I couldn't get housing, I just went out and got a place on my own. I pay a lot more than I would for housing, but I just couldn't take it anymore. I manage. I'm not complaining. I have the peace of mind. I have all this space, so that makes it nice. I just go home at night. Like I say, I'm going to start back in January to school.

I finally got a place to live, renting the basement of a house. I was homeless for nine months. I stayed all over. I stayed at Angeline's. I stayed at the Wells, just a lot of different shelters at night. And it seemed like when the nine months hit, it was like a pressure cooker. I just had to get out. I was waiting for housing, and they sent me the housing interview for the low-income housing, and I didn't pass it. They refused me. Because I had Section 8 before, and I messed up. My one apartment, I had got involved in drugs, and I had a lot of traffic and stuff like that. It's my fault.

The next time I saw Flower, she was in a rehabilitation facility, recovering from another stroke. When I arrived, she was playing cards out in the garden with two women, one of whom, "Erica," I recognized as another regular at Mary's Place. When we went back up on the floor, we ran into a young woman who regularly visited another woman on the ward. During her last visit, she'd given Flower some of the daisies she'd brought for her friend, and Flower voiced deep appreciation for the gift. She went on to tell me about the circumstances of her stroke.

"Getting on the bus, going all that way, walking, trying to find the place. It was hot. I'm in the middle of a stroke. I'm having a stroke."

Last month I had brain surgery, and it went well. They gave me some pills that are called Plavix, and you're supposed to take them when you have heart surgery or brain surgery. It thins your blood out. I had ran out of them. I sent my sister's roommate to get my prescription, and she said my insurance wouldn't pay for it. It was, welfare—DHSH—or whatever it's called. One prescription cost one hundred and forty some dollars, and I guess they don't pay for it. So the next day I asked the pharmacist to call my doctor and get a pill that's equivalent to Plavix that my insurance would pay for, and they said that it would take a day, 'cause they couldn't just call. They had to fax. It has to be in black and white, you know, the paper shuffle stuff. And so when the next day came, that's when I had the stroke, because I didn't have these pills in me, and I guess, a blood clot formed, and it caused me to have a stroke.

I was on my way to Mary's Place. I left Third and Pike going to get on the bus, and my leg felt heavy, and so I caught the bus going down Third and got off on Third and Columbia and walked up the hill. It just got to the point where I couldn't use my leg at all—I had to drag it. So I dragged it up that hill. You know how far that is? That's a big hill, that hill. And it just wouldn't work. I had to drag it, drag it up there. So when I got in the door, Kim [a staff member] said, "What's wrong with your leg?" and I was like, "I don't know." It never dawned on me I was having a stroke. "Nurse" Kim—she don't know nothing—she said, "Well, just prop your legs up and it'll come back." That's what she said, "It happens to me all the time—sciatic nerve." And I was like, "I don't know what no sciatic nerve is, but if that will help, I'll prop it up." So I tried propping it up, and [Kim] said, "Well, the naturopathic will be here any minute."

My housing appointment was that day. That was my interview for King County Housing Authority. My memory—I wasn't doing too good before I had the stroke but now it's gotten pretty bad. So, what was I saying? So Kim said that she could sign me up first for the naturopathic. They've been seeing me off and on—they're very good—and they looked at me, and she said that she didn't think it was a stroke, but with my history I need to probably see a doctor 'cause I just had brain surgery last month.

Thank god for Kim and the naturopathic because I wasn't going to go to the hospital—I was going to go to my housing appointment. That was really important. They had to convince me. Sue—she sells *The Real Change* papers—she said she would go to the housing appointment with me. I said, "I'll just drag it. I need to go to this. I do not need to miss my housing appointment interview." And they was like, "No, she needs to go to the hospital." So Kim said, "That's it, I'm going to call the ambulance." Before I could say, "Wait a minute," Kim was out the room, and I couldn't run, get up, and run and chase her and stop her. And next thing I know [*Flower imitates a siren*], I'm like, "Oh, my god, here come everybody looking and stuff. I get embarrassed with that stuff, you know. Be on the stretcher and all that stuff." I was so embarrassed I didn't know what to do.

But it was a good thing that they were there 'cause it was a hot day. Getting on the bus, going all that way, walking, trying to find the place. It was hot. I'm in the middle of a stroke. I'm having a stroke. I would probably be a lot worse off than I am now, so it's a good thing I got to the hospital immediately when I did. So it worked out good that I stopped, and for Kim not listening to me and just going on her own wits. It has a lot to do with her and the naturopathic that I'm here, cause I sure was going to my appointment, my housing appointment. 'Cause I want to get my housing.

I was in the hospital for seven days. I'm having physical therapy and occupational therapy so, I don't know how long that's going to be. The feeling's back in my toe. My equilibrium is really bad right now. I fall all the time. And it affected my peripheral vision. It affected the leg, but it's coming back slowly. I just have to work hard on that, not try to rush it. But you know, it's coming.

Yesterday I snuck out. I was so tired of sitting up in here. I started down yesterday and went down to Mary's Place, and boy, I won't do that again. They're having a big party down there, so I'm so mad I missed that. I was sad and depressed about not going to the party, but the party came to me. I was really depressed, you know. I had anticipated getting out of here. They had me on restriction, so finally they let me go out. The only thing that they're concerned about is with me falling, you know.

I finally got to go out yesterday. I went down to Mary's. Girl, it was so hard for me getting back here. It was the hardest. I never knew that it was going to be so hard on me.

"There's death around you all the time..."

We spoke about the recent—July 26, 2007—stabbing of a staff member at Angeline's, which Flower frequented along with Mary's Place.[1]

It's not the best of places, but Angeline's does help a lot of women—hundreds and hundreds of women. That would be horrible if the stabbing would affect them closing that place. She was stabbed five or six times in the back. The woman asked her for about a shower. She told the woman that you have to sign up for it, and then she turned her back, and she just started stabbing her. I don't know who it was. I don't know anything, but I know she needs to be punished big time—to the max for it. The lady that she stabbed is a really, really good friend of mine...

These flowers are so pretty, they remind me of walking in one of those wild patches—fields where wild flowers grow. The colors—this color right here, I just love it. They're beautiful. I love them. I love them. It's not easy to accept being here. I've been sick for awhile, but I never thought in a million years at this age and at this point I'd end up in a nursing home. You see what I'm saying? Look at my stupid self! [*laughs*].

...That one girl Tonya that was brutally killed, she was a good friend. That really affects me tremendously. Just before she died, we went to a group upstairs that's called Women's Empowerment Group, and she was saying she wanted to go and see her son, but her face was real beat up, and she said she didn't want her son to see her like that, but she had an appointment to see him. And we said, "Well, you can just call him." And then I think the next day was when she was killed. So that really affected me tremendously. I've been in them jungles before, and you know that could have been me. So it was very devastating. Just for her to die like that—so tragic, so violent. That was too much.

Since I've been homeless, I've had a lot of friends die. Sheila Frazier, when she died, that took a lot out of me. And you know, by me already being sick and stuff, and so long, it's not good for my health to stay upset all the time like that. I did Tonya's Women's in Black memorial, her cleansing and stuff. I did that, but it took a lot out of me. It's been so often, it's been too much on me. I would be more involved in [the WHEEL/Women in Black vigils], but it's just too morbid. I can't do it. I got to the point now, my nerves—my blood pressure—is so bad I can't physically and mentally do it.

I try to remain a happy person. It's real easy for me to slip into a depression and stay in that depression mood, especially when it comes to death, you know. Because by me being an outgoing person and a loving kind of person, I have acquired a lot of friends, so a lot of the women that has passed on were good friends of mine. I'm a people person—people kind of magnetize towards me and I them, because I like people. And so it drains me—it's really hard on me. And now with the brain surgery and a lot of the cancer stuff, I just have a lot of stuff going on physically, healthwise.

And I'm not too sure of my mental stability. At times I feel like I'm really stable, but going through the domestic violence abuse stuff that I went through this last year has been really rough on me. Going through that with that guy and trying to get strong enough mentally from that, that took a lot out of me. I'm just trying to get strong. Trying to stay in a happy mood, which is really hard to do when everyone's dropping dead around you, you know. Especially close friends, and I've lost a few good friends this year.

That was a horrible thing with Tonya's death. She had to die so brutally—that was just awful. And then Sheila, she had a stroke, and then I even had a stroke. I was thinking about that the other day. I believe I was thinking about that yesterday. I can't remember which day it was. But you know, this is my second stroke. And I'm not so sure how I feel about death right now. When I had to face this aneurism—stroke—and knowing the reality of me being homeless and getting out of the hospital and not knowing where I'm going, and having to deal with that is very hard.

Go figure, with all the luck, the day of my stroke, I had a housing appointment. And what do you pick—go to the hospital or go to your housing appointment? I don't know. You just hope for the best and hope that things work out. And you know, I got a roof over my head, but nobody wants to sit up in a nursing home [*laughs.*] There's death around you all the time too. Most the people here are dying. They're terminal. I'm pretty sick too, but there's still hope. I'm not terminal.

Erica has been here since January. She had a room. She was cleaning her room and she fell. I guess she had mixed some cleaning chemicals and she passed out, and the stuff got on her skin, and she's not healing. If you look at her legs, they're in bad shape. They're not healing. So that's what happened to her. She had just got housing too.

I could have been down at Angeline's and been walking around and not even knowing anything was wrong with me. Could have been in such a state of mind, 'cause I have a lot of pain pills. I'm just trying to look at the bright side, versus just looking at it like everything's doomed and stuff. I think this weekend the weather's going to be nice. If somebody'd come get me I could probably go down there for the Parade tomorrow—the Torchlight Parade. I like the floats. They have some very beautiful floats.

CHAPTER 15

Arnette Adams

Figure 6 Photograph of Arnette Adams

*I met Arnette at Mary's Place in the summer of 2006, and she readily agreed to be inter-
viewed. I interviewed her twice that year, and once again in 2008. Fifty-nine when we
first met, Arnette is a striking woman, close to six feet tall, with short graying hair. She has
a commanding physical presence, and when I first encountered her, I would never have
guessed that she had been in anything but perfect health her entire life. Her sometimes
stammering speech and the way she shakes her head in a mix of frustration and amuse-
ment as she searches for a familiar word were the only clues that Arnette had suffered a
stroke in 1987.*

As a child, Arnette clearly defied the normative gender roles for women in the late 1950s and early 1960s, but her mother had obviously been a central figure in her life growing up. Some fifty years later, Arnette verged on tears as she recalled her mother's hurt and frustration at discovering that one of her children had pilfered her last five dollars from her purse. In remembering the incident, Arnette seemed to confront, as if for the first time, the depth of her mother's exhaustion, and the struggles she must have endured to keep the family afloat. If Arnette internalized for a time the racist aesthetics of 1950s and early 1960s popular culture to the point where she contemplated suicide as a adolescent, it seems in no small measure due to the love and respect she felt for and from her mother that she survived and recognized in herself over time the kind of beauty she so clearly saw in her mother.

Arnette spoke of the central importance of spirituality and gospel music in her life, from her childhood listening to Mahalia Jackson, whose songs and life spoke about keeping the faith in the midst of poverty, racism, and oppression, to the prayer that she credits with enabling her to survive her husband's assaults and on at least one occasion, a near brush with death at his hands. However violent her husband may have been at times, like many of the women I interviewed, following the death of her husband, Arnette's attempts at self-medicating to cope with loss led her to fall headlong into addiction. Falling behind on the rent, she was evicted from public housing. Arnette was fortunate in that she was able to secure shelter and then transitional housing, kick her addiction, and ultimately regain a spot in Section 8 housing after two years of homelessness. Housed continuously since 1992, Arnette still regularly seeks out the community of homeless and low-income women at Mary's Place, and on Saturdays when Mary's Place becomes the Church of Mary Magdalene, Arnette is up front with the choir, praising and moving.

"When she sung, the words it pierced my heart. And I think back to the times that God was there but I didn't know it."

Do you know where King County Hospital is?[1] I was raised up that way. I lived across the street from the hospital, on Alder Street. When I was nine or ten, I'm going to run home every afternoon at 3:25 to see Mahalia Jackson on TV. She come on at 3:25 for five minutes. God wasn't alive at that time, and I didn't know nothing about that. All I knew, there was something about that woman, and I felt her presence through the TV. She's a strong woman, and I believed she loved God. That's my first drawing to God, through this woman. When she sung, the words it pierced my heart. And I think back to the times that God was there, but I didn't know it. God wanted me here, because there was a couple of times that I didn't want to go on because of things that happened.

When I was about nine or ten, I was in the bathroom looking in the mirror at myself and I was, "Arnette, you're ugly." And the mirror said, "You're ugly, you're ugly." So I went down stairs and got a butcher knife and was going to kill myself, 'cause I thought I was an ugly duckling. I was the biggest one in the family. So I took the butcher knife and hold it to my stomach, and then it started hurting too bad. Thank

God, I didn't know about no guns, I didn't know about no suicide. I didn't know how to do it. I didn't know the word to call it anyways. Suicide, that's one forgiveness that God does not [give].

I was raised by my mother. I didn't have no father. My mother was a pretty woman. She's dark skinned. I look like my mother now. I feel good about it. I never heard my mother use foul language. She didn't smoke. She drank, but she didn't drive. We always said our prayers at night.

We went to church, Sunday school. But the first [time] I saw the spirit hit somebody, it was my mother. I was about nine years old then, and I believe that when the Spirit hit my mother, he was chastising her. She was shaking, and she was saying, "Yes, Lord. Yes, Lord," over and over again. And "Is that what you mean?" Since then God has whooped me, and when the spirit been hitting me, I knew, I knew I was supposed to be doing something, and I wasn't doing it. It hit me for about four or five minutes, and I knew that God was blessing me, blessing me and chastising me.

"When I was in the sixth grade, I was the king of the school. My friends told me there's nobody would fight me."

I grew up a tomboy, and dressed like the boys. When I was in the sixth grade, I was the king of the school. My friends told me there's nobody would fight me. Sandy Jo and Bradley—they're dead now—and Bradley's brother Larry, we were partners. If friends got squashed, we'd all huddle together, and we'd beat one of them up. One time, we're going walking by the railroad tracks and Larry and Sandy Jo's cousins came with someone and then all of a sudden they got a whiff of me, and they was in a group talking about jumping me. They tried, but they couldn't handle me. There was four. Larry told me what they were trying to do. I don't even know how it came up. Where did they get that idea from?

But the cops stopped us, and we ran from the cop. He caught me and Larry. Bradley and Sandy Joe and his cousin, they were pretty fast and ran off, but the cop put me and Larry in the car. Larry was crying and crying. He was scared. I also got a little bit scared too. I wasn't crying, though. And Larry said, "You took us to jail. You took us to jail," and I said, "I ain't going to do nothing." But the cop, he thinks I'm a boy. I said, "I ain't a boy, I'm a girl" [*laughing*]. They got up towards Jackson and Sixth, and they got a call on the radio. Someone got shot or something so he let us out of the car. So we walked back home to the projects.

We go to Denny Store on Jefferson and 9th or 10th and we said, "There's the cops—the same one's that picked us up." The guy that got shot—he died. But the cops came and the ambulance. We're on this side of the street in the bushes, and before they took him to the morgue, they threw his pack of cigarettes—Camel cigarettes. So we went and got the cigarettes. We paid "dead man's tax" with the cigarettes: it come from a dead man; you see the thing, you touch it, you're it. I was about eleven and that was a big day for us. There's three incidents: the boys, and the cops, then the dead man.

One time I took five dollars from my mother. I spent it. I run home to see Mahalia Jackson on TV. I was standing by the stairs, and I heard my mother on the phone. She was crying. She said, "Girl, one of my kids took my last five dollars. It was my *last* five dollars." I said, "Oh, I should tell my mother. But if I tell my mother, Mama going to whoop me." I don't think no man could whoop me worse than my mother can whoop me. She hung up the phone, and I'm scared now, and I said, "Mama, I want to tell you something." "Yeah, what is it baby?" I said, "But mama, you're going to whoop me, and I don't want no whooping, mama." She said, "I no whoop you." And then, "Oh, mama I took your five dollars." She said, "Baby, why, why you do that?" I didn't have no reason. "I'm sorry mama, I will never do that again." And I didn't. I thought it didn't mean nothing. She won't miss it, you know? *But [it was] her last five dollars.*

I loved my mother. She worked in nursing homes, and then finally it was welfare. But I didn't know that's what it was, because every Easter we had a Easter basket with eggs and bunny. And Christmas time in the projects, no chimney, but the back door would be open when we got up. The back door be open, and she'd make a good scratch cake, a chocolate swirl cake, with chocolate icing and vanilla, and pies. And a big piece out of the cake. Santa probably ate that, you know [*laughing*].

We never saw the presents until we got up. One time my mother's boyfriend, he bought some [toy] guns, a whole bunch of guns. I was so proud, like I'm a cowgirl. But we never owned guns before. Someone took it from me, because girls don't have those things. They gave me a doll—I didn't like dolls, you know, so I was really hurt. And [my mother] gave my holster gun to a little boy, and for a long time I disliked him because he had my gun.

"So I told him, I said, 'Jerry, you almost killed me last night, and today you don't know nothing about it?'"

I was seventeen when I married my husband. There was fourteen years difference between us. The club opened about ten, and he'd be, "You be home at twelve o'clock." I told him once, I said, "Jerry, you can't keep a bird in a cage so long. It get out, it's going to fly away." That's me. I don't want to be tied down. For a year I planned on leaving him, because he treated me too much like a child.

But he's a good man. He graduated second in his class. He joined the Navy after that. He got like an allotment [and] wanted to send that to his mother. It was in 50-something, and they wouldn't do that. So he told his officer, he said, "No disrespect sir, but if my mother don't get that money, I'll be no good for this man's Navy." He was in the Navy four years. When he passed away, he was in electronics.

When we met, the only Black history I knew was minor. He taught me, and I was shocked to learn some things. I thought, "You know, he's a good man." He was into Muslims, until they killed Malcolm X, and then he dropped it, 'cause he believed then that his people killed him. He would tell them, "I don't believe in that because you all killed Malcolm X." That's what he said. Nowadays, as time went on, I believe[d] that, 'cause Malcolm was busting out from the Black Muslims. I believe God loves all Muslims. All kinds of colors, not just one. Anything I wanted to know, I asked my husband [*laughing*].

But my husband was an alcoholic. One day, he was slapping me, and I started saying, "Thank you, Jesus," every time he hit me. "Thank you Jesus!" And after a minute or so, I didn't feel it. He went and got the gun. He said, "Shut up! Don't say that!" That was the devil, because the word "Jesus" is powerful. He went and opened the window and shot the gun out onto the corner of 23rd and Washington, and he said, "Shut up!" The more I said it, I felt so peaceful. I felt like full of feathers. That was one of the best feelings I ever had. But he was drunk. Thank God for Jesus! His name would save me [*laughing*]. And the next day, my husband, he didn't even remember. That really bothered me too, you know. So I told him, I said, "Jerry, you almost killed me last night, and today you don't know nothing about it?"

One time, my husband, he was drinking, and he was throwing a butcher knife. I came home, and he was in the bed. His hand's tied up, and there's blood. I unwrapped his hand, and I started to pray for him. I put my hand on his hand. No mark. God had touched him and healed him.

He used to say, "You don't need to go to church. You just went this morning." But my praying did affect him. One time this lady, she asked him, "What are you thinking while you're wife is in church?" And I've never heard him say this before, he said, "My wife had a glow about her." It made me feel good that my husband said it, but then my butt backslid. And to have my husband say something like that! I said, "Thank you, God," because I didn't think he would notice nothing. I didn't think he ever did. Then he passed.

He died in '75. Me and my friend was at the store. It was New Year's Eve—my daughter's birthday. Jerry wanted gumbo for New Year's, so we left and went to the store. I don't know why, but I looked at the clock, and it was five minutes to seven. I didn't take medicine then; I didn't take nothing, but I bought some Pepto Bismal, because it says it's supposed to settle your stomach. I left the store and went to another store, and I looked at the clock. It was seven o'clock. I believe I was feeling my husband. He was playing dominoes with his brother and his two sons, and his last words were to my son: "You joined the Mexicans, son." Because my son made a bad play [*laughing*]. And that's the last thing he said. And the Pepto Bismal didn't do anything for me.

So I went in the house, and I seen my husband—he was passed already. I knew from when I was a kid, and I saw somebody die. But I didn't want to believe it. So I pushed him up on the couch. I said, "Oh, he's alright." Then I called the ambulance. Before he passed away, [my husband] told me a lot of things. He wanted to be cremated. I forgot that. I buried him. And he wanted me to ride to with him. I didn't. If I had, the ambulance men wouldn't have just robbed him. He just got paid, but I wasn't thinking about money then.

"I went inside and I saw all the people. I saw a lot of people laying on the floor. I never saw that before, and I said, 'I can't do this. I can't.'"

I started using about a year after my husband died. Since my husband passed away, there's probably not too many things I haven't done. I took pills and then Sharm came out.[2] Thank God it didn't last but three or four years. I thank God. I know one girl in particular, her mind's gone. It didn't happen to me. I thank God. Okay, heroin, girl, I did it, but I never did get skinny, the nodding, the slurred words. But thank God I'm free now. I thank God, 'cause God has a purpose for me. I love the way God makes me feel. Ain't nothing like it, and I like to keep that feeling [*laughing*]. I ain't seen God recently you know, but I know he's around. I thank him for that.

Drugs took a lot of money out of my pocket. I had five kids and looking back, it wasn't me. I would say sometimes, "Why Lord? Why?" Now I don't ask why. I can see why. Now that I've put it aside, I can talk to women [who are using]. And I don't have to lie about nothing.

I became homeless in '91. Nobody could have told me I would be homeless. I had a nice place—fifty-three dollars a month. I didn't pay one fifty-dollar month, and the next month I didn't pay fifty dollars again. I knew they had a bunch of people who owed four hundred dollars rent. But I didn't call nobody. I didn't remember to tell anyone, "I missed my rent, I'll pay next month." I didn't say anything.

I went to work one day, and my niece calls, and she says, "Auntie, they're moving your stuff out." I said, "What you mean?" "They're moving you out." I left the job—just left work and came home—and sure enough, they was moving me out. It's embarrassing, but I did it to myself. I had no place to go. I gave my furniture to my neighbors. They gave me some money, and one gave me storage for my belongings.

Me and my niece came downtown to Second and Cherry. They had a shelter there. I went inside, and I saw all the people. I saw a lot of people laying on the floor. I never saw that before, and I said, "*I can't do this. I can't.*" But my sisters and brothers, I couldn't go to none of them. I was on my own.

My niece called a friend of mine, and we went and stayed there until he got to be wanting to be too friendly, and I had to leave there. Thank God, I called [the Lutheran Compass Center] and told them I needed a place, and they said, "Yes, come on down." It's a blessing.[3] We lived there for six weeks, and before my time was up there, I got a call from the Y, and then I moved upstairs [to the transitional housing floor] and I stayed for about a year and a half. They told me to apply for [Seattle Housing Authority], so I called them, and they told me all I had to do is pay what I owed for that rent: the original one hundred ten—one hundred fifteen dollars. I couldn't wait. I paid that right away, and then I got a place.

They gave me three choices. The second place they took me to, it made my skin crawl. I had one more choice, and I liked it. A lot of them didn't have a bedroom, but this one had a bedroom in it. The door closed, and it wasn't painted up yet, but I liked it.

"Street people, lovely people, all kind of people. There's a lot of kind folks in the world, a lot of kind folks in the world."

But I still couldn't stop thinking about the women here. So, I get into my place, and I still came downtown to Angeline's, and I heard about Mary's Place. And then when I came down here, there's some Native Americans, Indians, Jews, all kinds of people, different colors. And I like that, you know, because I see all God's people, different colors, and I like the church. Sister Kim was minister then. She's a wonderful lady. When I first saw her, I said, "Little Chinese lady!" I'm Black, and all I've been ministered to is by Caucasians. But she was so peaceful. She was calm, and she spoke plain, and I listened to her, and she was saying the Word. She preached the Word plain, and everything she was saying was true. It was the truth. So I liked it. I liked her. I had to get it out of my mind about being Black. I was a blind person, as far as the Word.

This was about thirteen years ago since I come in here, and I've been coming ever since. There's one thing that I realize: I love God's word. I believe anybody needs to come on to church sometime because you get strength there. No need to stand in the wind by myself. I know those people here. They will help me. One time I went to another place and I didn't come for about a month. And the first person I see is Sister Pat, and she said, "Ain't seen you in a while. You coming to church Saturday?" I said, "Yeah," and I said to myself, "Doggone it." 'Cause my word means a lot to me. I don't want nobody to say, "She's a liar." The Lord knows everything, and he knew during this time how it was and was telling me I need to go back. So, I came the next Saturday, and I prayed for what I'm doing bad: smoking cigarettes. I didn't feel like coming here then 'cause I ain't doing right. But that's the time to be here, because the more I stay away, the more I get into. And I know this for a fact for myself. I need a place to worship with other people and to talk to. And now I thank God for this place, and I believe my calling, my work, is among these people.

Sister Rachel, about a month ago, I'm on my way to go out, and I was worried about money, and she told me, "Matthew"—I forgot what verse. She told me, "Don't worry about money, 'cause if you're doing for me, I'm going to take care of you." So I said, "Yes, Lord." It's a fear for me to think to leave now with no money in my purse, but I know, God is going to take care of that. I believe he will. I know he will. As long as I stay in the presence of God and go around where his work needs to be done.

They come in, the ones that come from a new town, the ones that won't talk to nobody. They're scared. I go up to them, "I haven't seen you before. You're new here." I started talking to them, and I just be me, because that's all I can be, and we get along. There's some people that probably don't like me, but for what reason? Somebody comes tell me, "So and so said so and so about you." But folks will lie, you know. I hate to be called a liar. I hate to lie. I can't. It hurts. I tell my kids, "Whatever you do, don't lie to me. Don't lie to me. Don't steal from me, and no fighting. That hurts me." It goes for anybody. Especially in church.

Two weeks ago, there was a fight. It brought tears to my eyes. One thing I felt bad about, I didn't pray. I just got up and start to stop it. There's eight, ten people trying to break it up, and through all of that, I don't remember praying at all. I should have been praying, "Lord, bless these hands. Help, and rebuke the devil too." It's good to pray without ceasing. God was on my mind, and you know, it just came to me again: "Pray without ceasing." At night when I'm in bed to sleep, I say, "Thank you, Jesus. Thank you, Jesus." I have to do something that keeps Christ on the mind. I learned that.

When I came to [Mary's Place] I had to get used to people leaving, cause a lot of people die, you know, and I got used to that. It makes me feel proud standing for someone I knew, the ladies I saw pass away. I believe it will make them feel proud [that we] stand for all of them. At first, like I went on 16th and Fir to the bus, and I went with a bunch of sisters and wore only black, and I was standing on the corner and this one lady rolled up her window. She's scared! I'm not going to hurt you! I want homeless people to know someone care. You see them all the time in Black—Women in Black. Sometimes we pass out those flyers [that] will have [the deceased person's] name on it, you know, and show the people: "You're here today. Tomorrow you don't know." When I'm gone, I want people to smile and then have nothing bad to say about me. That's what I want. That's what what's driving me forward. My heart goes out to whoever died, and my heart goes out to everyone else, and people who stop because of concern.

Every morning on the bus, I say, "Good afternoon. How you doing? God bless you." My spirit told me to say it. And I'm glad he put it on me. Sometimes I say it, and sometimes they don't say nothing. But in 2002, I left home close to 1:28, and when the bus came, [God] said, "Say 'Good morning.' *Loud.*" I said, "Yes, Lord." So I get on the bus, and I say "Good morning." I think it's sad for God—I feel sad myself—it hurts me when nobody say anything. One time I got on the bus, and a man said to me, "I'm so glad you said 'Good morning' to me, because I needed someone to say something to me." Sometimes they remember me saying that, and they took time to say it to me. Made me feel good. I met a man, homeless, dirty, and I hugged him, and you know, I ain't never saw that man again. I said, "Maybe he was an angel." Sometimes I see somebody and see the presence of God, and when I see the presence, I want to hug them, to get some of that. Street people, lovely people, all kind of people. There's a lot of kind folks in the world, a lot of kind folks in the world. Some of them need a person to start a conversation with them. It's a blessing from the one that came from above. He needed somebody to use and he picked me, and it's a blessing. Sometimes on the bus I think about all this goodness that he bestowed upon me, and I thank God. Thank you Jesus, cause nobody could do that but you, and I know that for a fact, I got a good God.

CHAPTER 16

Marlowe

I met Marlowe when she came and sat down next to me and opened up a conversation outside Mary's Place in July 2006. Had I not met her under these circumstances, like many of the homeless women I've spoken with over the years, I would have had no clue that Marlowe was homeless. She, however, made the logical assumption, given our location, that I shared the experience of homelessness and almost immediately launched into a critique of the dehumanization of homeless people in the United States, pointing to the need to expand the struggles of the civil rights movement to address the basic human rights of homeless people. I was immediately struck by her mix of poise, dignity, and soft-spoken indignation, and I knew that I wanted to interview her for the book, and she was more than happy to find a public venue for her critique.

Marlowe had just arrived in Seattle and had neither friends nor family in the city. Forty-eight years old at the time of our first interview, Marlowe had reached the average life expectancy for women suffering from sickle cell anemia and was painfully aware of the toll that homelessness was taking on her health. Marlowe also suffered from fibromyalgia and had been living on Social Security disability payments in Atlanta, where she'd lived for two decades. Evicted from her apartment in a dispute over a cable bill, Marlowe had flown to Los Angeles to try to make a new start, before she ran through the last of her money and became homeless.

After a time, Marlowe moved into transitional housing in North Seattle on the grounds of a decommissioned naval base. Marlowe continued to struggle with her health and worried about the health impacts of possible asbestos exposure. During one visit, we sat at the table and drank coffee in front of a window in Marlowe's tidy apartment, a photo of her niece pinned to the refrigerator door, and thriving plants perched on the counters here and there, while Marlowe read through a penultimate draft of the chapter.

For all the physical pain and challenges that Marlowe confronted as a homeless person, the psychological wounds she incurred while homeless seemed to run significantly deeper. I spoke with her intermittently by phone, and she frequently returned to her struggle to come to terms with the side of American life she'd witnessed during her period of homelessness. Marlowe had been particularly shocked by her exposure to the warehouse-like conditions of shelters in Los Angeles and cried at the memory of having seen children sleeping outside with their mother.

"There's an aspect of me that I refuse to allow anyone to take from me. They cannot take my integrity. They cannot take my dignity..."

We have a system that looks at homeless people as being trash. They're trash. You're not contributing to society; you're not doing anything for yourself and society. [With] the first words that come out of your mouth, "I'm homeless," you're automatically invisible to them. Well, I'm not invisible. I know I came here as someone and somebody, and I'm still someone and somebody, regardless of what society thinks of me or any other person that's homeless. We have rights too. We deserve a home.

Everywhere you walk—I don't care what city you're in—you see overpriced housing. That tells us that the people that has the resources to live in housing like that are more deserving than we are. And there's no truth to that. There is so much abundance here—everyone should have. We don't have to be depleted or talked down to because we're in a situation that anyone at any given time can face. I don't care what job position you're in. I met doctors, I've met lawyers, I met accountants, I met scientists, I met people that had top-notch jobs and they're homeless. Anyone can be homeless. We're all a paycheck away from homelessness.

There's an aspect of me that I refuse to allow anyone to take from me. They cannot take my integrity. They cannot take my dignity, and they cannot take the truth that I bring, because I'm not a person that's submissive. My dad always told me, "Marlowe, your mouth is going to get you in trouble." It may have, but I realize there's a source higher than man. I don't depend on man for nothing, and I keep going because there's a source out there that can turn all of this around. That's my belief. Man is manipulative. Man is controlling. Man is deceitful, and I don't give them that power.

"I have always been spiritual. I was born with a gift. From the time I can remember, from the time I was born, I saw things."

There's a saying of people of color that it takes a village to raise a child. I grew up in a village. I was everyone's child. My friends in the neighborhood, they was my parent's children too. So those values are still embedded in me. And they're going to continue to be embedded in me until I take my last breath. I know as a person if I had the resources, I would help a lot of people. I'm always hopeful that one day I'll get to help.

My grandmother was the type of woman, she didn't take no mess off of no one. But she had a big heart. She was strong, and she stayed strong until the very end of her life. She was an entrepreneur. She used to be a maid for a woman—a southern woman—and the woman taught her. My grandmother didn't have a high school diploma, and she didn't graduate from high school and went to college, but she had a master's degree in common sense, and she applied her common sense in establishing a business for the family with the store, and then she went on to buying real estate. A very spiritual, very grounded person, but she didn't take no mess. She loved her kids, all her children and grandchildren and great grandchildren. She instilled a lot of values in all of us, all of us. Some of us kept them and some of us didn't, [but] she instilled them.

Growing up, my mom, she always allowed me to make personal decisions that will allow me to be the person that I am today. I had met people like Duke Ellington, Sandra Dee, and people from foreign countries. And I'm glad that that's what I grew up with, because it allowed me to be not closed-minded about people and diversity. I could talk to anybody about anything. I had that pleasure, and I am seeing it in my life—even being homeless. Japanese women, Chinese women, Korean women, Mexican women, everyone talks to me as if I'm a friend. You make a lot of friends that way. A lot of friends.

I have always been spiritual. I was born with a gift. From the time I can remember, from the time I was born, I saw things. I saw futures and events in people's lives; I saw past events in people's lives. I was invited to go on radio, travel, to help people develop their intuitive gifts to a higher self. In Atlanta, I was a guest on the nonprofit radio [station], on a metaphysical radio [show]. I'd tell people what they need to change about them. I didn't cut any corners. I didn't bite my tongue. I just told them what I saw. So, I guess that my gift is I see things. I don't hold it back. I verbalize [it and] a lot of people don't agree with that.

I've been a Buddhist since 1986. I got tired of going to churches and watching the fashion show. It was too phony, and I wanted something that was going to allow me to enhance myself, to change. I realize it doesn't matter what religion, what culture, people still treat you the same when you're homeless. They don't want to care. The only kind thing that they can say to you is "Good luck." Well, nothing you can do with wishing good luck. You can't do nothing with those things. They're not even a commodity, they're just words.

I always have a problem with the way people word things. I think that as human beings certain words should not be used in the vocabulary. Like when they talk about "poor." The most profound riches a person can gain is wisdom, spirituality. In this society because you are without material things, you're considered poor. One thing I was taught [is] that love does not deplete. Love does not hate. Love does not label. When we start adding all these adjectives and additives, trying to put someone in a category, I think that's when we're not human anymore.

When I was little, growing up having sickle cell, they used to call us "sicklers," until one day, I asked the doctor, "Sicklers? What's that?" He said, "You know, you people with sickle cell." I said, "Wait a minute, so you're telling me you call people with sickle cell disease 'sicklers'? What do you call people with high blood pressure? With MS?" He didn't have no names for them, and he immediately apologized. And I said, "Right, and you're a professional, and you're labeling people because there's a group of people that have this, but you're not looking at their individuality." He said he got the message.

I don't care what no one says, we need each other more than we need our stupid ego, our pride, my so-called material possessions. Because there will be times on this planet when we're going to need each other, and all that other stuff, it's not going to mean nothing.

"After all those years of being a model tenant, I end up homeless."

I have always paid my rent on time. I have always been the model tenant. But in [the eyes of the management company] I wasn't because I stood up for myself. [The management company] didn't like the fact that I'm a person that stands up for myself, so they took it upon themselves that they were going to help me become homeless, and they did. The cable was supposed to be turned off. And they was coming at me for money. It was their incompetence. I tried to resolve it by letting them know that that wasn't my problem, that it was their problem because of their lack of communication with each other. It was like the revolving door at Macy's. If you can't keep employees there, then there's something definitely not working. It just so happened that they thought I was too arrogant, or I was too cocky, that they couldn't deal with my personality—sticking up for myself, standing up for myself. So they decided to forge my name on a letter I never received. At court, the judge wouldn't hear my side. He told me I had to evict the premises after how many years of being there? From 1988 to 2003. That's a long time. I had to evict the premises within seven days. And I looked at the judge, I said, "Thank you very much," and left the courtroom and never looked back. This is the society we live in; it's cold; its calculating; its heartless. After all those years of being a model tenant, I end up homeless.

If you ask me if I miss the place, because I'm homeless right now, I would tell you, "No, I don't miss it." The reason I would say "no" is because there was no kindness there towards me. So I don't miss living there, but I miss having my own space. I visualize the next home that I want for myself. I love bookcases because I read a lot. I want a wall-to-wall bookcase. I want a fireplace, a real fireplace where I can actually put wood inside the fireplace and burn it. And I want hard wood floors and a beautiful, well-designed kitchen. Because I like to juice and I like to cook. I want a nice screened patio where I can have lots of flowers and sit and meditate and connect with nature. Somewhere where it's quiet and peaceful, that's what I want my next home to be. I don't want a mansion. I think that will be enough for me. That would be enough.

"It's not easy having sickle cell and being homeless. But I'm grateful because my body has not given up on me."

Right now I feel like I need to be in a hospital, because I'm having pain in my joint area, and I'm relating it to pulling heavy bags, and [having to] keep going everyday, moving, always consistent movement that's very stressful to me, not only physically but mentally as well. The way things are designed in these shelters, they have indicated to us that if we left our bags there overnight, they would throw them away into the trash dumpster. Why would you hurt someone if they're already down and out by throwing away something that could be so special to them? It could be a sweater. It could be a picture. You would throw that away knowing that's all that person has left of a life that they used to have? How cold and calculating.

I know it's harder on an elderly person's body because they don't have the strength. I have sickle cell and my blood pressure is low, and the elderly person, they're low also because of age, circumstances. It's hard, and it shouldn't have to be that way. If there's lockers or anything available for storage, why not open it up so someone can utilize it? What you saving it for when you're not using it? So, you're saying you'd rather be so hateful, and so mean-spirited and uncompassionate where you can't help a person to stop them from suffering in any form or in any way? But that's how the masses of these private entities and so called "shelters" are. They don't want to help you at all. Because if they help you, they're afraid that you're going to be successful where they don't want you to be successful at all. They want you to just go away and become a part of the earth.

Me, there's certain things I travel with: I travel with herbs; I travel with toiletries, and I travel with clothes that will keep me environmentally comfortable. I can't get cold, because my joints hurt. I can't get overheated, because I become dehydrated. Carrying the clothes that I need, it's hard on me right now. My right side is so full of pain, if I raise this arm and try to reach, there's pain all in here. And there's a bone I can touch—every time I touch that bone, it hurts. I don't know if there's a blood clot sitting there because I have been doing a lot of moving about where my blood is causing blood clots. They call it hematomas. It's hard not being sure where you are going and not being stabilized in one place.

I deal with sickle cell differently than most people that may have sickle cell. I have to approach my health in a holistic way. I take herbs, and I try to sleep, and I try to drink as much water as I can. But when you're homeless, you have to sometimes drink water that is not healthy for the body as far as flushing [toxins]. There was a time when I had housing, I always drank distilled water, and I notice my hemoglobin breaking up, and my eyes become jaundiced if I'm not drinking the water. It's not easy having sickle cell and being homeless. But I'm very grateful because my body has not given up on me. I don't have sores. I don't have lacerations. I am grateful now that it's been this long that I have not been in a hospital, and I don't know where it's coming from, but I sense my body is breaking down and a crisis is building. But you know, if I ate balanced meals, and if I was able to take my herbs on a regular basis like I used to, I could probably overcome this.

To be honest, there's a sadness there and a great disappointment, because I know that many cities has sickle cell clinics and they're supposed to be there to help people that are living with sickle cell overcome everyday adversities, whether it is health-related, financial or mental. That's what these clinics are designed for. But it is painful because they don't seem to target people with sickle cell that are homeless. It's like, "We can help you get to the hospital, or we can help you get some money for your electric bill, but we can't help you if you become homeless."

I was hospitalized in Los Angeles because my body did wear down, and when I went to Cedar-Sinai, they was very good to me. Those people at Cedar-Sinai was so good to me, they treated me like I deserved to be treated, like a human being. They asked me, "Well, what's your circumstances?" I said, "I'm homeless. " I was look-ing for some type of prejudging from them, but they didn't. They treated me well. They treated me like I was royalty. And the doctors was so compassionate. They said, "You're homeless?" I said, "Yes." They said, "You don't look like a homeless person." And I immediately asked him, "Well, what is a homeless person supposed to look like?" And he said, "Well, you don't have any sores on your body." And I said, "Doc, I'm not going to have any sores on my body." He said, "You don't even look your age." I said, "Well, maybe I'm taking care of myself. I'm trying to take care of myself being homeless." And he told me, "If there's anything you want or need, you let me know." While I was there, I tried to rest, and I tried to heal, and I did.

When it came time for me to leave, I had no idea where I was going to go. And then a friend—supposed to be a friend—I slept in their van when I got out of the hospital. And then they told me I couldn't sleep in their van no more. I had to go. I did not realize they weren't my friends. I kept on trying to find a place. Slapped me in a couple of hotels, and I realized that hotels, they're there just to take from you. A lot of my money was reserved in that hotel 'cause I needed a roof over my head. I needed some place to be quiet, to be still, to heal. That was the only place I could go, was a hotel. Nothing in society is designed to make life comfortable for you. Nothing. It seems like the richest man in the world, he gets all the comfort, and the reason he can is because he has something that somebody else wants, which is his money. And if he has it, then they're capable of kissing his behind and doing whatever else he said he wants them to do because they want that back. So, I would say he sold his soul to the devil. Figure of speech.

"I know that there are a lot of people that are losing their minds. You lose your mind and you just don't surface. You're not yourself anymore."

I'm packing bags and going up and down streets, and going here one night, and going somewhere across town the next night. It's too much. Not just physically, but mentally, because at night, you have somewhere to lay your head and be under a roof, and then you go with the same cycle the next day.

Because I was in California and here, I notice that it's a system. It's a system to keep you down. It's a system that keeps you going in a circle so you either become exhausted or you just give up. Some people, they just give up. They commit suicide, or they take an overdose. They just give up because it's too overwhelming to deal with. I've felt that way a few times, but somehow, everyday seems like I gain more and more strength by knowing that this is a very corrupt society. I know that there are a lot of people that are losing their minds. You lose your mind and you just don't surface. You're not yourself anymore.

Believe it or not, there are some people that don't care about becoming stable. They're enjoying their freedom. They just love what they're doing, but that's not my case. Because I know I came here for a very significant reason on this earth plane. And I'm not going to leave this earth plane until I have done my part. And my part could be my voice because I do speak up to injustice. I see what's in front of me. Homelessness is right here; it's right here in this country. But you know, they propagate [that] it's always over in India. It's over in Africa. But it's right here. It's right here. You take care of home first and then you worry about somebody else. What speaks truly about homelessness—look at people's faces, that tells you a lot. There's so much pain there. There's so much anger there. There's so much disappointment there. Their faces tell you.

The shelter I stayed at in Los Angeles was one large warehouse. It reminded me of an old airplane hanger for abandoned airplanes. They had 400 army cots. Two hundred for the men, and 200 for the women. And the women, they used to personalize those army cots. They would decorate it as if it was their permanent housing. If they were near a wall they put all their pictures underneath. They had their toiletries and their personal items, as if they was making permanent residency there. I met women from all walks of life: doctors, lawyers, you name it, they was there. Engineers, scientists, somebody's mother, somebody's aunt, somebody's grandmother. There was all kinds of women there. But they was hard, and they was mean. And I don't know if their hardness came during the time they became homeless or prior to the time they was homeless. They was always angry and fighting amongst each other. And when I saw that, I said, "I am not going to be here tomorrow morning." It was like two-thirty in the morning. I slept all of about two hours. When four-thirty came, I got up and I never looked back. I said, "I am not going through this. I am not." I just walked the streets, but I wasn't going to be in that environment.

"When I saw them children, I realized that we live in a very cold, cold, society and society doesn't care about life."

The thing that really hurt me the most when I was in California was when I was downtown pulling bags, and I came across these two children. These children was outside, sitting on a cardboard box, and they was playing as if their life was good. I just broke down and cried, because them babies didn't have a roof over their head. They're sleeping under a cardboard box on a city street, but they was able to wake up and not have hatred, not be angry because of the way their lives were. It touched me so much, because when you see children homeless, it puts something in you that you cannot suffer through. It makes you become more humble. But when I saw that, I had to break down because—because they was so pure and they was in the position they was in. It was like they weren't angry and maybe because they wasn't quite sure of their circumstances—of being homeless.

And every time I think about them, I always end up crying because the society had failed the children. It had failed me, and it had failed many of us, but how do you fail children? How come children have to suffer? The elderly—nobody should have to suffer. When I saw them children I realized that we live in a very cold, cold, society, and society doesn't care about life. How can we do that to someone that haven't even started to live yet? God, of everything I've been through, that hurts. Here we are, a society of people where we can't unify ourselves to come as one to help each other out. Am I my brother's keeper? Good question, huh?

"[T]his is why there is so much turmoil in this country. There will never be peace, there will never be love, because of the fact that there are too many people without."

Charlie Chaplin said, "Our knowledge has made us cynical; our cleverness has hardened us, and made us very unkind. More than machinery, we need humanity. More than cleverness, we need each other and kindness and gentleness. Without these qualities, life would be very violent." And that's what it is, very violent now. And I say dictators are very unhappy people. The greatest happiness belongs to those who walk with the people.

[Homelessness] is an embarrassment to the good old U.S. of A. Here you are, the richest and most abundant in the world, and there's homelessness. Wouldn't you be embarrassed? You should be. You can't stand to know that your brother is homeless [and] you're supposed to be his keeper. So you turn your head and you walk past that person as if they're invisible. Like you didn't even see them. Otherwise you would have to feel compassion, and compassion is hard right now for a lot of people. They don't want to feel nothing; they don't want to see anything that is going to be a constant reminder of where they could be tomorrow or next week or in a month or a year.

Civil rights pertains to all people's rights. What civil rights means is treating a human being as a human being, that's what civil rights is. And I say that because I know my history. My forefathers have come here, have built this country, and 'til this day, I feel that everyone should have housing and all the things that are necessary to sustain life, to sustain peace, to sustain us as human beings, to sustain us from having to go and be in poverty. And I think because of situations like this, this is why there is so much turmoil in this country. There will never be peace; there will never be love, because of the fact that there are too many people without. The universe is full of abundance, and everyone should have the necessities.

They told me that [the] Section 8 [lottery] was in May and they will not open that up until another three years. I think the housing lottery sucks. It shows humanity's inhumane side. To have a lottery for housing? To show what? "Oh, let's watch them fight all over each other. Let's give such and such to this one, and that one don't get. Let's see what happens." There's something sick with the society that creates things like that. Everyone should have housing. Everyone. A mass of people homeless and they have to wait three years for housing? That's twisted—very twisted. Nobody deserves that. If they can give billions of dollars to make a freaking weapon, why can't they take care of people?

. . . I want people to know I have a tenacious spirit, and I'm not going to die until its time for me to die. And there's no one or nothing's going to kill my spirit off, to convince me that I am dead. The sun is going to come up every day, and the wind is always going to blow to the east and to the west and the south, and somewhere in the midst of all of that I'm still standing. That's what I want people to know.

CHAPTER 17

Conclusion

"The Homeless Place of Remembrance"

Marlowe's assertion that "[E]veryone should have housing and all the things that are necessary to sustain life, to sustain peace, to sustain us as human beings, to sustain us from having to go and be in poverty," resonates strongly with core tenets of the Universal Declaration of Human Rights. Among those rights enshrined in the 1948 UN document are the rights to food, housing, health care, "to security in the event of unemployment, sickness, disability, widowhood, [and] old age,"[1] to a living wage,[2] and collective bargaining.[3] In 2011, in the face of escalating assaults on Social Security, Medicare and Medicaid, public housing, public education, and the right to collective bargaining, it's easy to doubt Martin Luther King's article of faith, drawn from the nineteenth-century abolitionist minister Theodore Parker, that "the arc of the moral universe is long but it bends toward justice." With the Bush-era tax cuts for the rich extended once again under the auspices of stimulating the economy and creating jobs, the rest of us are called upon to bear the cost of "austerity" measures in the form of cuts to public schools, health care, social services, housing, pensions, and Social Security. We are witnessing, in short, "the global race to the bottom" that was the focus of the 1999 WTO protest. Seattle activists involved in the continually unfolding global democracy movement recognized that under the logic of neoliberalism, corporate profits are treated as sacrosanct, while workers' rights, and the very right to life of all but a narrowing corporate elite are treated as disposable commodities, the acceptable collateral damage of "Free Trade."

As of 2011, more than 400 women and men have died homeless in the city that spawned Starbucks, Microsoft, and Boeing, as well as the 1999 WTO protest. WHEEL/Women in Black's dream of a site that would recognize the deaths—and honor the lives—of those who died homeless was touched upon in my interviews with several women. The vision of a "homeless place of remembrance" struck a particular chord with Mona, who transformed her personal grief into activism as she struggled to come to terms with the unsolved murder of her fiance José Lucio, whose ashes were interred in a mass grave, alongside the ashes of nearly two hundred homeless and indigent people in the "Emerald City."

In 2010, WHEEL/Women in Black's modest dream of honouring the city's homeless dead finally came to fruition, following years of dialogue, organizing, design development, grant-writing, and collaboration with community stakeholders. In 2009, the Homeless Remembrance Project Committee (HRC), composed of activists from WHEEL and Women in Black and a team of architects and designers, submitted a proposal to the Pike Place Market Historical Commission. While the Historical Commission rejected the proposal, the decision was overturned by the Hearing Examiner of the City of Seattle. The controversy that the proposal generated exemplifies the ongoing marginalization of homeless people in public spaces and policy decisions. At the same time, the arguments that the HRC's lawyer mounted in defense of the "Place of Remembrance" illustrate the ongoing importance of recording the voices of marginalized and oppressed communities, whose history of struggle is continually threatened with erasure.

Given the Historical Commission's guidelines discouraging "memorials," the proposal that the HRC brought forward was for a "public art installation" to be cited in Victor Steinbreuck Park alongside the Pike Place Market and overlooking the Puget Sound. The proposal represented the installation as a thirteen-foot tall "tree of life" surrounded by glass panels illuminating the roots.[4] The tree, the proposal indicated, would depict "the interconnectedness of life" and "celebr[ate] the idea of community."[5] The proposal specified that there would be no mention of the dead, "no plaques or names on the sculpture," and no "reference to the identity, background or intent of the donors."[6] Still, the proposal was rejected by the Market Historical Commission on grounds that included claims that the design was in fact "a memorial," and that it would detract from the "character of the district" and "depart[ed] from the character of the park's design."[7]

The HRC's pro bono attorney Richard Hill went on to appeal the decision to the Hearing Examiner of the City of Seattle, in a legal brief that excavated the history of poverty, exclusion, and displacement in the Pike Place Market District. Victor Steinbreuck Park, Hill noted, is planted over top a parking garage constructed on the site of the old Washington State National Guard Armory built about 1909. "A red-brick turreted structure that looked like a fort ready to protect Elliott Bay and the city from invading naval forces," the Armory, Hill argued, "had a uniquely relevant use" historically.[8] It had served as a "gathering place for victims of the Depression, with food-handout lines" and "free baths for down-and-outers when health authorities deemed that such facilities were needed."[9] Though "[a]fter 1939, the old Armory was allowed to lapse into decay," as Hill noted, "even as late as the 1960s, the property was used to provide social services to the homeless and the indigent."[10] The armory, in fact, was "partially destroyed in a fire in 1962, at the time when the historic Pike Place Market District was doomed by business and city government for replacement with high rise apartments, hotels and offices."[11]

The brief noted that the Pike Place Market District had been radically altered by an "urban renewal and historic renovation plan" executed in the 1970s that resulted in the closure and demolition of thirteen "residential hotels, which originally served sailors on shore leave and farmers in town to sell their goods at the Market," and later served as a "permanent residential community...consisting largely of low-income single men, half of whom were 60 years of age or more, with an average household income of $190 per month."[12] And, as Hill also observes, while

> there were plans and hopes to build some, at least replacement housing...It is unknown what happened to these men...What is known is that an "unavoidable" consequence of the renovation of the Pike Place Market in the 1970s was the displacement of hundreds of low income elderly men and the subsequent homelessness of at least some of them.[13]

Hill went on to note that all prior applications for "free-standing artwork in the Market" had been approved by the Historical Commission, including "the installation of a bronze sculpture of a life-size swine to be used as a piggy bank to collect donations for the Market Foundation," another sculpture of a pig, and a sculpture of a "Seattle Squid."[14] Hill contested the MHC's claim that the installation, which "includes no text, no reference to any person or group of persons,"[15] violated the Historical Commission and Parks and Recreation prohibitions against memorials.

Hill noted, moreover, that the MHC, had, in fact, unanimously approved four memorials. Among those memorials approved in recent years, Hill observed, was a "set of murals and memorial plaques" sponsored by the Japanese American Citizens League (JACL) "commemorating...Japanese American farmers" barred from the Market during World War II, following Executive Order 9066.[16] Following the order, as the JACL recounted once again in a recent press release, "the United States forcibly removed virtually the entire population of 120,000 Japanese Americans from their homes on the West Coast and incarcerated them in concentration camps in America's interior."[17] Pike Place Market, Hill argued,

> ...is a reflection of our City. Wonderful as it is, it also reflects our faults. This has always been the case. In 1941, two thirds of the 513 farmers selling produce in the Market were Japanese American. As of May 1, 1942, all Japanese American farmers were banned from the Market. Two thirds of the stalls became empty. White businesses moved in.[18]

Hill cited a 1942 article in the *Seattle Star*, which "quot[ed] the general manager of the market as saying: 'The market in general is enjoying an excellent increase in business because white patrons like to buy from white farmers.'"[19] One JACL-sponsored plaque on display at the Market reads, "In 1941 approximately two-third of the farmer's stalls in the Pike Place Market were occupied by Japanese Americans. Today none." Another JACL plaque reads, "The United States Order 9066 forever changed the Pike Place Market and the lives and families of 120,000 citizens of the United States of America."[20]

In June 2010, the Hearing Examiner ruled in favor of the Homeless Remembrance Committee, approving the installation of the "Tree of Life" in Victor Steinbrueck Park. By a prior agreement struck between the Homeless Remembrance Committee and the Seattle Department of Transportation, throughout the downtown core, the sidewalks of Seattle will be scattered with tiles in the shape of "bronze 'leaves' "[21] bearing the names of people who have died homeless in one of the "most livable cities" in the United States.

In 2011, as we stand at the crossroads between Martin Luther King Jr.'s "beloved community" and Glenn Beck's Brave New World, it's hard to feel hopeful. More and more Americans are falling into bed dead tired from working two or more jobs to try to stave off homelessness. Many are lying awake at night wondering how they're going to pay the bills and keep a roof overhead, while others sleep—and die—in terror on the street. Over the past two decades, literally trillions of dollars have gone to pay for corporate bailouts, bloated military budgets, and a "War on Terror" that in Iraq alone has resulted in more than 100,000 civilian deaths and 4.5 million refugees and internally displaced persons.[22] Democrats and Republicans on Capitol Hill seem increasingly indistinguishable in their embrace of immigrant detention, torture, and the global "war on terror," and more and more indifferent to the struggles, and the very "right to life" of all but a narrowing economic elite. The antidote to the current economic crisis, we're told, lies in more of the same: relaxation of safeguards against corporate greed, tax breaks for corporations and the rich, and permanent war. The "trickle down" effects of these policies are wholly predictable. And while the beneficiaries of corporate bailouts and corporate largesse are sailing away in their yachts, we are asked to decide once again whom we will throw out of the lifeboat.

Middle- and working-class Americans—and white Americans in particular—have historically been taken in by these arguments, subscribing to the logic of social Darwinism masquerading under myths about American meritocracy. In the United States, as Arun Gupta has recently argued, movements that focus on preserving an American dream founded in consumerism and on the narrow rights and privileges of the middle class, "rather than trying to build an alliance of single mothers, the poor, immigrants and the elderly" are doomed to fail.[23] "If," as Gupta observes, "labor is not acting out of real solidarity by fighting vigorously for everyone who is dispossessed, then different social groups will be demonized and pushed into low-wage work that can supplant union jobs."[24] Our best hope for the future lies in recognizing the short historical leap from the "I got mine, you get yours" attitude of the 1980s, with its racist demonization of "Welfare Queens," to the demonization of public sector workers in the present. We need to recognize that a strong social safety net that includes public housing, universal health care, and quality public schools and institutions—enshrined in European social democracies—is not only essential to protecting the most vulnerable members of society, but living wage jobs across the board.

Whether history bends toward justice will depend upon whether we focus on the narrowing choices afforded us in an electoral process that is bought and sold by corporations, or on the unfolding history of social movements for economic and racial justice locally, nationally and globally. If stepping over the bodies of other human beings on the street or enacting laws that sweep them out of sight or into prisons and detention centers is the only way that we can stave off our own fears about the future and preserve our faith in the American dream, then dreaming will continue to be a dangerous business. None of the women I interviewed for this book chose to become homeless, but many of them have found hope and meaning in working to end poverty, homelessness, and oppression. History will bend toward justice if enough of us are willing to join in the struggle.

CHAPTER 18

Afterword

In February 2008, Marlowe wrote and told me that she'd read Victor Frankl's *Man's Search for Meaning*, a seminal text in the field of existential psychology. The book draws on Frankl's own experiences and those of other Holocaust survivors who struggled to find meaning in life in the face of the atrocities they experienced and witnessed in Nazi concentration camps. Marlowe wrote that she'd cried at the accounts of people "rob[bed] of their personal keepsakes and most of all" of the "illusion of what we call freedom." Marlowe wrote that the book had enabled her to "take notice of how small my suffering is," and inspired her to run for a position on the executive committee of her building. She was helping tenants access furniture and kitchen sets as they transitioned into permanent housing. In 2009, she moved back east. Despite the women's best attempts to keep me organized, I lost Marlowe's phone number and haven't been able to locate her. I listen sometimes to the last message she left on my answering machine before she moved. "Des," her voice reminds me, I haven't heard from you in a while."

I met up with Arnette on November 18, 2009, immediately following WHEEL's annual Homeless Women's Forum, to go over the chapter focused on her life. Arnette's hair was a bit grayer, and she was walking with a cane. We made our way to the closest restaurant, a couple of blocks away, with Arnette stopping now and then to catch her breath. In reading through the chapter, Arnette once again seemed most moved by the sections that focused on her mother. After our meeting, we were headed down Third Avenue, when Arnette suddenly asked me, "Who's that Black writer...?" I thought that she was trying to recall a passage that had resonated with her own experience, when I looked up to see Cornel West coming out of KIRO TV about a half a block away. Arnette had seen him only the week before on *The Mo'Nique Show*. Professor West and Arnette greeted each other with such warmth, familiarity, and for lack of a better word—delight—I thought perhaps they were old friends.

As the deadline for submission of this manuscript neared, I tried once again, as I had at various points over the last several years, to reach some of the other women I had interviewed in the 1990s. I managed to locate a phone number for Pam's brother through an obituary for a family member. Within minutes of speaking with him, Pam called me. She was still living just a few miles from me in Portland, and we met up the day after Christmas so she could read through the chapter. Pam's son, who lived down in Florida, died of cancer a few years ago.

During our meeting Pam recalled once again the experience she had at the age of seventeen of being coerced into signing adoption papers while she was still under the effects of sedation from giving birth. Several years ago, Pam's daughter located her. They communicate regularly. Having suffered a number of strokes—most, though not all of them, transient ischemic attacks (TIAs)—since we last spoke, Pam uses a mobility device to get around. She has been married for six years, but during a period of separation, she became involved in another battering relationship that resulted in her eviction from her apartment. Though she spends days with her husband, who lives in public housing, he's barred from having overnight visitors for more than two weeks out of the year. She is staying at a women's shelter for the present, but she reports that for two weeks this winter, with the shelters all filled, she spent two weeks sleeping outside in downtown Portland. She has been sober since 1981.

The day after I met with Pam, I flew down to San Francisco to meet with Roxane to go over the edited chapter. Roxane and I had kept in contact by phone and e-mail since she moved to San Francisco in 2008. She had written at various points to tell me about her life there, including her participation in a weekly Mission District street corner "guerilla-style poetry slam" coordinated by the Collaborative Arts Insurgency.[1]

Roxane and I met up for breakfast not far from the SRO where she lived, and afterward we walked to San Francisco Public Library. On our way to check in to an ADA-equipped carrel, Roxane stopped in the periodicals section. Holding a magnifying glass against the stacks, she strained to read the titles and call numbers, until she found what she was looking for and handed me the volume. It was a copy of *Sinister Wisdom, A Journal by and for Lesbians*. There in the special edition titled, "Women Loving Women in Prison" were two prose poems by Roxane Roberts.[2]

Inside an ADA-equipped carel, I read Roxane's chapter to her. In places she laughed out loud, and when we got to the passage about her life in the "little summer place" she had shared with Tommy, she found Chicago's "Wake up Sunshine" on the computer, cranked up the volume, and sang along in the sound-proof booth. Before we boarded the BART train to the airport so I could catch a flight back to Portland, we visited Roxane's SRO. Among the books in Roxane's sparsely furnished room were copies of Bertrand Russell's *A History of Western Philosophy*; *Jung, Jungians and Homosexuality* by Robert H. Hopcke; and W.H. Adkins's *Moral and Political Behavior in Ancient Greece, from Homer to the End of the Fifth Century*.

Back home in Portland, I exchanged e-mails and arranged a phone interview with Ramona Drake, who received services from Youth Advocates in Seattle when Roxane worked there in the 1970s. The two of them had maintained sporadic contact over the years via e-mail. Roxane, Ramona told me, "had a huge impact on my life." "In 1974," Ramona went on to observe, "I was fourteen and I was a wild child. I was a runaway, crazy wild, mostly gay, but maybe bi. I was an addict in the making at that time. Roxane taught me not only love, but respect in a deep and profound way. I had been molested by a family member and no one else could reach me. Nobody could control me, but that woman who became like a parent to me." Ramona, who is white, is married to an African American woman. They are raising a family together. A certified counselor, Ramona manages a nonprofit for people in recovery in Los Angeles.

A few days later I headed up to Seattle for a final visit before submitting the manuscript. After being released from the rehabilitation facility where I'd last seen her in downtown Seattle, Flower had suffered yet another stroke. She was living now in a nursing home a forty minute bus ride from downtown. Flower is confined for the present, at least, to a wheelchair. We sat in the courtyard, and I quietly read the first few pages of the chapter focused on her life. After a few minutes, Flower asked me to stop reading. She trusted that I had accurately rendered her story, but for the present, at least, she didn't want to hear anymore.

Flower's complex medical needs make it impossible for her to visit Mary's Place anymore. "I miss it a lot," she tells me. "I miss everybody down there. But it's just one of them things, I guess." Flower spends her evenings reading and studying the Bible with another woman at the facility. "This [body] is just a shell that God gave us," she tells me. "When we die, if we're obedient to God we're promised eternity. We're promised owning a house, a mansion, no suffering, nothing like that. No evilness can touch us any more. We wonder why some people are rich and everything is perfect for them and others are homeless, never been loved except by the Father, and go through all this tragedy. It was just our destiny."

A few hours later, I met up with Elizabeth Thatcher in a café not far from her apartment, where we had met once before in the summer of 2010 after reconnecting in 2009 on Facebook. Elizabeth arrived pushing a walker draped in the front with small plushy toys. They were gifts that her daughter brought to her in the hospital, after she suffered a major heart attack on the street in 2002. Elizabeth has cardiopulmonary disease (COPD) and relies on an oxygen tank to breathe. She hasn't had any legal problems since her release from Purdy in the 1980s before her stay at the Compass Center. She reports having been homeless again for nine months in 2004 and having slept in a corner of a friend's house during the day and spent nights standing up in a phone booth on the corner. She has been sober since 2005. Elizabeth shares an apartment with her 32-year old son, who is her caregiver. Her former boyfriend who battered and stalked her, she tells me, has been sober for twelve years. They live now in the same apartment building operated by Seattle Housing Authority. They sometimes see each other on the elevator, but beyond that they have no contact. Elizabeth made the decision to put her real name on the story and told me, "I'm the last of my crowd: the junkies and the hustlers and the people that I grew up with. They taught me a lot of things in and out of prison. They've all died but me, and it's kind of amazing that what I have is life threatening, and I'm going to die from it, but it's not that bad. I've really had a wonderful life and I'm really blessed."

Afterwards, I met up with Annamarie Tailfeathers. A few days earlier I'd located her on Facebook and we had spoken by phone. Anna distinctly remembered the interviews. She told me she'd done a lot of healing since, and I could easily hear the change in her voice. She was eager to read through the chapter. I e-mailed it to her and the next day she replied on Facebook: "I read it. I love it. Totally."

We met up for an hour in an apartment in a North Seattle suburb. Anna has been sober since 1996. She credits Washington State Mental Health Court with having saved her life. The motto of the Washington State Mental Health Court is "treatment instead of incarceration for the mentally ill offender."[3] In the last few years, she reconnected with two of her children and they regularly communicate with each other. Anna makes and sells dream catchers, beadwork, and leather crafts at fairs and flea markets. She was married for two years, but her husband died of colon cancer in 2002. She remarried a few years later. She told me, "I have no anger or malice toward anyone. I've learned from everybody in my life. I'm glad for all of it. This is the first time in my whole life I've felt this elated and happy."

She spoke briefly of the death of the wood carver John T. Williams, whom she counted as a friend, and observed that "countless people I've known over the years have died. A person dies in their house, it's all over the news. A homeless person dies in their camp from exposure, does anyone mention him or her? Each and everyone of us is a soul worth saving." She and her husband started a street ministry several years ago and continue to deliver food and coffee on the weekend to people sleeping on the streets of downtown Seattle.

Though I had tried unsuccessfully over the years to contact Deb Martinson through the listserve she launched back in the 1990s, I finally managed to locate her on Facebook. In the evening, on her way home from work, Deb met me at a coffee shop and drove me to her apartment, where she read through the chapter, while I glanced through the books—including Barbara Ehrenreich's *Nickel and Dimed and* Molly Ivins' *Shrub—* that jammed a row of floor to ceiling bookshelves. Deb stopped reading intermittently to speak about her life, and try to fend off her cat Schadenfreude. Deb has been working "in tech" for "fifteen or twenty years," She has held the same job full-time for several years. She got promoted last year and has a "quasi-supervisory position." She has automatic deductions from her paycheck donated to Foodlifeline, "a nonprofit food distribution agency working to provide nutritious food to hungry, low-income people in Western Washington state."[4] Looking back on her childhood, she recalled it as an "armed camp." She still struggles to come to terms with the experience of being homeless, observing, "We have this myth of the rugged individual, the self-made man, and if you can't make it, if you're a failure, you deserve whatever happens to you." The website that Deb launched is still going strong though Deb has pulled back a bit from its daily operation. I asked her if she would mind if I spoke with Armando Favazza, author of *Bodies under Siege,* about the impact of her online advocacy, and she agreed.

I interviewed him by phone a few days later. Debra, he told me, "was a real pioneer in the field of self-harming, with the website that she started to get the information out. She deserves a tremendous amount of credit for bringing the problem of deliberate self-harming into public consciousness. Hers was really the first website to provide coherent, meaningful and helpful information to people who self-harm, to not only remove the stigma, but provide professionals with guidelines for how to deal with individuals who deliberately harm themselves." He asked me if I'd seen the document she'd drafted that is still broadly used, "The Bill of Rights for People Who Self Harm."[5] I hadn't. The first principle in the document is, "The right to caring, humane medical treatment," and stipulates that "self-injurers should receive the same level and quality of care that a person presenting with an identical but accidental injury would receive. Procedures should be done as gently as they would be for others." March 1 is National Self-Injury Awareness Day, an event Debra Martinson was instrumental in launching.

Notes

I Introduction

1. "Discover the Needle: Fun Facts," http://www.spaceneedle.com/discover/funfacts.html (May 17, 2011).
2. Jack Broom, "Sprucing up the Space Needle, Age 37—20$ Million Face Lift," *Seattle Times*, September 11, 1999, http://community.seattletimes.nwsource.com/archive/?date=19990911&slug=2982421 (May 17, 2011).
3. Tyrone Beason, "Space Needle: Forty years after World's Fair, Seattle's symbol still stands tall," *Seattle Times,* April 12, 2002, http://seattletimes.nwsource.com/html/seattlecenter/2004338231_seacentericon09.html (May 17, 2011).
4. Mildred Tanner Andrews, ed., *Pioneer Square, Seattle's Oldest Neighborhood* (Seattle, WA: University of Washington Press, 2005), 21.
5. Ibid.
6. Ibid.
7. Seattle Housing Authority, http://www.seattlehousing.org/development/yesler/Yesler.html (May 17, 2011).
8. Andrews, *Pioneer Square*, 95.
9. Ibid.
10. Ibid, 30–33.
11. "Seattle's Downtown: Pioneer Square," *History.org, the Online Encyclopedia of Washington History*, http://www.historylink.org/?keyword=pioneer+square&DisplayPage=results.cfm&Submit=Go.; see also Andrews, *Pioneer Square*, 94–104.
12. Andrews, *Pioneer Square*, 120–121.
13. See David Harvey, *A Brief History of Neoliberalism* (New York: Oxford University Press, 2005), 39–63. For a theoretical overview of neoliberalism, see 64–86.
14. An extensive body of literature exists on the spike in homelessness during the Reagan administration; see, for example, Martha Burt, *The Growth of Homelessness in the 1980s* (New York: Russell Sage, 1992); and Kim Hopper and Jill Hamberg, *The Making of America's Homeless: From Skid Road to New Poor, 1945–1984*. Report prepared for the Institute of Social Welfare Research (New York: Community Service Society, 1984). For a theoretical and historical overview of neoliberalism, see Harvey, *Neoliberalism*, 64–86 and 152–182.
15. In recent years, memoirs of people who have experienced homelessness first hand have included Tiny, aka Lisa Gray-Garcia's *Criminal of Poverty, Growing Up Homeless in America* (San Francisco, CA: City Lights, 2006); Michelle Kennedy's *Without a Net: Middle Class and Homeless (with Kids) in America: My Story* (New York: Viking, 2005); and Lee Stringer's *Grand Central Winter, Stories from the Street* (New York: Washington Square Press, 1998). See also Alexander Masters' biography of homeless activist Stuart Shorter, *Stuart a Life Backward* (New York: Delacorte Press, 2006).

16. David Wagner, *Checkerboard Square, Culture and Resistance in a Homeless Community* (Boulder, CO: Westview Press, 1993), 3. While Wagner's observation is not specific to homeless women in particular, it is, I believe, a particularly apt description of representations of homeless women. David Wagner's *Checkerboard Square* was something of a watershed text in contemporary studies of homelessness. Wagner represents homeless people as resistant political subjects, challenging American individualism and "dominant cultural norms of work and family," 3. For an overview of the literature on women and homelessness, see, Sylvia Novac, Ph.D., Joyce Brown, M.S.W., M.E.S. and Carmen Bourbonnais, B.A., No Room of Her Own, *A Literature Review on Women and Homelessness,* November, 2006, available at http://www.nrchmi.samhsa.gov/(S(qlnxv2zgyur1n545h2cfj2yn))/Resource/No-Room-of-Her-Own-a-Literature-Review-on-Women-and-Homelessness-35131.aspx (May 17, 2011).

17. Mitch Duneier's *Sidewalk* (New York: Farrar, Strauss & Giroux, 1999) focuses on the intellectual and political interests, entrepreneurial activity, and cultural work of homeless and marginally housed magazine and book vendors in New York City. The classic study by Elliott Liebow, *Tell Them Who I am, The Lives of Homeless Women* (New York: The Free Press, 1993), remains one of the compelling and influential portraits of single homeless women. Talmadge Wright's *Out of Place: Homeless Mobilizations, Subcities and Contested Landscapes* (Albany: State University of New York Press, 1997) focuses on political organizing, communal ties, cultural and artistic production among homeless communities. See also Susan Finley and Marcelo Diversi, "Critical Homelessness: Expanding Narratives of Inclusive Democracy, *Cultural Studies, Critical Methodologies* 10 (2010): 4–13; and Finley, "From the Streets to the Classrooms: Street Intellectuals as Teacher Educators, Collaborations in Revolutionary Pedagogy," in *Democratic Curriculum Theory and Practice: Retrieving Public Spaces* (New York: Educator's International Press), 113–126. The most comprehensive oral history of homeless people to date is *Voices from the Street, Truths about Homelessness from Sisters of the Road* (Portland, OR: Gray Sunshine Publishing, 2007).

18. "Status Report on Hunger and Homelessness in America's Cities, a 24-city survey," United States Conference of Mayors, December 2005, 5, www.usmayors.org/hungersurvey/2005/HH2005FINAL.pdf (May 17, 2011). The report estimates that the number of individuals suffering from some form of severe and persistent mental illness at 22 percent and those with significant substance abuse issues at 30 percent. These figures do not account for the overlap between the two groups, which suggests that individuals with either issue may comprise significantly less than half of the homeless population as a whole.

19. See Peter Marcuse, "Neutralizing Homelessness," *Socialist Review* 88, no. 1 (1988): 69–97. Marcuse's assessment of the prevalence of mental health and substance abuse issues among homeless communities has been challenged in more recent studies. See also, D. Stanley Eitzen, Kathryn D. Talley, Doug A. Timmer, *Paths to Homelessness Extreme Poverty and the Urban Housing Crisis* (Boulder, CO: Westview, 1984), esp. 10–30.

20. E. D. Sclar, "Homelessness and Housing Policy: A Game of Musical Chairs" *American Journal of Public Health* 80, no. 9. (September 1990): 1039–1040. See Paul Koegel, M. Audrey Burnam, and Jim Baumohl, "The Causes of Homelessness," *Homelessness in America,* ed. Jim Baumohl (Phoenix, Oryx Press, 1996), 24–33.

21. "Universal Declaration of Human Rights," http://www.un.org/en/documents/udhr/index.shtml#a25 (May 15, 2011).

22. See, Peter Marcuse, "Neutralizing Homelessness," *Socialist Review* 88, no. 1: 69–97; See for example, Peter Rossi, *Down and Out in America, The Origins of Homelessness* (Chicago, IL: University of Chicago Press, 1989); James. D. Wright and Beth A. Rubin, Is "Homelessness a Housing Problem?" *Housing Policy Debate* 3, no. 2 (1999): 987–56; James D. Wright and Julie A. Lam, "Housing and the Low-Income Housing

Supply," *Social Policy* 17, no. 4 (1987): 48–53; Kim Hopper, "'More than Passing Strange': Homelessness and Mental Illness in New York City," *American Ethnologist* 15, no. 1 (February 1988): 155–167; David A. Snow, Susan G. Baker, Leon Anderson, and Michael Martin, "The Myth of Pervasive Mental Illness Among the Homeless," *Social Problems* 33, no. 5 (1986): 407–423; Arline Mathieu, "The Medicalization of Homelessness and the Theater of Repression," *Medical Anthropology Quarterly* 7, no. 2 (1993): 170–184.

23. Vincent Lyon-Callo, *Inequality, Poverty and Neoliberal Governance, Activist Ethnography in the Homeless Sheltering Industry* (Toronto: Higher Education Press of Toronto Press Inc., 2008); see esp. 57–96 in Jean Calterone Williams, *"A Roof Over My Head," Homeless Women and the Shelter Industry* (Boulder, CO: University of Colorado Press, 2003); see also, Kurt Borchard, *The Word on the Street, Homeless Men in Las Vegas* (Reno: University of Nevada Press, 2005), 103–132.

24. Lyon-Callo, *Neliberalism*, 111.

25. Ibid, 86–107.

26. Anthony Marcus, *Where have all the Homeless Gone? The Making and Unmaking of a Crisis* (New York: Berghahn Books, 2006), 152–53.

27. Arloc Sherman and Chad Stone, "Income Gaps Between Very Rich and Everyone Else More Than Tripled In Last Three Decades, New Data Show," Center on Budget and Policy Priorities, June 25, 2010, http://www.cbpp.org/cms/index.cfm?fa=view&id=3220 (May 17, 2011).

28. Thomas M. Shapiro, Tatjana Meschede, and Laura Sullivan, "The Racial Wealth Gap Increases Fourfold," Institute on Assets and Social Policy Research and Policy Brief, May 2010, 1.

29. Dwight D. Eisenhower, Military Industrial Complex Speech, 1961, http://www.h-net.org/~hst306/documents/indust.html (May 17, 2011).

30. Ibid.

31. Rev. Martin Luther King, "Beyond Vietnam: A Time to Break Silence," April 4, 1967, http://www.hartford-hwp.com/archives/45a/058.html (May 17, 2011).

32. "The Cost of War," The National Priorities Project, www.nationalpriorities.org/costofwar_home (May 15, 2011).

33. Joseph Stiglitz and Linda Bilmes, *The Three Trillion Dollar War* (New York: W.W. Norton & Co., 2008), xv. For a conservative estimate, see Amy Belasco, "The Cost of Iraq, Afghanistan, and Other Global War on Terror Operations Since 9/11," Congressional Research Service, July 16, 2010, 1–2.

34. The War Resisters League, "Where Your Income Tax Money Really Goes," http://www.warresisters.org/pages/piechart.htm (May 17, 2011).

35. "Facts and Media," The National Coalition for Homeless Veterans, http://www.nchv.org/background.cfm (June 15, 2010).

36. See the Western Regional Advocacy Project, *Without Housing: Decades of Federal Housing Cutbacks, Massive Homelessness and Housing Policy Failures,* 2006, www.wraphome.org/pages/downloads/high_school_workbook.pdf (May 17, 2011).

37. See Tara Herrivel and Paul Wright, *Prison Profiteers, Who Makes Money From Mass Incarceration* (New York: New Press, 2007).

38. Marc Mauer, "The Impact of Mandatory Sentencing Policies in the United States, Prepared for the Standing Committee on Legal and Constitutional Affairs," The Sentencing Project, October 28, 2009, 2 (May 17, 2011).

39. John Schmitt, Kris Warner, and Sarika Gupta, "The High Budgetary Cost of Incarceration," Center for Economic and Policy Research, June 2010, 1, www.cepr.net/.../the-high-budgetary-cost-of-incarceration/ (May 17, 2011).

40. Michelle Alexander, *The New Jim Crow, Mass Incarceration in the Age of Color Blindness* (New York: The New Press, 2010), 39.

41. *One in 31, the Long Reach of American Corrections*, Public Safety Performance Project, Pew Center on the States, March 2009, 12, www.pewcenteronthestates.org/... /PSPP_1in31_report_FINAL_WEB_3-26-09.pdf—Similar (May 17, 2011).

42. "Options to Stabilize Prison Populations in Washington: Interim Report," January 2006, Washington State Institute for Public Policy, 2, http://www.scribd.com /doc/11202216/Options-to-Stabilize-Prison-Populations-in-WashingtonInterim-Report (May 17, 2011).

43. Figures on 2010 tuition provided by Carol Diem, U.W. Director of Institutional Research, July 13, 2011. The 2010 figure applies to the 2009–2010 academic year.

44. Ryan S. King and Marc Mauer, "The War on Marijuana: The Transformation of the War on Drugs," *Harm Reduction Journal*, 3, no. 6 (2006): 3, http://www. harmreductionjournal.com/content/3/1/6 (July 13, 2011).

45. See Neil DeMause, "The Recession and the 'Deserving Poor' Poverty finally on media radar—but only when it hits the middle class," March 2009, Fairness and Accuracy in Reporting (FAIR), http://www.fair.org/index.php?page=3726 (May 17, 2011).

46. See esp. 35–62 and 138–53 in Marcus, *Where have all the homeless gone?*

47. *Homes Not Handcuffs: The Criminalization of Homelessness in U.S. Cities*, the National Law Center on Homelessness and Poverty and the National Coalition for the Homeless, July 2009, 10–11. See also Barbara Ehrenreich's op-ed piece I in the wake of the report's release, "Is it Now a Crime to Be Poor?" *New York Times*, August 8, 2009, http://www.nytimes.com/2009/08/09/opinion/09ehrenreich.html (May 17, 2011).

48. See Don Mitchell, *The Right to the City, Social Justice and the Fight for Public Space* (New York: The Guilford Press, 2003) 16–17, and Anthony Marcus, *Where have all the homeless gone?* 136–137.

49. Mitchell, *The Right to the City*, 167.

50. Timothy A. Gibson, *Securing the Spectacular City, The Politics of Revitalization and Homelessness in Downtown Seattle* (New York: Lexington Books, 2004), 86. See also Stacy Warren, "Disneyfication of the Metropolis: Popular Resistance in Seattle," *Journal of Urban Affairs* 16, no. 2 (1994): 89–107.

51. The 2009 Annual Homeless Assessment Report to Congress, U.S. Department of Housing and Urban Development Office of Community Planning and Development, June 2010, i, www.hudhre.info/documents/5thHomelessAssessmentReport.pdf (May 17, 2011).

52. See Martha R. Burt, Laudan Y. Aron, America's Homeless II, Populations and Services, the Urban Institute, January 1, 2000.

53. "United States Conference of Mayors Status Report on Hunger in Homelessness in America's Cities" (December, 2009), 1, www.usmayors.org/pressreleases/.../USCM HungercompleteWEB2009.pdf.

54. See Danilo Pelletiere, Ph.D., *Renters in Foreclosure: Defining the Problem, Identifying Solutions*, National Low Income Housing Coalition, January 2009, www.nlihc.org/ doc/renters-in-foreclosure.pdf (May 17, 2011). Pelletiere estimates that 20 percent of properties foreclosed on during the crisis have been rentals. Given, moreover, that many are multi-unit properties, the report estimates that "renters make up roughly 40% of the families facing eviction," 4.

55. *Foreclosure to Homelessness: the Forgotten Victims of the Subprime Crisis*, April 15, 2008 report by the National Coalition for the Homeless, 4, www.nationalhomeless.org/... /foreclosure/foreclosure_report.pdf (May 17, 2011).

56. In March 2010, the Congressional Budget Office estimated the cost of TARP at $109 billion, down from an estimated high of $356 billion. Annalyn Censky, "Price Tag of TARP bailout $109 billion," March 18, 2010, CNN Money, http://money.cnn. com/2010/03/17/news/economy/CBO_TARP/index.htm (May 17, 2011).

57. "Out of Reach," the National Low Income Housing Coalition Report of 2007–2008, 4, www.nlihc.org/oor/oor2008/ (May 17, 2011). Data on efficiency and one-bedroom apartments were supplied by Megan DeCrappeo, NLIHC research analyst in a 6/23/11 phone interview. Calculations of hours needed to work to support FMR rents are my own.

58. These figures do not take into account the fact that the "roughly 8.8 million renter households—almost one-quarter of all renters—reported household income below what a full-time job at their state's current minimum wage would pay today," "Out of Reach," 5.

59. "Hunger and Homeless Survey, A Status Report on Hunger and Homelessness in America's Cities, A 23-City Survey," The United States Conference of Mayors, December 2007, 15, www.usmayors.org/hhsurvey2007/hhsurvey07.pdf (May 17, 2011).

60. "Social Security Fact Sheet, 2008 Social Security Changes," Social Security Administration, 2, www.ssa.gov/pressoffice/factsheets/colafacts2008.pdf (15 July 2011). Of 7.5 million recipients nationwide, "More than half (56 percent) had no income other than their SSI payment"; only "[t]hirty-five percent of SSI recipients also received Social Security benefits" (Social Security Online, Research, Statistics and Policy Analysis Data, http://www.ssa.gov/policy/docs/statcomps/ssi _asr/2008/index.html).

61. Brent Walsh and Bryan Denson, "Getting disability payments can be a fight to the death," *Oregonian,* August 3, 2008, http://www.oregonlive.com/special/index. ssf/2008/08/getting_disability_payments_ca.html (May 17, 2011).

62. Cydney Gillis, "Governor, legislator disagree on disability reform," *Real Change,* January 27, 2010, http://www.olympianews.org/2010/01/27/governor-legislator -disagree-on-disability-reform/ (May 17, 2011).

63. For an overview of the declining HUD budget and its impact on homelessness, see the 2006 Western Regional Advocacy Center, *Without Housing;* and "HUD Fiscal Year 2008 Budget Summary," 1, www.hud.gov/about/budget/fy08/ (May 17, 2011).

64. "HUD Fiscal Year 2008 Budget Summary," 3.

65. *Without Housing,* 38–9.

66. *Without Housing,* 1.

67. James D. Wright and Beth Rubin, "Is Homelessness a Housing Problem," 943.

68. Sarah Olkon, "Chicago Housing Authority to hold lottery for Section 8 voucher waiting list," April 16, 2008, *Chicago Tribune,* http://articles.chicagotribune.com/keyword /vouchers/recent/4 (May 17, 2011).

69. Ibid.

70. Seattle Housing Authority Press release, June 12, 2006, http://www.seattlehousing. org/Newspage/newsarticles/Section8waitclosed.htm.

71. A survey of literature on homelessness among the elderly is available via a National Coalition for the Homeless fact sheet at www.NationalHomeless.org /factsheets/elderly.html (May 17, 2011). A 2003 report by the Health and Human Resources and Services Administration, "Homeless and Elderly: Understanding the Special Health Care Needs of Elderly Persons who are Homeless," http: //www.nrchmi.samhsa.gov/Search.aspx?tagId=45381&search=elder+homelessnes s (May 17, 2011), sites a variety of factors that contribute to homelessness among the elderly, including long waiting lists for affordable senior housing, as well as

"lack of information about resources and eligibility requirements," 8. The report also foregrounds the range of acute and chronic medical issues and risks of victimization among elderly homeless people, many of who may feel safer sleeping outdoors than in shelters or may be unable to access shelters due to mobility issues. The National Coalition for the Homeless fact sheet also notes that people in their fifties and sixties who have experienced protracted periods of homelessness may suffer from health issues more commonly found in much older people.

72. HUD defines a person as chronically homeless if he or she is "an unaccompanied homeless individual with a disabling condition who has either been continuously homeless for a year or more or has had at least four episodes of homelessness in the past three years," who has "been on the streets or in emergency shelters (i.e., not in transitional or permanent housing) during these episodes." "Third Annual Homeless Assessment Report to Congress," U.S. Department of Housing and Urban Development, Office of Community Planning and Development, 13, www.hudhre.info/documents/3rdHo melessAssessmentReport.pdf (May 17, 2011).

73. *Without Housing*, 2006, 9.

74. The 2009 "U.S. Mayors' Report on Hunger and Homelessness in American Cities" indicates that 16 cities or "64% of respondents, reported a leveling or decrease in the number of homeless *individuals.*" The report also notes, however, that "[n]ineteen cities, 76 percent of respondents reported an increase in family homelessness," 1.

75. A two-part series in the *Seattle PostGlobe* (Eric Ruthford, "Officials plan to end Homelessness by 2014. Can it Happen?" June 25, 2010, http://seattlepostglobe. org/2010/06/25/plan-to-end-homeless-not-meeting-the-needs (May 17, 2011) includes interviews with a number of Seattle service providers offering bleak assessment of progress in the plans.

76. See George Lakoff, HUD is Trying to Privatize and Mortgage off All of America's Public Housing," *Huffington Post*, May 21, 2010, http://www.huffingtonpost.com /george-lakoff/hud-is-trying-to-privatiz_b_585069.html (May 17, 2011).

77. *Homes Not Handcuffs*, 10.

78. *A Dream Denied: The Criminalization of Homelessness in U.S. Cities*, a report by the National Coalition for the Homeless and the National Law Center on Homelessness and Poverty, January 2006, 11, www.nlchp.org/content/pubs/ADreamDenied1 –11-06.pdf (May 17, 2011).

79. Ibid, 9.

80. *Homes Not Handcuffs*, 10

81. *A Dream Denied*, 11.

82. Kim Hopper, "More than Passing Strange," 163.

83. Frances Fox Pivens and Richard Cloward, *Regulating the Poor, the Functions of Public Welfare* (New York: Pantheon Books, 1971, Repr. 1993), 15.

84. For one of the most comprehensive studies of the link between poverty and mental illness, see Christopher G. Hudson, Ph.D., "Socioeconomic Status and Mental Illness: Tests of the Social Causation and Selection Hypotheses," *American Journal of Orthopsychiatry*, 75, no. 1(2005): 3–18.

85. "Why sleep is important and what happens when you don't get enough," American Psychological Association, www.apa.org/topics/sleep.why.aspx. As recently as 2001, the Bush administration deemed sleep deprivation a form of torture, condemning it in a US State Department report on torture techniques practiced in Turkey, Israel, and Jordan. See " 'Stress and Duress:' Drawing the Line between Interrogation and Torture," Virginia Ladisch, *Crimes of War Project*, April 24, 2003, www.crimesofwar.org/onnews/news-stress.html (May 17, 2011).

86. Ashley Fantz "Teen 'sport killings' of homeless on the rise," CNN.com, 20 February 2007, http://www.cnn.com/2007/US/02/19/homeless.attacks/index.html (May 17, 2011).

87. *Hate, Violence and Death on Main Street USA: A Report on Hate Crimes and Violence Against People Experiencing Homelessness 2008*, National Coalition for the Homeless, August 2009, 10, www.nationalhomeless.org/ . . . /hatecrimes/hate_report_2008.pdf (May 17, 2011).

88. "Teen 'sport killings' of homeless on the rise." See also "Hate, Violence and Death on Mainstreet USA in 2005," 35.

89. "Florida leads nation in attacks on homeless," *Orlando Sentinel*, April 30, 2008, articles.orlandosentinel.com/ . . . /homeless30_1_homeless-people-attacks-on-homeless-homeless-men (May 17, 2011).

90. Dave Birkland, "One Less Bum on the Face of the Earth," *Seattle Times*, August 18, 1999. A memorial webpage for David Ballenger can be found at http://www.findagrave.com/cgi-bin/fg.cgi?page=gr&GRid=17976575 (May 17, 2011).

91. "Barely getting by: a special appeal, we need your support to get *Real Change* on stable Footing, http://www.realchangenews.org/index.php/site/printer-friendly/3398 / (May 17, 2011)

92. The characterization of Seattle's mainstream media, the *Seattle Times* and the *Post-Intelligencer* is Timothy Gibson's, 264.

93. See Gibson, *Securing the Spectacular City*, especially 171–181.

94. "SHARE/WHEEL reach shelter agreement, Homeless shelter organization will participate in Safe Harbors system," Seattle City Government News Release, April 12, 2006, http://www.cityofseattle.net/mayor/newsdetail.asp?ID=6054&dept=40 (May 16, 2011).

95. "Homeless Management Information Systems (HMIS) HUDHRE.info, U.S. Department of Housing and Urban Development Homelessness Resource Exchange, http://www.hudhre.info/hmis/ (May 16, 2011).

96. "SHARE/WHEEL reach shelter agreement."

97. http://www.sharewheel.org/ (May 17, 2011).

98. Ibid.

99. Adam Hyla, "Vital Service, Vital Talks" For SHARE and city, there's light at the end of the tunnel, *Real Change*, April 13, 2006.

100. On the history of the Women in Black Movement, see http://www.womeninblack.org.uk/ Who%20are%20we.htm (May 17, 2011).

101. "Who are Women in Black?" Women in Black for Justice. Against War. http://www.womeninblack.org/en/about (May 17, 2011).

102. Ibid.

103. "King County Homeless Death Review," Public Health—Seattle & King County, 2003, 4, www.kingcounty.gov/healthservices/health/ . . . /health/publichealth/ . . . /hchn_death_review.ashx (May 17, 2011).

104. For an examination of the range of views of homeless women on social policies impacting homelessness see Meredith L. Ralston, *"Nobody Wants to Hear Our Truth," Homeless Women and Theories of the Welfare State* (Westport, CT: Greenwood Press, 1996).

105. See Catherine Silva, "Racially Restrictive Covenants: Enforcing Neighborhood Segregation in Seattle," Seattle Civil Rights and Labor History Project, http://depts.washington.edu/civilr/covenants_report.htm (May 17, 2011); Quintard Taylor, *The Forging of a Black Community, Seattle's Central District from 1870 through the Civil Rights Era* (Seattle, WA: University of Washington Press, 1994);

and Douglas S. Massey and Nancy A. Denton, *American Apartheid, Segregation and the Making of the Underclass* (Cambridge, MA: Harvard University Press, 1993).

106. The National Fair Housing Alliance reports a spike in housing discrimination complaints in 2008, which it attributes to the foreclosure crisis and "internet advertising that violates fair housing laws." Fair Housing Trends Report, "Fair Housing Enforcement: Time for a Change," May 1, 2009, 3, www.nationalfairhousing.org/LinkClick.aspx?fileticket...tabid (May 17, 2011). On the impact of subprime lending on African Americans, see Monique Morris, "Discrimination and Mortgage Lending in America: A Summary of the Disparate Impact of Subprime Mortgage Lending on African Americans," NAACP, 2009, action.naacp.org/page/-/resources/Lending_Discrimination.pdf (May 17, 2011).

107. See David Bacon, *Illegal People: How Globalization Creates Migration and Criminalizes Immigrants* (Boston, MA: Beacon Press, 2008).

108. Jordan, B.K., Maarmar, C.R., Fairbank, J.A., & Schlenger, W.E., "Problems in Families of Male Vietnam Veterans with Post-Traumatic Stress Disorder," *Journal of Consulting and Clinical Psychology*, 60, no. 6 (1992): 916–26. Cited in *Gulf War and Health*, Volume 6, *Physiologic, Psychologic, and Psychosocial Effects of Deployment-Related Stress,"* Committee on Gulf War and Health: Physiologic, Psychologic, and Psychosocial Effects of Deployment Related Stress (Washington, D.C.: Institute of the National Academes, 2008), 285. See also Michelle R. Ancharoff, James F. Munroe, and Lisa M. Fisher, "The Legacy of Combat Trauma, Clinical Implications of Intergenerational Transmission," *Intergenerational Handbook of Multigenerational Legacies of Trauma*, Yael Danieli, ed. (New York: Plenum Press, 1998), 257–276.

109. As summarized by Peter J. Mercier and Judith D. Mercier in *Battle Cries on the Home Front, Domestic Violence in the Military Family* (Springfield: Charles C. Thomas Publisher, 2000), 4. On the impact of war and militarism on women and children in war zones, see Ann Jones, *The War's Not Over When It's Over, Women Speak Out from the Ruins of War* (New York: Metropolitan Books, 2010).

110. On battering and normative gender roles, see Ginny Nicarthy, *Getting Free, You Can End Abuse and Take Back your Life* (Emeryville, CA: Seal Press, 2004) 1–49; and Ann Jones, *The Next Time She'll be Dead* (Boston: Beacon Press, 2000),106–128.

111. Adverse Health Conditions and Health Risk Behaviors Associated with Intimate Partner Violence—United States, 2005," Morbidity and Mortality Weekly Report, Centers for Disease Control, February 8, 2008 / 57(05);113–117, http://www.cdc.gov/mmwr/preview/mmwrhtml/mm5705a1.htm#tab1 (May 16, 2011).

112. Ibid.

113. Ibid.

114. See, for example, L. Bensley, J. Van Eenwyk, and K. Wynkoop Simmons, "Childhood Family Violence History and Women's Risk for Intimate Partner Violence and Poor Health," *American Journal of Preventive Medicine* 25, no. 1 (2003): 38–44.

115. Center for Disease Control epidemiologist Michele Black, Ph.D., in an interview, following the release of the 2005 CDC report on IPV. Daniel Denoon, "CDC: 1 in 4 Women, 1 in 9 Men Suffer Intimate-Partner Violence," WebMD Health News, February 7, 2008, www.ncdsv.org/images/CDC_1in4Women1in9MenSufferIPV_2-7-08.pdf.

116. On the arbitrary distinction between homeless and battered women, see Jean Calterone Williams, "Domestic violence and poverty," *Frontiers* 19, no. 2 (1998): 143–165.

117. Suzanne L. Wenzel, Barbara D. Leake, and Lillian Gelberg, "Risk Factors for Major Violence Among Homeless Women," *Journal of Interpersonal Violence* 16, no. 8 (2001): 739–752, 744; the definition of "major violence" can be found on 740.

118. Ibid, 744.

119. Suzanne L. Wenzel, Ph.D., Barbara D. Leake, Ph.D., Lillian Gelberg, MD, Ph.D., "Health of Homeless Women with Recent Experience of Rape," *Journal of General Internal Medicine* 15 (2000) , 265–268, 266.

120. Much has been written on homeless women's strategies for appearing housed. Marjorie Bard treats the issue at length in *Shadow Women: Homeless Women's Survival Stories* (New York: Sheed and Ward, 1990).

121. "2008 Annual One Night Count of People who are Homeless in King County, WA," Seattle King County Coalition on Homelessness, 5, www.homelessinfo.org /downloads/2008_ONC_Report.pdf (May 17, 2011).

122. Melissa Farley, Ph.D. and Howard Barkan, Dr., Ph.D., "Prostitution, Violence Against Women and Post-Traumatic Stress Disorder," *Women and Health* 27, no. 3 (1998): 37–49, http://www.prostitutionresearch.com/ProsViolPosttrauStress.html (July 13, 2011).

123. "Green River Killer Gary Ridgway pleaded guilty," *Seattle Times*, November, 19, 2004, www.seattletimes.nwsource.com/html/greenriverkillings/.

124. Marc Mauer, "The Changing Racial Dynamics of the War on Drugs," The Sentencing Project, April 2009, 1, www.sentencingproject.org/search/dp_raceanddrugs.pdf (May 17, 2011).

125. John Schmitt, Kris Warner, and Sarika Gupta, "The High Budgetary Cost of Incarceration," Center for Economic and Policy Research, June 2010, 2, www.cepr. net/.../the-high-budgetary-cost-of-incarceration/ (May 17, 2011).

126. Ibid., 3.

127. Cited by Robin Levi and Judith Appel, "Collateral Consequences: Denial of Basic Social Services Based Upon Drug Use," Drug Policy Alliance, July 13, 2003, 1, www. drugpolicy.org/.../Postincarceration_abuses_memo.pdf (May 17, 2011).

128. Mauer, "Changing Dynamics," 8.

129. "Cocaine and Crack," The Drug Policy Alliance, http://www.drugpolicy.org/facts /drug-facts/cocaine-and-crack (May 15, 2011); see Marc Mauer, "Beyond the Fair Sentencing Act," *The Nation*, December 27, 2010, http://www.thenation.com /article/157009/beyond-fair-sentencing-act (May 15, 2011). The law, reduced, but did not eliminate the sentencing disparities and does not apply retroactively.

130. Stuart Taylor, Jr. "America's Prison Spree Has Brutal Impact, The Trend Toward Long-Term Imprisonment of Nonviolent Offenders has Made Us No Safer While Ruining Countless Lives," *National Journal Magazine*, November 14, 2009, http://conventions. nationaljournal.com/njmagazine/or_20091114_7374.php (May 17, 2011).

131. "Schools and Prisons: Fifty Years After *Brown v. Board of Education*," The National Sentencing Project, 2004, 1, www.sentencingproject.org/pdfs/brownvboard.pdf (May 17, 2011).

132. Michelle Alexander, *The New Jim Crow, Mass Incarceration in the Age of Colorblindness* (New York: The New Press, 2010), 225.

133. Ibid., 83.

134. Robin Levi and Judith Appel, "Collateral Consequences," 1.

135. *United States of America, Rights for all, "Not part of my sentence," Violations of the Human Rights of Women in Custody*, Amnesty International, March 1993, 3, www. amnesty.org/en/library/info/AMR51/019/1999 (May 17, 2011).

136. Tara Herivel, "Wreaking Medical Mayhem on Women Prisoners in Washington State," in *Prison Nation, The Warehousing of America's Poor*, ed. Tara Herivel and Paul Wright (New York: Routledge, 2003), 174.

137. Robert L. Jamieson, " 'Trash' fire turns out to be a man," *Post-Intelligencer*, July 1, 2006, www.seattlepi.com/default/article/Trash-fire-turns-out-to-be-a-man -1207801.php.

138. See Amy Rolph, "Women in Black hold vigil for slain woman, Tonya Smith, 42, was on path to recovery," *Seattle PI*, July 19, 2006, www.seattlepi.com/.../Women-in -Black-hold-vigil-for-slain-homeless-woman-1209382.php -(May 17, 2011).

139. Michael Frisch, *A Shared Authority, Essays on the Craft and Meaning of Oral and Public History* (Albany, NY: Suny Press, 1990), 84.

140. For an indepth critique of "academics construct[ing] knowledge about oppression from the comfort of a privileged life," see Marcelo Diversi and Claudio Moreira, *Betweener Talk, Decolonizing Knowledge Production, Pedagogy and Praxis* (Walnut Creek, CA: Left Coast Press, 2009).

141. Alessandro Portelli, *The Death of Luigi Trastulli and Other Stories* (Albany: SUNY Press, 1991), 52.

142. Ibid.

143. Ibid.

144. Sandy Polishuk, *Sticking it to the Union, An Oral History of the Life and Times of Julia Ruutila* (New York: Palgrave Macmillan, 2003), 9.

145. Portelli, *The Death of Luigi Trastulli*, 52.

2 "Mama Pam"

1. Texas, it is worth noting, is at the forefront of the push for abstinence-only sex education, which recent studies have correlated with rising rates of pregnancy, abortions, and sexually transmitted infections. See Tamar Lewin, "After Long Decline, Teenage Pregnancy Rate Rises," *New York Times*, January 26, 2010, http://www.nytimes. com/2010/01/27/us/27teen.html (May 15, 2011).

2. See "Herstory of Domestic Violence: A Timeline of the Battered Women's Movement," Minnesota Center for Violence and Abuse, http://www.mincava.umn. edu/documents/herstory/herstory.html (June 16, 2011); see also R. Emerson Dobash and Russell T. Dobash, *Women, Violence and Social Change* (New York: Routledge, 1992).

3 Annamarie Tailfeathers

1. Terry Hansen, "Seattle Police Slay Native Woodcarver and an Outraged Community is Asking Why," *Indian Country Today*, September 7, 2010, http://www. indiancountrytoday.com/national/Seattle-police-slay-Native-woodcarver-and-an -outraged-community-is-asking-why-102346199.html (May 17, 2011).

2. Ibid.

3. "County pays $925,000 to settle part of Chasse lawsuit," *Portland Tribune*, July 2, 2009, http://www.portlandtribune.com/news/story.php?story_id=124656161331502700 (May 16, 2011).

4. Phone interview with John Fox, June 2008.
5. A south Seattle neighborhood.

4 Elizabeth Thatcher

1. *HistoryLink.org*, The Free Online Encyclopedia of Washington State, http://www. historylink.org/index.cfm?DisplayPage=output.cfm&file_id=3837 (May 17, 2011).
2. Ibid.
3. Ibid.
4. Good Shepherd Center Artist Spaces Near Completion," *Seattle Press Online*, January 17, 2002, http://archive.seattlepressonline.com/article-9427.html (June 15, 2010).
5. Knute Berger, "Breed and Weed: In this biotech center, it's time we came to terms with Washington's role in the terrible history of eugenics," *Seattle Weekly*, Wednesday, April 16, 2003, http://www.seattleweekly.com/2003-04-16/news/breed-and-weed.php/.
6. While Elizabeth's teeth were extracted at Walla Walla, as Herivel notes in her article, "Wreaking Medical Havoc on Women Prisoners in Washington State," WCCW employed a dentist, Dr. Carl Weaver, who was "infamous for his fetishistic preference for extractions," and whose "vanity plates" read, "Dr. Yank," 178.

5 "Sweet Pea"

1. In an op-ed piece by a writer identified only as "South Seattle Top Cop," that purports to dispel widely held myths about gangs takes note of the fact that there are, in fact, white crips. See "South Seattle Cop on Kids, Gangs, Violence & Self-Hate," *Rainier Valley Post*, October 2, 2009, http://www.rainiervalleypost.com/south-seattle-cop-on -kids-gangs-violence-self-hate/ (May 17, 2011).

6 Debra Martinson

1. For more background on the practice, see Armando Favazza, M.D., *Bodies Under Siege, Self-Mutilation and Body Modification in Culture and Psychiatry* (Baltimore, MD: Johns Hopkins University Press). The 1990s saw a significant rise in prevalence among adolescents in particular, spurring broader reevaluation of the practices, particularly as strategies for coping with depression and posttraumatic stress related to child and adolescent sexual abuse. According to Julie Mehta, An estimated "3 million people in the United states engage in self-injury." "Hurts so Bad." *Current Health* 31.4 (Dec. 2004), 2, juliemehta.com/site/health_files/CHdepression.pdf (May 17, 2011); Joan Brumberg observes that "[O]nce a highly isolated group, people who practice self-harm and self-injury now participate in a virtual community, incorporating more than 400 internet message boards to share thoughts and experiences. The Internet provides support—sometimes to stop the behavior, sometimes to continue it." "Are We Facing an Epidemic of Self-Injury?" *Chronicle of Higher Education* 53, no. 16 (2006), http://chronicle.com/article/Are-We-Facing-an-Epidemic-of/5820 (May 17, 2011).

2. A psychiatric ward at Harborview Medical Center in Seattle.
3. Debra subsequently graduated from the University of Texas Arlington.
4. Dusty Miller, *Women Who Hurt Themselves, a Book of Hope and Understanding* (New York: Basic Books, 1994); Judith Herman, *The Aftermath of Violence, From Domestic Violence to Political Terror* (New York: Basic Books, 1992, 1997).

7 Anitra Freeman

1. Fellowship of Reconciliation is an interfaith, international organization with branches in more than forty countries with the mission of "replac[ing] violence, war, racism, and economic injustice with nonviolence, peace, and justice." See the Fellowship of Reconciliation website at http://www.forusa.org/ (May 17, 2011).
2. The Seattle Grannies identify their mission and goals respectively as "promot[ing] global peace, justice, and social and economic equality by raising public awareness through the medium of song and humor," and "challeng[ing]...audiences to work to bring about the social changes that are required in order to end economic oppression, particularly of women and children, and to end racial inequality, environmental destruction, human rights violations, and arms proliferation." See the website for the Seattle Raging Grannies at http://www.seattleraginggrannies.com/ (May 17, 2011).
3. See "Woman found dead at camp is identified," *Seattle Times*, June 1, 2000. http://community.seattletimes.nwsource.com/archive/?date=20000601&slug=4023982 (15 May 2011); and Robert L. Jamieson, Jr., "Ceremony honors slain homeless Bearing silent witness to unseen casualties of violence and tragedy," *Seattle PI,* April 18, 2001, http://www.seattlepi.com/news/article/Ceremony-honors-slain-homeless-1052514.php#ixzz1MYpKbexH (May 15, 2011).

8 Roxane Roberts

1. Rachel Smith, "CORE's Drive for Equal Employment in Downtown Seattle, 1964, *The Seattle Civil Rights and Labor Project,"* http://depts.washington.edu/civilr/core_deeds.htm (May 17, 2011).
2. Ibid.
3. "The Defender Association, providing public defense in Seattle and King County Since 1969," www.defender.org (May 17, 2011).
4. Phone interview with Jackie Rye, January 26, 2011.
5. "Holds Ups Jail Mother," *Spokane Daily Chronicle*, December 20, 1979, 6, http://news.google.com/newspapers?id=xK0SAAAAIBAJ&sjid=MfkDAAAAIBAJ&pg=7218%2C1370819 (June 16, 2011); "Woman Bank Robber Gets Aid," *Tri-City Herald*, January 4, 1980, 33, http://news.google.com/newspapers?id=2r00AAAAIBAJ&sjid=e4cFAAAAIBAJ&dq=helyn%20walton&pg=2982%2C1356580 (June 16, 2011).
6. Clark Brooke, "The Seattle School Boycott of 1966," Seattle Civil Rights and Labor History Project, http://depts.washington.edu/civilr/school_boycott.htm (May 17, 2011).
7. Ibid.
8. Mark Robinson, "The Early History of the UW Black Student Union," *Seattle Civil Rights and Labor History Project,* http://depts.washington.edu/civilr/BSU_intro.htm (May 17, 2011).

9. Ibid.
10. Ibid.
11. Ibid.
12. I have not been able to substantiate this claim.
13. Roxane's mother had worked on the psychiatric ward at Harborview.
14. Roxane attended the National Lawyer's Guild People's College of Law for a brief period in the 1970s.
15. In a December 27, 2010 phone interview, Bill Hilliard, vice president of the Office of Minority Affairs at the University of Washington from 1968 to 1975, indicated that there was a funding crisis due to the unexpectedly high rates of recruitment in the newly emerging SEP Program and that while they scrambled to fill the funding gap, and succeeded, some students may have felt compelled to take out loans in the meantime.
16. *The State of Washington v. Roxane Elizabeth Roberts*, Superior Court of Washington for King County, No. 99-1-50418-2 KNT.
17. State of Washington v. Raymond Edward Bartley and Roxane Elizabeth Roberts, Superior Court of Washington for King County, No. 00-C-06979-7.

9 Delores Loann Winston

1. Raised in Chicago, Till was visiting relatives in Money, Mississippi, when he was killed. When Till's body was recovered from the Tallahatchie River, a seventy-five-pound cotton-gin fan tied around his neck with barbed wire, one eye had been gouged out and he'd been beaten severely enough to sustain several broken bones, and then shot in the head at point blank range. Roy Bryant and his J. W. Milam, who were tried and acquitted for the crime, subsequently recounted the killing in an interview with *Look* magazine. See Mamie Till-Mobley's account (with Christopher Benson) in *Death of Innocence: The Story of the Hate Crime that Changed America* (New York: Random House, 2002); see also *The Lynching of Emmett Till, A Documentary Narrative*, ed. Christopher Metress (Charlottesville: University of Virginia Press, 2002).
2. The history of the Black Panthers in Portland is extensively documented in "The Seattle Black Panther Party History and Memory Project," part of the Seattle Civil Rights and Labor History Project, http://depts.washington.edu/civilr/BPP.htm.
3. Henry W. McGee, Jr., "Gentrification, Integration or Displacement: the Seattle Story," at "BlackPast.org, Remembered and Reclaimed: an Online Reference Guide to African American History," Quintard Taylor, editor, http://www.blackpast.org/?q=perspectives/gentrification-integration-or-displacement-seattle-story. The complete article was originally published in "Seattle 1990–2006: Integration or Displacement," *The Urban Lawyer* (ABA) 167:39 (2007).
4. Ibid.
5. Ibid.
6. Ibid.
7. In an August 29, 2009, phone interview, Elmer Dixon, cofounder of the Seattle Black Panther Party, noted that weapons were stored on the second floor of the two-story duplex that housed the Panthers' first free medical clinic and main headquarters at the corner of 20th and Spruce Streets. While the building has since been demolished, the "Panther Wall," a mural bearing images of Angela Davis, Bobby Seale, Huey Newton, and "the New York Twenty-One" still marks the old site. Dixon noted that in 1969, when the building came under attack by Seattle Police, weapons were passed from the

second to the first floor of the building via a trapdoor, but that that no children were on site during any of these episodes.

8. According to a July 2, 1985 story in *The Seattle Times,* "Man Not Guilty of Wife's Death, Jury Concludes after 6-day Trial," Ovetta Green died of stab wounds to her neck on April 20. As the Times story reports, her husband was tried for second-degree murder and acquitted.

9. W.E.B. DuBois makes reference to the "veil" in *The Souls of Black Folks.* In a footnote to an excerpt in the collection *Race and Racialization, Essential Readings* (University of California, 1994), Tania Das Gupta notes that "In African American folklore, a child born with a caul, a veil-like membrane that sometimes covers the head at birth, is said to be lucky, to be able to tell fortunes, and to be a 'double-sighted' seer of ghosts," p. 147n6.

10. Seattle's Total Experience Gospel Choir was "organized in September 1973 at the Mt. Zion Baptist Church of Seattle. The core group represented members of the "Black Experience Gospel Choir of Roosevelt High School and the Franklin High School Gospel Choir of Seattle." Since 1986, the choir, whose members now range in age from 10 to 65, has toured and performed internationally ("Total Experience Gospel Choir, History," http://www.totalexperiencegospelchoir.org/press.html, May 17, 2011).

11. Tessie Comeslast St. Pierre was a Blackfeet woman from Montana, who died in 1999. According to Michelle Marchand, a friend who visited Tessie's grave in a cemetery in St Ignatius, Montana, reported that on the left side of the flat marble headstone is an etched feather, and on the right side is an image of the space needle and the Seattle skyline. Michele recalled a conversation with Tessie one evening the summer before she died, in which Tessie told Michele she had "seen the owl" and that she knew she was dying.

10   Mona Caudill Joyner

1. See Polly Keary, "A Dream Interred, Why couldn't Mona Joyner bury the ashes of the man she loved," Real Change, December 24, 2003, http://www.realchangenews.org /old_site/2003/2003_12_24/current/features/dreaminterred.html (May 17, 2011).

2. Fred Harris, "Burning Up People to Make Electricity," The New Atlantic, July, 1974, www.theatlantic.com/doc/197407/harris-mining (May 17, 2011).

3. Harlan County, Kentucky, U.S. Census, State and County Quick Facts, http: //quickfacts.census.gov/qfd/states/21/21095.html (May 17, 2011).

4. "Son Charged in Father's Murder," Enterprise Staff Report, Harlan Enterprise, June 16, 1978.

5. A nonprofit organization founded in 1921 by Seattle businessman Martin G. Johanson, the Millionair Club operates a center for day laborers that also provides meals, hygiene facilities and social services, http://www.millionairclub.org/ (May 17, 2011).

11   Jessie Pedro

1. For more information on the Tokelauan islands, see *Matagi Tokelau: History and Traditions of Tokelau,* trans. Antony Hooper and Judith Huntsman (Apia: Office of Tokelau Affairs, 1991).

2. The center was established in 1984 as part of a nationwide network of Client Assistance Programs authorized and funded by 1984 Amendments to the Rehabilitation Act (P.L. 98–221).
3. The History and Mission of the Hawaii Disability Rights Center can be found online at http://www.hawaiidisabilityrights.org/Services_Overview.aspx (May 17, 2011).
4. In *Tokelau, People, Atolls and History* (Wellington: First Edition Ltd., 2007), Peter McQuarrie provides an example of British colonists using the term "king" to refer to "hereditary high chief[s]." He emphasizes the communal nature of traditional Tokelauan culture, noting that "fish catches, as well as village water supplies and revenue generated by any community activities" are shared among villagers, "each according to his or her needs," 65.
5. Jessie identified the program as "BIACO," or "Boredom is a Copout," which is administered by the Tri-City Mental Health Center: www.tricitymhs.org (June 26, 2011).
6. In a December 10, 2010, phone interview, Jane Miyahara, administrative specialist at the Hawaii Center for Disability Rights, and likely their longest running employee, confirmed in a brief phone interview that Jessie served on the PAIMI Advisory Council, but indicated that her "memory doesn't go back that far" and she couldn't provide any more specifics on the work that Jessie did at PAIMI.
7. The Downtown Emergency Service Center "serves disabled and vulnerable homeless adults, and [is] one of the largest multiservice centers for homeless adults in the Pacific Northwest," with "programs including permanent supportive housing, clinical services and emergency services and overnight shelter," http://www.desc.org/mission.html (May 17, 2011).
8. According to NAMI's website, " NAMI's support and public education efforts are focused on educating America about mental illness, offering resources to those in need, and insisting that mental illness become a high national priority," http://www.nami.org /template.cfm?section=About_NAMI's (May 17, 2011). In "Grading the States 2009: A Report on America's Health Care System for Adults with Serious Mental Illness," http://www.nami.org/Content/NavigationMenu/Grading_the_States_2009/Findings /Findings.htm (May 17, 2011), NAMI rated the overall state of mental health services in the United States at the D level. In the 2009 ranking, Washington was one of twenty-one states to earn a D. Eighteen states were awarded C's, six states B's, with no A's awarded.

12 "Marie"

1. The Village is the focus of a documentary entitled, *Doorways to Dignity*, produced by Wendy Kohn and Heather Mosher of Kwamba Productions, in collaboration with Villagers; see Dignity Village's website at http://www.dignityvillage.org/; Susan Finley, "The Faces of Dignity: Rethinking the Politics of Homelessness and Poverty in America," *Qualitative Studies in Education* 16, no. 4: 509–531.
2. On the links between fibromyalgia and trauma, see, for example, C. Heim, U. M. Nater, E. Maloney, R. Boneva, J. F. Jones, and W. C. Reeves, "Childhood Trauma and Risk for Chronic Fatigue Syndrome and Association With Neuroendocrine Dysfunction" *Archives of General Psychiatry*, 66, no. 1 (2009): 72–80; see also Gabor Mate, *When the Body Says No, Understanding the Stress-Disease Connection* (Hoboken, NJ: John Wiley & Sons, 2003).

14 "Flower"

1. See Rosette Royale, "Unsafe of the Streets, Violence at Homeless Center," *Real Change*, August 1, 2007, http://www.realchangenews.org/index.php/site/archives/2614/ (June 27, 2011).

15 Arnette Adams

1. King County Hospital was subsequently renamed Harborview Medical Center.
2. A cigarette dipped in PCP.
3. At the time of the interview, Arnette was unaware that I had worked and done interviews at the Compass Center.

17 Conclusion

1. "Universal Declaration of Human Rights," Article 25, Section 1, http://www.un.org/en/documents/udhr/index.shtml#a25 (May 15, 2011).
2. Ibid., Article 23, Section 3 (May 15, 2011).
3. Ibid., Article 23, Section 4 (May 15, 2011).
4. McCullough Hill, P.S., "In the Matter of the Appeal of the Homeless Remembrance Project," City of Seattle Hearing Examiner, File R-10–001, 2.
5. Ibid.
6. Ibid., 3.
7. Ibid., 3.
8. Ibid, 7.
9. *Seattle Times*, December 12, 1978, cited in Hill, Appeal, 7.
10. Hill, 8.
11. "Victor Steinbrueck Park," http://www.seattle.gov/parks/park_detail.asp?ID=338.
12. Hill, "Appeal of the Homeless Remembrance Project," 6.
13. Ibid., 6.
14. Ibid., 10.
15. Ibid., 3.
16. Ibid., 5.
17. "JACL Response to the Texas Board of Education," March 19, 2010, 1.
18. Hill, Appeal, 5
19. *Seattle Star*, May 6, 1942, cited in Hill, Appeal, 5.
20. Ibid, 5.
21. Information on the Homeless Remembrance Project can be found at "http://www.fallenleaves.org." The website, now in development, will include memories and photos of the deceased.
22. For figures on Iraqi civilian deaths, see www.iraqbodycount.org, which bases its estimates on "cross-checked media reports, hospital, morgue, NGO and official figures." A report published in the British medical journal *The Lancet* in 2006 ("Mortality after the 2003 invasion of Iraq: a cross-sectional cluster sample survey," 368, no. 9548: 1421–1428) estimated 654,965 "excess" Iraqi deaths of combatants and noncombatants

between the start of the war in 2003 and June 2006. The estimate includes victims of gunfire, car bombings, etc. as well as more indirect casualties resulting from the destruction of infrastructure, including water treatment plants, etc. An August 2008 report published by the Congressional Research Service (Rhoda Margesson, Jeremy Sharp, and Andora Bruno, "Iraq: Refugees and Internally Displaced Displaced Persons: A Deepening Humanitarian Crisis") estimates that two million refugees have fled to Jordan, Syria, "and other neighboring state," while another 2.7 million people have been displaced within Iraq (2).

23. Arun Gupta, "The American Dream As We Know it is Obsolete, Why progressives need to think beyond the mantra of 'middle-class America,'" Alternet, April 9, 2011, http://www.alternet.org/economy/150555/the_american_dream_as_we_know_it_is _obsolete (May 14, 2011).

24. Ibid.

18   Afterword

1. "See Julia Scott, "Street poets The Collaborative Arts Insurgency takes over one of the toughest corners in the Mission," http://www.sfbg.com/39/09/art_performance_ streetpoets.html (July 4, 2011).

2. *Sinister Wisdom*, 61 (2003–04): 65–7.

3. Mental Health Court, Counseling Washington State, http://www.counselingseattle. com/WSADCP/mental-health-court.htm (May 17, 2011).

4. The website for Food Lifeline can be accessed at http://www.foodlifeline.org/ (May 17, 2011).

5. "Bill of Rights for People who Self Harm," http://www.palace.net/llama/psych/brights. html (May 17, 2011).

Index

abortion, see *Roe v. Wade*
Abu Ghraib, 12
Adams, Arnette, 18, 165–71, 189, 210
Afghanistan War, 7
AIDS, *see* health issues
Alcoholics Anonymous, 37, 42, 144
alcoholism, 12, 30–2, 37–8, 42–3, 47–8,
    55–6, 77, 80–1, 87, 90, 97–9, 117,
    119, 133, 169
Alexander, Michelle, 21, 198n40,
    203nn132, 133
Amnesty International, 22
Ancharoff, Michelle R., 202n108
Anderson, Leon, 197n22
Andrews, Mildred Tanner, 195nn6, 8–10, 12
Angeline's, 82–3, 116, 122, 130, 150–3,
    161, 163–4, 171
Appel, Judith, 203nn127, 134
Aron, Laudan Y., 198n52
arthritis, *see* health issues
Assets and Social Policy, Institute of, 6
asthma, *see* health issues

Bacon, David, 202n107
Baker, Susan G., 197n22
Ballenger, David, 14, 16, 204n137
Bard, Marjorie, 203n120
Barkan, Howard, 203n122
battering, *see* intimate partner violence
Baum, Rex, murder of, 13
Baumohl, Jim, 196n20
Beason, Tyrone, 195n3
Beck, Glenn, 186
Belasco, Amy, 197n33
*Beloved Community: the Sisterhood of
    Homeless Women in Poetry,* 16
Bensley, L., 202nn114
"Beyond Vietnam: A Time to Break Silence,"
    197n31

Bilmes, Linda, 197n33
Birkland, David, 201n90
Black Panthers, 105, 110, 207n7
Black Student Union (BSU), of University
    of Washington, 95
Borchard, Kurt, 197n23
Bourbonnais, Carmen, 196n16
Broom, Jack, 195n2
Brown, Joyce, 196n16
Brown v. Board of Education, 21, 94, 203n131
Burnam, Audrey, 196n20
Burning Bed, 30
Burt, Martha, 195n14, 198n52
Butte, Montana, 18, 49

Cashio, Debbie, 90
Centers for Disease Control, 19
Central Area Civil Rights Committee
    (CACRE), 95
Central District, 18, 95, 105–6, 111, 201n105
    Chasse, James, 40, 204
Child Protective Services (CPS), 60
Chinatown, 18
Church Council of Greater Seattle, 89
Church of Mary Magdalene, 17
    see also Mary's Place
Civil Rights Act of 1964, 94
civil rights movement, 6–7, 80–1, 94–6,
    173, 201n105, 206nn1, 6, 8, 207n2
Cloward, Richard, 200n83
Congress of Racial Equality (CORE), 94
Connelly, Janice, 16, 18, 147–56

Danieli, Yael, 202n108
Dawson, Douglas, 22, 26, 120, 121, 154
death and dying, coping with, 22–6, 55,
    72–4, 91, 96, 157–8, 160, 163–4,
    169–70
    see also Women in Black, Seattle

Decatur, USS, 1
DeMause, Neil, 198n45
Denson, Bryan, 58
Denton, Nancy A, 202n105
DESC, *see* Downtown Emergency Service
    Center
Diary of Anne Frank, the, 59, 61
Dignity Village, 14, 137
Diversi, Marcelo, 196n17, 204n140
Dixon, Elmer, 207n7
Dobash, R. Emerson, 204n2
Dobash, Russell T., 204n2
domestic violence, *see* intimate partner
    violence
Downtown Emergency Service Center, 90,
    130, 209n7
drug use, *see* "War on Drugs"
Dubois, W.E.B., 208n9
Duneier, Mitch, 4, 196n17
Duwamish Tribe, 1

education, 8, 29, 34, 61–2, 67, 69–73,
    95–7, 100–4, 108–9, 111, 138–9,
    141, 142
Ehrenreich, Barbara, 192, 198n47
Eisenhower, Dwight D., 6, 197nn29, 30
Elliott Bay, 1
epilepsy, *see* health issues
Equal Opportunity Employment
    Commission, 94
eugenics, 50, 205n5

Fairbanks, J.A., 202n108
Fair Housing Act of 1968, 94
Fair Sentencing Act of 2010, 21
Farley, Melissa, 203n122
Favazza, Armando, 69, 192
federal budget, 7, 12, 186
Fellowship of Reconciliation (FOR), 80
fibromyalgia, *see* health issues
Finley, Susan, 196n17
Fisher, Lisa M., 202n108
"Flower," 18, 23–4, 157–64, 191
foreclosure, 8, 9, 18, 198n54, 202n106
foster care, 12, 19, 23, 59–60, 62, 101–3,
    118, 157–9
Franklin High School, 104, 110, 208n10
Freeman, Anitra, 4, 6, 16, 23–4, 79–92
Frisch, Michael, 25, 204n139
Fugitive slave laws, 12

gangs, 59–61, 64–5
Garfield High School, 94–5, 97, 100, 159
Gelberg, Lillian, 203nn117, 118
general assistance unemployable (GAU),
    9–10, 70, 74, 144
gentrification, 8, 10, 105–6, 122–3, 133–4,
    207nn3–6
Gibson, Timothy, 8, 198n50, 201nn92, 93
Gillis, Cydney, 199n62
Gray-Garcia, Lisa, aka Tiny, 195n15
grief, *see* death and dying; health issues;
    mental health issues, trauma
Guantanamo, 12
Guiliani, Rudy, 8
Gujar, Nanad, 200n85
Gupta, Arun, 186, 211n23
Gupta, Sarika, 197n39, 203n125

Hamburg, Jill, 195n14
Hansen, Terry, 204n1
Harborview Hospital, 22, 70
Harlan, Kentucky, 18, 116–17
Harvey, David, 195nn13, 14
Hawaii, 128–30
Health Care for the Homeless, Seattle-King
    County, 17
health issues
    AIDS, 36, 46, 56–7
    arthritis, 13, 19, 40, 83
    asthma, 19
    epilepsy, 13, 42, 45, 71, 73–4, 87
    fibromyalgia, 13, 137–9, 173
    heart disease, 19
    hypertension/stroke, 11, 13, 19, 29,
        34–5, 40, 83, 113, 157–65, 190–1
    nutrition, 140–1, 145
    sickle cell anemia, 13, 173, 176–8
Herivel, Tara, 197n37, 204n136
Hill, Debra, 14
Hill, Richard, 184–5
Holocaust, 21, 189
Homeless Management Information System
    (HMIS), 16, 201nn94, 95
Homelessness
    causes of, 4–14, 18–22, 80–1, 85–7
    criminalization of, 8–10, 11–13, 15–16,
        200nn77–80
    dehumanization of, 3–5, 39–43, 76–8,
        88–91, 119–25, 133–5, 142–5, 154–5,
        172–81

elderly, 9–10, 83, 177, 199n71
encampments, "sweeps" of, 11
estimates of, 8–9, 20, 203n121
pathologization of, 3–5
violence against, 13–15, 18, 20, 22–4; *see also* Smith, Tonya "Sonshine"
Homeless Remembrance Project, 16, 112, 135, 183–6
Homeless Voice, 14
Home of the Good Shepherd, Seattle, 49, 51
Homes Not Handcuffs, 198n47, 200nn77, 80
Hooverville, 2, 15
Hopper, Kim, 11, 195n14, 197n22, 200n82
Housing
    discrimination in, 18, 84–5, 202nn105, 106
    Fair Market Rents, 9–10
    Housing Authority, Seattle, 23, 195n7
    lottery for, 10, 132, 181, 199n68
    Section 8, 10, 30, 122, 132, 161, 166, 181, 199nn68–70
Housing Act of 1937, 2
Housing and Urban Development, Department of (HUD), 10–11, 16, 199nn63, 64
Hudson, Christopher G., 200n84
Hyla, Adam, 201n99

immigrants (targeting of), 2, 18, 185, 186
immigration, 202n107
interviewing, *see* methodology
intimate partner violence, 19, 30–1, 34–6, 43–5, 55–6, 117, 119, 139, 149, 160, 163, 166, 169, 202nn109–116, 204n2
Iraq, war in
    civilian casualties in, 197, 210n22
    cost of (financial), 7, 186, 197nn32–34
    displaced persons in, 197
    see also Military, families in; veterans

Jamieson Robert L., 22, 204n137
Japanese-American internment, 185
Jones, Ann, 202n109
Jordan, B.K., 202n108
Joyner, Mona Caudill, 16, 18, 22–4, 27, 115–26, 184, 208
juvenile detention, 49–58

Kennedy, Michelle, 195n15
Kim, Reverend Jean, 17
King, Martin Luther, Jr., 6, 7, 43, 183, 186, 197n31
King, Ryan, 198n44
King County Homeless Death Review, 100
Koegel, Paul, 196n20

labor, 2–3, 7, 9, 8–19, 34, 59, 86–7, 116–18, 183, 186
    see also work
Ladisch, Virginia, 200n85
Lam, Julie, 196n22
Lang, Rev. Richard, 89
Leake, Barbara, 203nn117, 118
Levi, Robin, 203nn127, 134
Lewin, Tamara, 204n1
Liebow, Elliott, 4, 196n16
loitering laws, 8, 11–12
Los Angeles, 15, 42, 173–4, 178–9, 191
Lucio, Jose, 18, 116, 119–20, 128, 184
Lutheran Compass Center (LCC), 1, 2, 4, 10, 17, 24, 29, 39, 40, 49, 55, 57, 59, 69
Lyon-Callo, Vincent, 5, 197nn23–25

Maarmar, C.R., 202n108
Magdalene, Mary, Church of the, 17, 166
    see also Mary's Place
Marchand, Michele, 15, 23, 79, 208n11
Marcus, Anthony, 5, 8, 198nn46, 48
Marcuse, Peter, 196nn19, 22
"Marie," 137–46
Marlowe, 6, 24, 173–82, 189
Martha Washington School for Girls, 49, 51
Martin, Michael, 197n22
Martinson, Debra, 6, 14, 24, 69–78, 192–3
Mary's Place, 17, 23–4, 80, 93–4, 105, 107, 124–5, 127–34, 157, 161–3, 165–6, 171–3, 191
Maslow, Abraham, 3
Massey, Douglas S., 202n105
Masters, Alexander, 195n15
Mate, Gabor, 21
Mathieu, Arlene, 197n22
Mauer, Marc, 197n38, 198n44, 203nn124, 129
McKay Apartments, 41
McKinney-Vento Act of 1987, 10
McLaughlin, Reverend Marcia, 23

mental health issues, 4–5, 12, 33–4, 40,
196nn18, 19, 197n22, 200n84
bi-polar disorder, 80–3, 104, 202n108,
203n122
non-suicidal self-injury, 69–70, 74–6
post-traumatic stress disorder (PTSD),
19, 80, 104, 202n108, 203n122
sleep deprivation, effects of, 12, 200n85
suicide attempts, 33–5, 47, 69, 95, 97–
100, 116, 118, 129, 149, 166–7, 179
trauma, 5, 19–21, 25–7, 45, 49–50, 59,
76, 80, 104, 128–9, 131, 137–41, 157,
202n108
mental health treatment
critiques of, 33–5, 63–4, 70, 74–5, 130–2
empowerment models in, 127–9, 193
lack of access, 12, 21
Patient's Bill of Rights for People Who
Self Harm, 193
Mercier, Judith D., 202n109
Mercier, Peter J., 202n109
meritocracy, myths of, 8, 186
Meschede, Tatjana, 197n28
methodology, 24–8
Microsoft, 58
Military
expenditures for, 77, 197nn31–34
families in, 19, 29–30, 34, 71–2, 80, 168,
202n109
see also Afghanistan; Iraq
minimum wage, 9
mining, 18, 49
Mitchell, Don, 8, 198nn48, 49
Model Cities Program, 94
Moreira, Claudio, 204n140
Morrell, Jessica, 196n17
Morris, Monique, 202n106
Munroe, James F., 202n108

NAACP, 95, 202n106
National Coalition for Homeless Veterans,
197n35
National Coalition for the Homeless, 4, 8,
11, 13, 17, 198n55, 199n71, 200n78,
201n87
National Fair Housing Alliance, 202n106
National Homeless Persons' Memorial Day,
17
National Law Center on Homelessness and
Poverty, 8, 11, 198n47, 200n78

National Low Income Housing Coalition,
198n54, 199n57
National Priorities Project, 197n32
Neoliberalism, 2, 12, 18–19, 186, 195n13,
14
New York City, 2, 8, 15
Nicarthy, Ginny, 202n110
North American Free Trade Agreement
(NAFTA), 6, 8, 18–19, 202n107
Northwest Evaluation and Treatment
Center, 70
Novac, Sylvia, 196n16
Nuu-chah-nulth, First Nation, Vancouver,
B.C., 40

Obama, Barack, 9
Olkon, Sarah, 199nn68, 69
Operation Homestead, 40–1
organizing, 40

Pam, "Mama," 24
Panhandling, 8
pathologization, 197n23
Pedro, Jessie, 17, 127–36, 208–9
Pelletiere, Danilo, 198n54
Pioneer Square, 1–2, 195nn11, 12
Piven, Francis Fox, 200n83
Point Elliott, Treaty of, 1
police violence, 39–40, 42, 45
see also Chasse, James; Williams, John T.
Polishuk, Sandy, 27, 204n144
poor laws, Elizabethan, 11–12, 19, 200n83
Poor Magazine, 3
Portelli, Alessandro, 26–7, 204nn141–143,
204n145
Preservation, Enhancement and
Transformation of Rental Assistance
Act (PETRA), 11, 200n76
prisons, 7–8, 22, 53–4, 197–8nn37–44,
203nn125–135, 204n136
see also "War on Drugs"
prostitution, 20–1, 46, 203nn122, 123
Puget Hotel, 41
Purdy, *see* Washington Corrections Center
for Women

racial discrimination
in education, 18, 94–5, 108–9
in housing, 18, 94–5, 201n105
in mortgage lending, 18–19, 105–6

in physical violence, 105, 108–9, 207n1

in sentencing, 21

in treatment of homeless people, 81, 151

see also "War on Drugs"

Raging Grannies, 80

Ralston, Meredith, 201n104

rape, 12, 19–20, 22–3, 33, 37, 39–40, 45–6, 73, 90, 95, 101, 117–18, 122–3, 129, 138, 153, 157, 160

Rayville, Louisiana, 105–9

Reagan, Ronald, 2, 7, 77, 195n14

Real Change, 14–15, 24, 80, 84–5, 89, 96, 124, 162, 199n62, 201nn91, 99

redlining, *see* racial discrimination

religion, *see* spirituality

Roberts, Roxane, 16, 18, 22, 24, 27, 93–104, 190, 206–7

Roe v. Wade, 29, 204n1

Rolph, Amy, 204n138

Rossi, Peter, 196–7n22

Rubin, Beth, 196n22, 199n67

Ruutila, Julia, 27

Safe Harbors, 16, 201n94

see also Homeless Management Information System

San Francisco, 11, 20

Schell, Mayor Paul, 1

Schlenger, W.E., 202n108

Schmitt, John, 197n39, 203n125

Sclar, E.D., 196n20

Seattle Displacement Coalition, 40

Seattle Has a Resource Effort (SHARE), 14–16, 201nn86–88, 92, 94, 96–98

"Secret Shame," 69

see also mental health issues

sex education, 29, 204n1

sexual abuse, in childhood, 31–2

see also rape

Shapiro, Thomas M., 197n28

shelters

battered women's, 20, 29–30, 113, 204n2

conditions in, 5, 13, 70, 77, 83–4, 88–9, 149–53, 161, 170, 174, 177–9

shortage of, 9, 15–16, 20, 23–5, 59, 121, 190

see also Seattle Has a Resource Effort; Women's Housing Equality and Enhancement League

Sherman, Arloc, 197n27

Shorter, Stuart, 195n15

sickle cell anemia, *see* health issues

Silva, Catherine, 201n105

Simmons, K. Wynkoop, 202nn114

Simpson, Rev. Pat, 89

single homeless, 4

single room occupancy hotels (SROs), 10, 40–1

"skid road," 2

skid row, 43

Smith, Tonya "Sonshine," 22–4, 26, 91, 96, 121, 127, 157, 163–4, 204n138

Snow, David, 197n22

social security income, 2, 9–10, 199nn60, 61

social services, critiques of, 5, 10, 14–16, 23, 39, 53, 89–90, 179

see also shelters

spirituality, 17–18, 23–4, 47, 64, 78, 86, 97–8, 109–10, 113–14, 119–20, 124–5, 155, 166–7, 169–71, 180, 189, 191–2

St. Pierre, Tessie Comeslast, 112, 208n11

stalking, 55–6

Stiglitz, Joseph, 197n33

Stone, Chad, 197n27

street newspapers, 15

see also *"Real Change"*

"street people," 39, 42–3, 46

stress, 12, 19, 48, 70, 80, 86–7, 123, 128, 137, 142, 147, 151, 160, 177

Stringer, Lee, 195n15

strokes, 11, 13, 19, 29, 34–5, 40, 83, 113, 157–65, 190–1

substance abuse, 4–5, 48, 52, 196n19

suicide, attempts, 33–4, 47

Sullivan, Laura, 197n28

"Sweet Pea," 26, 59–68, 71

Tailfeathers, Annamarie, 24, 39–48, 192, 204–5

Taylor, Quintard, 201n105

Taylor, Stuart Jr., 203n130

Taylor, the Reverend Robert, 89–90

tent cities, 15–16, 84–5, 88–9, 137–8

Ten-Year Plans to End Homelessness, 10, 46, 89, 153, 200n75

Thatcher, Elizabeth, 18, 22, 24, 49–58, 191

Till, Emmett, 105, 207n1
Tokelau, 128, 209n4
Total Experience Choir, 111, 208n10
Troubled Relief Asset Program (TARP), 9,
   199n56

Universal Declaration of Human Rights, 5,
   183, 196n21, 210n1
Upward Bound Program, 95, 101–2, 138,
   142, 151
U.S. Conference of Mayors' Hunger and
   Homelessness Survey, 9, 196n18,
   199n59, 200n74

Vancouver, B.C., 21
Van Eenwyk, J., 202nn114
veterans, 7, 18–19, 197n35, 202n108
Veterans for Peace, 80
Veterans Housing Administration, 18

Wagner, David, 4, 196n16
Walla Walla State Penitentiary, 55
Walsh, Brent, 199n61
Walton, Helyn Doris, 94
War, *see* Afghanistan; Iraq; Military
Warner, Kris, 197n39, 203n125
"War on Drugs," 7–8, 21–2,
   197–8nn37–44, 203nn124–134
"War on Poverty," 2, 6, 7, 95
Warren, Stacy, 198n50
War Resisters League, 7, 197n34
Washington Corrections Center for Women
   (WCCW), 22, 54, 55, 104, 191
Washington State University Vancouver, 26
wealth gap, 6, 197n28
Wenzel, Suzanne L., 203nn117, 118, 119
West, Cornel, 189
Western Regional Advocacy Project
   (WRAP), 7, 10, 197n36
Western State Hospital, 30

white privilege, 77, 204n140
Williams, Jean Calterone, 5, 197n23,
   202n116
Williams, John T., 40, 192
Winston, Delores Loann, 18, 105–14, 207
Women in Black, Seattle, 14–17, 22–6,
   79–80, 90–1, 105, 112, 116, 120–2,
   153–4, 157, 163, 172, 183–4,
   201n101, 204n138
Women in Black Movement, International,
   16–17, 201nn100–102
Women's Housing Equality and
   Enhancement League (WHEEL),
   14–17, 22–6, 34–5, 79–80, 83–5,
   88–9, 105, 112, 116, 120, 127–8, 130,
   137, 147, 148, 152–4, 201nn94,
   96–99
work
   paid, 2–3, 7, 9, 8–19, 34, 36, 41, 46,
      49–51, 56–7, 59–60, 64, 74, 80, 82,
      86–7, 103–4, 107, 111–12, 117, 119,
      124, 129–30, 138–9, 147, 149, 151,
      153, 159–60, 168, 170, 190, 191, 192;
      see also labor
   volunteer, 17–18, 39, 79–80, 127,
      134–5, 144, 191, 192; *see also* Women
      in Black, Seattle; Women's Housing
      Equality and Enhancement League
World Trade Organization (WTO), 1, 123,
   183
Wright, James, 196n22, 199n67
Wright, Paul, 197n37, 204n136
Wright, Talmadge, 196n17

Yesler, Henry, 1
Yesler's Mill, 2
Yesler Terrace, 1
Yesler Way, 2
Yoo, Seung-Schik, 200n85
YWCA, 81, 153